Psychodrama: inspiration and technique

Working with people struggling to escape from the strait-jacket of unexpressed human emotion and thought, professionals often use an exploration of truth through dramatic method. This method is called psychodrama.

The twelve experienced psychodramatists who have contributed to this book were asked to write about that which inspires them in their work and about the techniques and psychological theories they use for creative clinical practice. They write in a personal and honest way about their attempts to help a variety of client groups including adolescents, autistic children, offenders, anorexics, the sexually abused, alcoholics, and those dying of cancer.

The majority of books on psychodrama in English describe the theory and practice of the classical method invented by J. L. Moreno and further developed by Zerka Moreno. This book describes how the boundaries of psychotherapy can be creatively stretched by the inspired use of technique (within the method of psychodrama) and by the use of other theories, including ideas from psycho-analysis. But above all, it describes how psychodrama can be used as an art to help human beings find their own spontaneity and creativity in living.

Psychodrama: inspiration and technique makes fascinating reading for experienced and trainee psychotherapists and will be essential reading for all those with a special interest in psychodrama. It will also inspire other pro-fessionals in their work with clients.

The book is illustrated by Ken Sprague, who has used the content of each chapter to inspire his print-making.

Contributors: Anne Ancelin Schützenberger; Anne Bannister; Elaine Eller Goldman; Paul Holmes; Jinnie Jefferies; Marcia Karp; H. J. Meillo; Zerka Toeman Moreno; Peter Pitzele; Gillie Ruscombe-King; Ken Sprague; Barbara Jean Quin; Sarah T. Willis; Kit Wilson.

DETAILED PROPS
NOT REQUIRED

Psychodrama: inspiration and technique

Edited by
Paul Holmes and Marcia Karp
Illustrated by Ken Sprague

Tavistock/Routledge
London and New York

First published 1991
by Routledge
11 New Fetter Lane, London EC4P 4EE

Simultaneously published in the USA and Canada
by Routledge
a division of Routledge, Chapman and Hall, Inc.
29 West 35th Street, New York, NY 10001

Typeset by LaserScript Limited, Mitcham, Surrey
Printed and bound in Great Britain by
Biddles Ltd, Guildford and King's Lynn

British Library Cataloguing in Publication Data

Holmes, Paul, 1947-
  Psychodrama: inspiration and technique.
  1. Medicine. Drama therapy
  I. Title II. Karp, Marcia
  616.891523

Library of Congress Cataloging in Publication Data

Psychodrama: inspiration and technique/edited by Paul Holmes and
  Marcia Karp: illustrated by Ken Sprague.
  p.   cm.
  Includes bibliographical references (p.   ).
  1. Psychodrama.   I. Holmes, Paul, 1947– .   II. Karp, Marcia,
  1942– .
  RC489.P7P76   1990   90-10817
  616.89'1523--dc20   CIP

ISBN 0-415-02672-5
ISBN 0-415-02673-3 (pbk)

This book is dedicated to Zerka T. Moreno who develops and embodies the ideas of J. L. Moreno

Contents

List of contributors   ix

Preface   xiii
Marcia Karp

1   **Inspiration and technique**   1
    Paul Holmes and Marcia Karp

2   **Classical psychodrama: an overview**   7
    Paul Holmes

3   **Adolescents inside out: intrapsychic psychodrama**   15
    Peter Pitzele

4   **Everybody's a somebody: action methods for young people
    with severe learning difficulties**   33
    Ken Sprague

5   **Time, space, reality, and the family: psychodrama with a
    blended (reconstituted) family**   53
    Zerka T. Moreno

6   **Learning to live again: psychodramatic techniques with
    sexually abused young people**   77
    Anne Bannister

7   **Psychodrama and piccalilli: residential treatment of a sexually
    abused adult**   95
    Marcia Karp

8   **Who goes there?: group-analytic drama for disturbed
    adolescents**   115
    Sarah T. Willis

9   **Issues of milieu therapy: psychodrama as a contribution to the
    treatment of a case of anorexia nervosa**   137
    Joke Meillo

Contents

10   **Hide and seek: the psychodramatist and the alcoholic**   155
     Gillie Ruscombe-King

11   **Doorway to the past: use of action techniques with adult
     children of alcoholics and co-dependants**   179
     Kit Wilson and Elaine Eller Goldman

12   **What we are doing here is defusing bombs: psychodrama with
     hard-core offenders**   189
     Jinnie Jefferies

13   **The drama of the seriously ill patient: fifteen years' experience
     of psychodrama and cancer**   203
     Anne Ancelin Schützenberger

14   **Healing the healers: psychodrama with therapists**   227
     Barbara Jean Quin

     Name index   245

     Subject index   248

Contributors

Anne Ancelin Schützenberger, PhD, TEP, Professor of Social and Clinical Psychology at Nice University, is one of the first twelve directors trained by Moreno and the organiser of the First International Congress of Psychodrama (1964, France). Her handbook on psychodrama has been translated into twelve languages. After working with schizophrenics, she now works with cancer and AIDS patients using psychodrama and genograms.

Anne Bannister, CQSW, RDTh, is a social worker who holds the Holwell Diploma in Psychodrama. She is also a registered dramatherapist. As a probation officer, she worked with groups of delinquent adolescents, which led to her special interest in child sexual abuse. Anne has managed the NSPCC & Greater Manchester Authority's Child Sexual Abuse Unit since its inception in 1987.

Elaine Eller Goldman, PhD, is a graduate of the Moreno Institute of Psychodrama, Sociometry and Group Psychotherapy. Currently, she is Executive Director of the Camelback Hospitals' Western Institute for Psychodrama, Head of the Psychodrama Department, Camelback Hospitals, Inc., Phoenix and Scottsdale, Arizona and is on the Faculties of Columbia Pacific University, San Rafael, California and Arizona State University. She has written a number of articles on psychodrama and is co-author of the book, *Psychodrama: Experience and Process.*

Paul Holmes, PhD, MRCPsych, is a child and adolescent psychiatrist, an analytically trained individual psychotherapist and a practitioner of psychodrama. He completed the Holwell diploma in 1989. For many years he worked as a psychiatrist in community-based units in deprived areas of inner London. He uses his knowledge of psychoanalysis to support his work as a psychodramatist. He is now based in Mexico City and London and is concentrating on his interests in psychodrama, psychoanalytic theory and writing. In 1988 he became the first formal chair of the British Psychodrama Association.

Jinnie Jefferies, MSc, trained in America and England, has a Master's Degree in Counselling Psychology and the Holwell Diploma in Psychodrama. She works as a psychodramatist for the prison service and for Guy's Hospital, London, and in a residential setting for emotionally disturbed adolescents. She has a private individual and group practice in Richmond, London, where she lives. In 1984 BBC Radio made a programme of her work with prisoners called 'I Love and Forgive You'. In 1989 she created and directed a series of six psychodramas for BBC Television called 'The Session'.

Marcia Karp, MA, TEP, was trained by Dr J. L. Moreno and Zerka Moreno and became a member of their faculty in the Institute of Psychodrama, New York City. She has worked in prisons, universities and hospitals in America, Canada and England and is primarily responsible for pioneering and developing classical psychodrama in Britain. In 1974 she founded the Holwell Centre for Psychodrama in North Devon, England. As Co-Director of training she conducts courses at the Centre and throughout Europe, South America, the USA and Finland. She is author of 'Living vs. survival: a psychotherapist's journey', in the book *On Becoming a Psychotherapist* (Routledge).

Joke Meillo, TEP, trained as a psychodramatist at the Moreno Institute, New York, between 1972 and 1975. She is a member and supervisor of the Dutch Association for Group Therapy and of the Association for Child and Adolescent Psychotherapy in the Netherlands. She has worked for over twelve years in a psychotherapeutic community for adolescents in the Provincial Hospital at Santpoort, the Netherlands, where she is also engaged in the supervision of reorganisation and in the training and supervision of multidisciplinary teams.

Zerka Toeman Moreno is the doyenne of psychodrama practice, who trained group psychotherapists and psychodramatists in many countries: the USA, Europe, Latin America, the Near and Far East and the Antipodes. Until 1982 she directed the Moreno Institute in Beacon, New York (founded by her husband, J. L. Moreno) – the original and world centre of psychodrama. She has served as President of the American Society of Group Psychotherapy and Psychodrama and is an honorary member of the Board of Directors of the International Association of Group Psychotherapy.

Peter Pitzele, PhD, TEP, is a Director of Psychodrama Services at Four Winds Hospital in Katonah, New York. He was trained at the Moreno Institute in Beacon, New York. He was awarded the Zerka T. Moreno award in 1986 for his outstanding achievement as a practitioner. He was elected as a Fellow to the American Society for Group Psychotherapy and Psychodrama in 1989.

Barbara Jean Quin (formerly Tideswell), MSc, AFBPsS, is a chartered clinical psychologist, qualified in 1974. She specialises in work with children, adolescents and their families and has worked in adolescent units, a social services community home, in education and in the community. She has been involved in staff training and support for many years and is currently involved in research into stress and breakdown in mental health professionals.

Gillie Ruscombe-King trained as an occupational therapist and has worked for the past eight years in the field of alcoholism at the Chilton Clinics – the Oxfordshire Regional Alcoholism Unit, based at the Warneford Hospital, Oxford. Since finishing her training twelve years ago, she has had a keen interest in creative therapeutic work. Latterly, she has been interested in the juxtaposition of the psychodramatic and group analytic process. She has trained at the Holwell Centre for Psychodrama and has had experience in individual and group analysis.

Ken Sprague is an accredited sociodrama director, psychodramatist and graphic artist. He is committed to the ongoing process of developing Morenian methods as life tools. He works to popularise action methods beyond the clinic and personal growth arena into the area of teaching, organisation or business management and community affairs. He teaches young people with severe learning difficulties and is Co-Director of the Holwell Centre, the only full-time residential training centre for psychodrama and sociodrama.

Sarah T. Willis graduated from Sussex University with a BA Hons degree in German and European Studies. She has worked as an actress in England, Europe and America, winning an OBIE award in New York, appearing with the National Theatre of Great Britain and touring abroad with her one-woman plays. She is Teacher-in-Charge of York Road Intermediate Treatment Centre, Battersea, London, a community project for disturbed adolescents. She is also a psychotherapist and group analyst, specialising in work with anorexics and their families.

Kit Wilson, ACSW, is a clinical social worker in private practice in Scottsdale, Arizona, USA. She is the former Director of Chemical Dependency at Scottsdale Camelback Hospital and a past President of the Arizona Board for Certification of Addiction Counsellors. She received her MSW at the University of Connecticut and did her psychodrama training at the Moreno Institute and the Western Institute of Psychodrama, Sociometry and Group Psychotherapy. Ms Wilson's expertise is in the area of recovery from chemical dependency and co-dependency.

Preface

Marcia Karp

What impressed me from my first encounter with psychodrama is its usefulness. The architect, Frank Lloyd Wright, said: 'Form and function are one.' The fusion of situation and behaviour in psychodrama is an indication of this statement. The setting for each scene is life itself (form) and the enactment of the scene (function) becomes fused in this type of psychotherapy. The client does not speak separately of his life, he or she creates it through enactment, using part of the therapy room as stage area on which the specifics of that person's life are represented.

Over twenty years ago I watched J. L. Moreno do psychodrama in a theatre in New York. He made it look simple. Since that time I have worked with a wide variety of people including prison inmates, stammerers, Catholic Brothers, university students and staff, teachers, the police, mental health workers and patients and autistic children. What strikes me as common ground in each population is the need to have encouragement and time to tell their truth about what happens in life; to risk looking at what didn't happen, to uncover opportunities and to test alternatives.

For example, when loved ones reach the end of their lives, we often don't say the things that need to be said. We may take for granted the fact that the person will always be there, the boundaries for expression are already circumscribed and not to be stepped over. Yet, when the person is gone, the boundaries seem limitless and many people yearn for a chance to have the real talk that didn't occur. Psychodrama gives that chance to people to release a dammed-up block of feeling or expression. It ranges from telling the person how much they were loved to sharing family secrets about abuse, which have been locked away for years doing silent damage. It is important for the subject of the session to reverse roles with the dead person. The living person may gain crucial insight into the dying person's reactions. In role the reaction may be very different to what was expected. The conspiracy of silence may be broken in this way.

As well as the parent who has died, the unborn child is an important figure in the lives of many. The foetus that was aborted, the baby who died at birth and the child which was never conceived may tie up people's emotions for years. Working with parents who have lost babies, it is rare that the hospital, the police or those around the parents completely deal with the complexities of the loss. Neighbours may avoid them, relatives don't know what to say, hospital staff may concentrate on what went wrong with the mechanics of the death, but in each instance the parents need to discuss and mourn the loss and simply talk about what it feels like. For some it can be psychodramatically helpful to talk to the lost child and to reverse roles with it. The special application in this situation can release the parent from the guilt of the death, even in the most severe situations – in one example, an exhausted mother who didn't check on her baby. The baby died during the night and was found in the morning. It was a cot death in which the mother was inconsolable and carried the guilt for years. When she took the role of the baby in a psychodrama she was able to say: 'Mum, even if you checked on me I may have died anyway. My lungs didn't work. That part of it you couldn't have helped.'

Several more examples from my own experience come to mind. In working with hard-core offenders, the hawk and the dove, the bold and the meek, the tough and the tender dramatically co-exist. From a high-security area in one prison, the inmates made a satin farewell card for me, dripping in roses and sequins. I mentally noted that the twenty-five signatures on the card were linked with a crime – murder, assault, arson or child molesting. The tenderness and love is often masked by layers of fear, resentment, anger and violence. Positive feelings may never have been expressed. The therapist must address this process of layering in order that the offender takes responsibility for his own process in the past and present.

One of the most memorable places where I worked as a psychodramatist was the California Medical Facility in Vacaville, California. I worked in a unit primarily with sexual offenders. A session that stands out in my mind was with a rapist who was in prison on six counts of rape. It is a good example of the dictum: 'Show me what happened, don't tell me.' It was because the young man showed us what happened in the earliest offence that he was able to see clearly for the first time how his criminal behaviour was linked to his childhood upbringing. The ability to understand some of the reasons for his pathology was a great relief to him. He felt he began to have some insight into why these crimes were committed.

In the scene he enacted he was sitting alone by a swimming pool. Nearby was a parked caravan in which lived a middle-aged woman. The woman was his mother's age, height and colouring and known to his mother. While sitting there, the protagonist showed us how he began to frighten the woman. He went to the caravan, moved around it, making noises. On hearing the noises outside, she put off the lights inside. She picked up a knife to defend herself. The young man saw the knife glinting in the moonlight. He decided, at that moment, to sexually overpower the woman. The connection he made at that point was that, up until the age of 19, his own mother constantly used to threaten to cut off his penis if he didn't stop wetting the bed. The knife association with the woman in the caravan helped him to see that he was symbolically overpowering his mother, and in each rape incident this was repeated.

We stopped the psychodrama at that point and allowed insight catharsis to be talked through. During more than six years of incarceration, the young man felt disconnected from these crimes, hardly feeling any involvement in them. The discovery that he must have done them was as crucial as the enactment itself. It allowed ownership into the treatment process. If he wanted to stop being a rapist, which he did, he had to begin to understand his responsibility for it. This makes special use of what Moreno called psychodramatic shock. When the protagonist experiences a shocked reaction to what is revealed through enactment, this shock can be a positive, pivotal point, touching him in a way other discussion and therapy have not done.

In a high-security area, safe boundary setting is crucial for people. The inmates are asked to each take responsibility for the total outcome so that it is not just the therapist's responsibility. The psychodrama takes place under conditions of control where the protagonist and other members are not hurt. To re-enact issues that are illegal takes a group morality that can openly discuss the issue. The group and the therapist must be careful not to condone the behaviour or, indeed, to rehearse it for future use by other inmates. I'm thinking here of a member of a bikers' club who showed how his gang entered a small village and took it over, terrifying some of the people in it. A caution with particular inmates is to spot the exhibitionists who simply want to show their peers how they behave. Rather than focus on how he did what he did, we focused on why, uncovering the motivation and looking at the root cause face to face. It was a tough job and was undertaken only because the protagonist asked to look at why he did it. The culture of wanting 'to get better', wanting to learn from what has happened so as not to do it again, has to be both worked on and maintained in special groups of this nature.

Autistic children take a particular application of action methods. Without classical psychodrama training I doubt that the following session could have taken place. Some children can take only partial application of the method. With some populations, using less of the psychodramatic tool ultimately gives more results. In this case I used the psychodramatic technique of 'doubling'.

Eddy was a 7-year-old autistic boy. He hadn't spoken in words for two years. I created a series of doubling sessions where there were just the two of us in a gymnasium. In becoming him, that is, following his movements carefully with my own body, the reality was created that he was not alone in the room. Every time he ran, I did. Every time he made a noise, I did. Slowly, he tested that mirrored image, which I deepened and expanded, taking small movements that he knew were different from his own. He began to observe and copy me with a firmer reality that he wasn't alone.

After ten of these doubling sessions, we were alone in the therapy room making figures in clay. The clay was particularly hard that morning. We held a piece between us and began to stretch it. As we exerted pressure together, the young boy yelled: 'Pull, Marcia, pull!' The earth seemed to move when he spoke. They were the first words I'd heard him say. He'd clearly begun to see himself separately from me and was able to invoke my help with the clay.

Working with Christian Brothers was another special application.

It was my job to run a weekly therapy group with young, religious Brothers. One of the Brothers came to the group extremely depressed. He felt he could never be as perfect as God so why should he keep trying? He began to play out a scene in which he could be as perfect as he wanted to be. He walked to the door, closing it with perfect sound and movement. In the session, he related to his classmates in a manner he considered to be 'God-like'. Little by little his peers turned from him, to talk to each other and to disregard him. He asked if he could re-do the scene as himself, wanting now to relate on some real basis with less perfection and more humanity. As he left the room the glass in the door shattered as he closed it energetically. What would normally have been an accident became a creative affirmation of the session.

Each psychodramatic application has to fit the moment. What is common to each of the examples given is that one could not have been substituted for the other. The application of the tools to each is unique to that situation. Though the artistry of psychodrama has, as its foundation, solid technique, it is the element of taking a calculated risk that makes the work inspired rather than simply routine. What is the act-hunger of the person working? What is the needed leap forward, and how can we help the person enact that? Both artistry and method are needed to produce change.

All our authors have been, in some way, pioneers in their field. We invite you to gain from the fruits of their work in this book of inspiration and technique.

Chapter one

Inspiration and technique

Paul Holmes and Marcia Karp

Lina was an attractive young woman whose physician had diagnosed a malignant sarcoma on her arm. She had been told that the only way to save her life was to have this limb amputated; she dreaded the thought of her life following this mutilating operation and sought other forms of therapeutic help that might help her survive as a physically and mentally whole person.

Chuck and Felix were warring adolescent brothers. Their father and stepmother had become concerned about the increasingly violent conflict and sought help for the boys and their family.

Tony was an effeminate Anglo-West-Indian boy who felt out of control and frightened. He had spent most of his life living in a series of different homes and institutions. Each placement had broken down because of his behaviour and he was locked in a cycle of rejections, about which he was at once both triumphant and despairing.

Irene was a 19-year-old whose weight had fallen to 37 kilograms and who had taken to hiding bags of her vomit in her bedroom. Her relationships with her peers were deteriorating and there was little affection within her family home.

Caroline, a married woman with several previous marriages and teenage children, has been known to the alcohol services for many years. When sober, she is always beautifully turned out, but when drinking has severe and frightening withdrawal symptoms. She has recently been detoxified and is desperate for a 'last chance', feeling guilt-ridden and angry about her failures.

These individuals and many others have been helped by psychodrama. At first sight they may not appear to be the easiest or most rewarding clients for a psychotherapist.

Traditionally, adolescents, anorexics and alcoholics are considered to be difficult to help; adolescents have a tendency to defend against emotional pain or anxiety by turning to action, such behaviour becoming very disruptive of any attempts to deal psychotherapeutically with their needs and difficulties. Indeed, some would argue that no therapeutic help can be given in any systematic way until the more dramatic phases of adolescence have passed. Young women suffering from anorexia nervosa also present therapists with an enormous challenge; their tendency to see the problems as entirely physical and related to weight and to eating denies the therapists the therapeutic footholds needed to make some headway with psychological treatment for an often life-threatening disorder. Alcoholics use their addiction as a way of numbing the pain of their past and their present; psychotherapy often (as part of the treatment process) increases a sense of pain and distress. The alcoholic will often revert to drink rather than face issues that, if resolved, may in the long term improve their ways of coping and the quality of their life.

The individuals and groups whose psychodramatic treatments are described in this book may be very different from the protagonists that psychodramatists have met in their training. Such groups usually consist of highly motivated and interested adults whose resistances and defences do not often deny emotional difficulties. The impulse controls of such individuals are well developed and they look upon the position of protagonist as a privilege during their training. Classical protagonist-centred psychodrama is easier to shape in these circumstances (see Chapter 2 for an overview of classical psychodrama).

What is it, then, that has allowed certain dramatists to move on from their classical training to work with clients whose problems and psychological difficulties make them notoriously difficult to help? A combination of factors shape destiny. Sometimes a job opportunity in an area not consciously chosen may begin a fascination that then turns into a challenge. Sometimes the personal impact of the therapist's own life can be a warm-up to the work. There may be an alcoholic member that one tries to help at an early age, or family problems that are never fully dealt with that lead to an individual pursuing a specialty area of work to address those issues. Sometimes there are professional warm-ups that lead one to the more difficult clients. Success with one type of client may produce interest in further clients and one becomes known as the person who can deal with that type of person, and so it goes on.

The authors of this book demonstrate that many pained and troubled individuals can be helped by a powerful combination of two factors: *inspiration* and *technique*. In her preface, Marcia Karp refers to the artistry of psychodrama and the need to take therapeutic risks. These processes crucially must be linked to a solid basis in the theories and techniques of psychodrama.

By inspiration we mean the process whereby creativity and spontaneity allow the individual to create something new for themselves and their clients. To inspire another person or group, the director needs to sow the seeds of change. Imagination, curiosity, playfulness, empathy, daring, self-knowledge, maturity and mastery of the method are required to ensure superior direction. The one who is inspired has been infused and enthused by others' thoughts and feelings. When inspired, it feels like breathing new air. Moreno used to say that the director should be the most spontaneous person in the room. Spontaneity is an infectious quality. In order to be spontaneous the director must first deal with his or her own warm-up. Then, as an inspirer, the director:

1. has an optimistic and affirmative view of the group potential;
2. is self-confident and gives the group the feeling that something positive will happen;
3. creates moments when all is possible: the director is able to create an atmosphere of potential magic;
4. creates an atmosphere where the unknown, the unspoken, the unborn, that which didn't happen is as important as what actually occurred in life itself. Psychodrama particularly is about what didn't happen, what life didn't give the opportunity to do.
5. must have a true sense of play, fun, freshness and embody the humour of life as well as the pathos;
6. knows Moreno's original ideas, hopes and inspirations and is able to transfer these into action;
7. must have the ability to take risks, to encourage, to stimulate and, at times, to provoke clients into therapeutic action;
8. must be able to engender in others the free-flowing of the creative and spontaneous spirit that promotes change.

Some of the most exciting and rewarding moments described in this book were not carefully planned, but occurred as the result of creative, spontaneous and inspired moments. Ken Sprague's descriptions of his groups with severely handicapped young people demonstrate how, with solid techniques at his disposal linked to his knowledge of psychodrama, he was able to inspire young people to new heights of pleasure and help them develop interpersonal skills. Anne Ancelin Schützenberger was able to make the inspired leap from the use of psychodrama as a treatment for psychological pain to a process that has life-saving potential for those dying of malignant physical disease. Her experience as a classical psychodramatist allowed her to take the risks of working with clients living with the fear and expectation of imminent death. In the chapters on psychodrama with adolescents, the authors demonstrate how by creative and inspired moves supported by their knowledge of this client group, they were able to adapt the processes of psychodrama and group analysis to the complex and demanding needs of the acting out adolescent. Peter Pitzele contains adolescent anxiety by using the calming distance of metaphor and the inner psychological world. Sarah Willis contains the same anxieties by keeping the drama at a slight distance from the adolescents' intense identification and thus allowing a fluid and creative therapeutic session to develop. Barbara Jean Quin uses her own experiences and self-knowledge to help her in her work supporting and encouraging other professionals.

All the psychodramatists who describe their work in this book have, at

3

different times in their therapeutic work, taken risks. They have allowed their own creativity and inspiration free rein such that their professional work has changed and developed and they have been able to assist clients that many would consider difficult if not impossible to help.

Preconceived notions about the best or only way to help should be discarded. The director must be open to the needs of the other in that particular session at that particular moment. If the therapist has to prove that something is true, separate from the perceived truth of the client, then the ability to work in tandem is lost. The mutual working rhythm of director and client is particularly important. Many people with special needs have a great loneliness that necessitates the therapist working *with* them and not *for* them. The director needs to use the group, which, if not used, will feel unseen. Psychodrama is a group process, not one-to-one therapy in a group setting. To honour the expressive capacity in the group helps individuals to honour their own ability to dare to express something from within themselves.

The therapeutic work described in this book demonstrates the need for technique to be supported by theory; together they underpin inspired and creative psychodramatic work. All the authors have had training in psychodrama. Without the ability to use classical techniques fluently, they would, no doubt, have stumbled and faltered in their attempts to work with their difficult clients. Without a psychological theory to explain human interactions, the directors may have become lost in their attempts to help.

Different techniques and psychological theories can be used to help and support the psychodramatists in their work. Ken Sprague uses his years of experience as a graphic artist to inspire his young autistic friends. Sarah Willis draws upon her experience as a professional actress in her ability to enthuse and direct the intense dramas in which her adolescents participate. Although a group psychotherapist, she never forgets that she is also an actress. Like any artist, one can only take risks if the basic skills are well and truly mastered.

In the intense and, at times, threatening context of a prison for men convicted of serious offences, Jinnie Jefferies may well have lost her professional and personal nerve had she not had her well-found and coherent abilities in psychodramatic method to rely on, supported by the theories of John Bowlby.

Joke Meillo draws upon her experience and training as an individual psychodynamic therapist to draw out her anorexic clients and help them 'work through' their difficulties. She argues that a professionally and therapeutically potent mixture can be created by the integration of the social aspects of living in a therapeutic community, the powerful intrapsychic aspects of protagonist-centred psychodrama and the potential for working through in the transference in individual psychoanalytic psychotherapy. Her ability to draw upon these various strands of her own personal professional life 'warm-up' to her work allows her to help disturbed young people like Irene.

Gillie Ruscombe-King also draws upon her theoretical knowledge of transference, demonstrating that certain individuals are likely (because of their past history) to enter very intense relationships with their therapists; relationships that may well deny reality and thus enter the transferential world with the repetition of early experiences. Her ability to keep this possibility in mind frees her from the danger of overintense, often negative and unproductive relationships developing between her clients and herself.

Anne Bannister and also Elaine Eller Goldman and Kit Wilson demonstrate that their inspiration is linked to their technical and theoretical knowledge of their particular client groups. The sexually abused child and the child of alcoholic parents have developed very specific ways of coping with the world. Knowledge of these ways and their rules of human interaction guide the inspired work of these directors towards their therapeutic goal. Ignorance of these rules might result in precipitate and unproductive confrontations resulting in groups collapsing and the individual's premature departure from treatment.

In this book, experienced practising psychodramatists describe how they have linked their own personal and theoretical warm-ups to their work with their ability to be inspired and creative. It is not an encyclopaedia; many of the contributors raise issues of theory and practice that can be discussed only briefly. It is hoped that the reader, if inspired, will pursue lines of thought that take their fancy. Our authors are by no means unique; there are many other psychodramatists who work in equally creative, inspiring and technically sound ways. We hope, however, that the selection of clinical work described in this book will inspire our readership, not only to develop their own technical prowess as dramatists, but also to integrate this with their professional experiences and with theories from other sources. With such skills, many pained, damaged and unhappy individuals may be helped. It is only when the individual is freed to be creative and spontaneous that productive, technically excellent and inspired therapeutic help can be developed.

Further reading

This list contains all the references on psychodrama. Other references are provided chapter by chapter.

Blatner, A. (1973) *Acting In – Practical Applications of Psychodramatic Methods*, New York: Springer Publishing.

Blatner, Adam and Blatner, Alec (1988) *The Foundations of Psychodrama. History Theory and Practice*, New York: Springer Publishing.

Feasy, D. (1984) 'Psychodrama is group psychotherapy', *The Midland Journal of Psychotherapy* (2): 30–7.

Goldman, E. E. and Morrison, D. S. (1984) *Psychodrama: Experience and Process*, Dubuque, Iowa: Kendal Hunt.

Greenberg, I. (1975) *Psychodrama: Theory and Therapy*, New York: Behavioural Publications.

Holmes, P. (1984) 'Boundaries or chaos: an outpatient psychodrama group for adolescents', *Journal of Adolescence* 6: 333–46.

Holmes, P. (1987) revised version in J. Coleman (ed.) *Working with Troubled Adoles-*

cents, London: Academic Press.

Leveton, E. (1977) *Psychodrama for the Timid Clinician*, New York: Springer Publishing.

Marineau, R. F. (1989) *Jacob Levy Moreno 1889–1974*, London: Tavistock/Routledge.

Moreno, J. L. (1953) *Who Shall Survive? The Foundations of Sociometry, Group Psychotherapy and Psychodrama*, Beacon, NY: Beacon House.

Moreno, J. L. (1960) *The Sociometry Reader*, Beacon, NY: Beacon House.

Moreno, J. L. (1972) *Psychodrama Vol. I*, Beacon, NY: Beacon House.

Moreno, J. L. (1973) *The Theatre of Spontaneity*, Beacon, NY: Beacon House.

Moreno, J. L. (1987) in J. Fox (ed.) *The Essential Moreno*, New York: Springer Publishing.

Moreno, J. L. and Moreno, Z. T. (1969) *Psychodrama Vol. III*, Beacon, NY: Beacon House.

Moreno, J. L. and Moreno, Z. T. (1975) *Psychodrama Vol. II*, Beacon, NY: Beacon House.

Moreno, J. L., Moreno, Z. T. and Moreno, J. D. (1964) *The First Psychodramatic Family*, Beacon, NY: Beacon House.

Moreno, Z. T. (1966) 'Sociogenesis of individuals and groups' in *The International Handbook of Group Psychotherapy*, New York: Philosophical Library Inc.

Moreno, Z. T. (1987) 'Psychodrama, role theory, and the concept of the social atom', in *The Evolution of Psychotherapy*, New York: Brunner Mazel.

Powell, A. (1976) 'Object relations in the psychodrama group', *Group Analysis* 19: 125–38.

Storr, A. (1977) *Psychodrama: Rehearsal for Living*, Chicago: Nelson-Hall.

Treadwell, T., Stein, S. and Kumar, V. (1988) 'A review of psychodramatic warm-up techniques for children, adolescents and adults', *Journal of the British Psychodrama Association* 13 (1).

Williams, A. (1989) *The Passionate Technique. Strategic Psychodrama with Individuals, Families and Groups*, London and New York: Tavistock/Routledge.

Yablonsky, L. (1976) *Psychodrama. Resolving Emotional Problems Through Role Playing*, New York: Basic Books.

Chapter two

Classical psychodrama

An overview

Paul Holmes

The authors in this book have adapted the methods of classical psychodrama to assist them in their work with different client groups. This chapter will present, for the reader unfamiliar with the technique, an overview of classical (or protagonist-centred) psychodrama, in which the action proceeds from the periphery of a situation to the roots of the cause of the difficulties of one member of the group. A list of further reading is given at the end of the chapter.

The authors of this book have described how they have developed (using their professional skills and individual creativity) the therapeutic method of psychodrama in their work with different client groups. I believe that the ability to work creatively and successfully in, at times, difficult circumstances is based not only on the individual practitioner's creativity and inspiration, but also on a firm understanding of and ability to practise the basic techniques of psychodrama. Adaptation or developments can only be successfully undertaken when the core skills are firmly under the belt of the practitioner.

Psychodrama is an action method of group psychotherapy created and developed by J. L. Moreno (born Jacob Moreno Levi in 1889 in Bucharest, Rumania). His family moved to Vienna when he was a child and he qualified there as a doctor in 1917. Initially he worked as a general physician with a particular interest in people's emotional and social relationships. In 1921 (the date Moreno records as the beginning of psychodrama) he developed a project he called Die Stegreiftheater (the Theatre of Spontaneity). From these roots developed his interest in the use of drama and social interaction as methods of psychotherapy. In 1925 he emigrated to America (changing his name to J. L. Moreno) and continued to develop psychodrama and group psychotherapy, opening his own private mental hospital in Beacon, New York in 1936. This hospital became the focus for development and training in psychodrama until its closure in 1982 (see Blatner and Blatner 1988).

Psychodrama is a method of group psychotherapy that uses a dramatic format and theatrical terms. Moreno also considered psychodrama to be a method of living not limited to the realm of therapy. He described five basic elements:

The protagonist – who is the focus of a psychodrama, being that member of the group to explore their personal issues in a particular session.

The director – who, in collaboration with the protagonist, directs and facilitates any individual drama. This individual might be considered to be the 'therapist'.

The auxiliary egos – members of the group (or co-therapists) who play significant individuals from the protagonist's life, thus helping the enactment of the drama.

The audience – consisting of other group members not directly involved in the enactment. Individuals, even if not directly involved in the drama, remain actively and positively involved in the process and may gain both enjoyment and benefit from the session.

The stage – in most cases simply a space in a room large enough to allow some physical movement, although at Beacon, Moreno built a more complex theatrical structure, which allowed the use of different stage levels in the enactment.

A classical psychodrama consists of three stages: warm-up, enactment and sharing. Each of these is essential to the complete psychodramatic process.

Warm-up

Warm-up has several significant functions:

1. To stimulate the creativity and spontaneity of group members. Moreno was particularly concerned that psychodrama should be seen as a process in which individuals (both group members and director) are encouraged to develop and use their own potential for spontaneity and creativity. He believed that these psychic processes enabled the individual to find their own ways forward (or solutions) to internal and external difficulties in their lives.
2. To facilitate interactions within the group, increasing a sense of trust and membership through techniques that encourage interactions between individuals (for instance, sharing of names, sharing of experiences, physical activities that involve some degree of touch or non-verbal communication). This process of warm-up develops the cohesiveness of the group, while at the same time allowing members to get some sense of the various strengths and qualities of individuals within the group. This phase of a psychodrama has many similarities to the processes that might be observed in an encounter group or a dramatherapy session, or as we 'warm up' to any daily activity.
3. To help members focus on personal issues on which they wish to 'do some work' in the psychodrama session. It is hoped that one (or more) people will emerge from the protagonist – (or individual need) –

centred, warm-up process and put themselves forward to become the focus of the enactment.

An experienced director will have a large repertoire of possible warm-up techniques. However, the director may also (using his or her own creativity) develop new warm-ups that seem particularly relevant to the group with whom he or she is working.

Selecting the protagonist

At the end of the warm-up, usually one or more members of the group will have identified (with varying degrees of precision and certainty) issues that they wish to pursue further in the session. They will be encouraged to put themselves forward to become the protagonist (from the Greek 'the leading or first actor'). The individual who will take on this central role for the session is then selected. It may be very apparent who the protagonist will be (one particular individual may demonstrate greater emotional readiness than the others), or it may be that several group members are sufficiently warmed up to put themselves forward. In this situation there are various techniques whereby the director and the group identify one individual who will be protagonist for the session that is under way (group members may vote on whom they wish to become protagonist, the potential protagonists may sort out the decision amongst themselves or the director may make his or her own decision about whom he or she wants to work with and is most appropriate for this particular session). Whatever the process, it is important that the protagonist is chosen in such a way that he or she has the approval and support of the group.

Enactment

The psychodrama then moves on to the process of enactment, in which the protagonist (with the support and help of the director) explores the issues highlighted during the warm-up. There is no script, the drama is spontaneous, created in the moment by the protagonist, the auxiliary egos and the director. This phase of the psychodrama will usually start with the protagonist and their director clarifying which issues are to be worked on, in a discussion that can be considered a form of contract between director and protagonist. The first statements by the protagonist must be listened to carefully (for example, 'I always have difficulties with the men in my life' or 'The warm-up reminded me of how upset I was about the TV programme on sexual abuse last night'). The 'contract' between director and protagonist gives a focus for the exploration of specific issues in the forthcoming session (Marcia Karp, personal communication).

Psychodrama is intrinsically a theatrical process and the enactment must move rapidly into drama. An initial scene is agreed upon between director and protagonist and the physical setting is described and laid out on the stage area.

Detailed props are not required; televisions, furniture and walls may all be indicated verbally or by the use of simple chairs and cushions. It is, however, essential that the protagonist describes the physical space in some detail, a process whereby he or she becomes increasingly in touch with the memories and emotions associated with that space. The protagonist is encouraged into action (talking in the present tense when referring to events from the past). The director discovers which individuals in the person's life are essential for the scene to be enacted (e.g. parents, brothers and sisters, employers) and will ask the protagonist to select other members of the group who could play these auxiliary egos. There is no doubt that the selection of individuals to play specific auxiliary egos is a far from random process. Through tele (the two-way flow of feelings between people – see Blatner and Blatner 1988: 129; Fox 1987: 40) a protagonist will sense which colleagues in the group have the potential to play important people in their drama. The boundaries of age and gender have little importance; the choice of people to play particular roles being based on subtler and more complex factors.

Once the scene is set and cast enroled, the drama continues. The interaction between protagonist and auxiliaries may initially attempt to recreate external (historical) reality, starting with a scene from the present (e.g. the protagonist and his wife). Once the psychological reasons for enacting this interaction have become apparent, the director may move to an earlier relationship in the protagonist's life (for example, by saying: 'Have you ever got into these difficulties before?'). The next scene may, for example, involve the protagonist and a girlfriend during adolescence. The psychodrama may then move on to an interaction from childhood (for example, the protagonist and his mother). Each scene is linked to the next by a logic specific to the protagonist's psychology and difficulties (see Goldman and Morrison 1984). Each scene from the drama must be consistent with the protagonist's memories of past events. Should the enactment stray from this course, the director must assist the protagonist and auxiliary egos to increase the apparent reality.

The director may, however (using clinical judgement), move scenes into an area of 'surplus reality'. In such interactions events may be staged and words spoken that never happened in reality (for example, experiencing care and good mothering in the psychodrama when in historical reality their family life was abusive and barren) or situations enacted that can never happen in the future (for example, the protagonist talking to a parent who died many years ago, or meeting someone with whom they may never have a close relationship).

In the final stages of the enactment the director may move the drama back to the interactions (in a scene from the present day) with which the session started. The protagonist will now have his or her behaviour informed by both feelings and thoughts from the preceding scenes, allowing the creation of different solutions to the difficulties in their present relationships. This process may be called 'role rehearsal' allowing the protagonist to become more confident in his or her handling of situations, although what is enacted is not necessarily a rehearsal for life. It may be a source of great relief to become very angry (in the psychodrama) to an employer or parent. Such expressions may, however, be less desirable in life outside the session; more appropriate ways of showing feelings may need to be developed.

The director may, however, decide that some other cathartic or dramatic episode may be developed that will leave the protagonist with a sense that their drama has been completed (at least for that day!).

There are various techniques at the disposal of the director to assist them with their task of helping the protagonist. These include:

1. *Role reversal*, in which the protagonist plays 'the other' with the auxiliary ego playing the protagonist is the engine which drives the psychodrama. This reversal has several uses in the psychodramatic process – it enables other group members to get a more complete picture of the protagonist's view of important people in their life through their dramatisation of these individuals; it enables the protagonist to experience the world from the viewpoint of the other and in this position to receive the impact of him/herself (now played by the auxiliary) as experienced by the world. This experience can be very powerful, salutary and therapeutic. Role reversal may also be used to encourage the protagonist to develop self-control, should a protagonist be experiencing intense and perhaps violent feelings towards 'the other'. Role reversal immediately puts the protagonist into an alternative role, a technique that encourages self-control and also gives the latter the experience of him/herself viewed more objectively. Role reversal is a way of transcending the habitual limitations of egocentricity (Blatner and Blatner 1988).

2. *Doubling*, a technique in which the protagonist is joined by another member of the group, who becomes an active participant in the enactment, standing close to the protagonist and getting body clues by adopting the same physical movements. The double's role is to function as a support in presenting the protagonist's position and feeling. Through his/her empathic bond, the double is able to express thoughts and feelings that the protagonist is repressing or censoring in the psychodrama. Once expressed, these thoughts and feelings may be accepted by the protagonist (in which case he or she will rephrase the sentiments in his or her own words) or rejected as being incorrect (in which case the double will retract certain statements and learn more about the protagonist).

   Such situations may, however, help the protagonist to reframe the comments: 'No, it's not that, it's ...', allowing him or her to develop self-knowledge. Indeed, with time, the protagonist may discover that the statements of the double were more relevant than was at first thought.

3. *Surplus reality*, defining those times in a psychodramatic enactment

when scenes and events are dramatised (in Zerka Moreno's words) 'that have never happened, will never happen or can never happen' (personal communication). The ability to experience these scenes (with the associated fears, emotions, fantasies and wishes) is one of the magical strengths of the psychodramatic process. The very act of having experiences in surplus reality is perhaps one of the unique therapeutic potentials of psychodrama.

4. *Mirroring*, a process in which the protagonist is replaced in the drama by another member of the group, allowing him or her to stand aside and watch the drama unfold. This encourages in the protagonist a more objective awareness of him/herself in interactions with others.

5. *Closure* (or completion), the process whereby the dramatic enactment of the protagonist's conflicts and life situations are brought full circle. Goldman and Morrison (1984) have described the structure of a psychodrama session as often starting with present issues, then recent experiences of the protagonist. As the drama progresses, scenes from the past are enacted, going back into childhood (or indeed infancy). In the latter stages of the psychodrama, the process may be completed by moving forward in time and repeating the scenes in the present that prompted the psychodrama, but now in a version informed and altered by the emotional and cognitive experiences of the psychodrama. For example, a man who may start his psychodrama discussing perpetual rows with his employer may, in the enactment, explore difficulties with his father. In the closure or completion of a psychodrama he will now repeat the scenes with this employer, hopefully managing this reality in a different way through his increased understanding and experience of the links between his relationship difficulties with his father (in the past) and with his employer (in the present).

Sharing

Sharing is the final stage of the psychodramatic group process, in which all the members are encouraged to share their thoughts and feelings, as well as their similarities and identifications with the protagonist. It is very important that in this process group members do not 'interpret' the behavioural or emotional difficulties of the protagonist, who (it must be accepted) may well be in a very vulnerable state. (In a discussion with Marcia Karp, J. L. Moreno likened the protagonist during the sharing to a patient in the recovery room following a major operation.) The sharing process also allows those who have been auxiliary egos to derole. It is a very powerful experience to play, for example, a dying or dead parent and it is crucial that the individual has a chance as him/herself to express certain feelings about having taken this role. It must be noted that these feelings may often be positive, even when having taken on a potentially negative or destructive role; it can be releasing to assume a role one does not usually adopt.

The process of sharing allows the protagonist (who may have felt very isolated in his or her dilemma) to feel links of commonality between him/herself and others. It also allows those in the group who may well have been very stirred up by the protagonist's enactments to share with the group their own powerful feelings and thoughts. This process allows the director (as group leader) to notice which members are still feeling particularly vulnerable, to support them and encourage further exploration, perhaps in subsequent psychodramas. The open sharing of these issues within the group encourages and facilitates support, caring and understanding between group members.

It is through the psychodramatic enactment of an individual's life (past, present and future) that the individual is able (using his or her own creativity and spontaneity) to come to terms with past life events or to develop future life skills. Zerka Moreno describes the process as 'a way of living without being punished for making mistakes' (personal communication).

J. L. Moreno defined psychodrama as the science which explores the truth through dramatic methods:

> One of its objectives is to teach people to resolve their conflicts in a microcosm of the world (the group), free of the conventional restraints by acting out their problems, ambitions, dreams and fears. It emphasises maximum involvement with others; in investigating conflicts in their immediate present form; in addition to dealing with the subject's early memories and perceptions.
>
> (J.L. Moreno 1963)

References

Blatner, Adam and Blatner, Alec (1988) *The Foundations of Psychodrama. History, Theory and Practice*, New York: Springer Publishing.

Fox, J. (1987) (ed.) *The Essential Moreno, Writings on Psychodrama Group Method and Spontaneity by J. L. Moreno MD*, New York: Springer Publishing.

Goldman, E. E. and Morrison, D. S. (1984) *Psychodrama: Experience and Process*, Dubuque, Iowa: Kendal Hunt.

Moreno, J. L. (1963) 'Reflections on my methods of group psychotherapy', Ciba Symposium II: 148–57.

Further reading

More detailed descriptions of the classical psychodramatic process may be found in the following books.

Blatner, A. (1973) *Acting In – Practical Applications of Psychodramatic Method*, New York: Springer Publishing.

Leveton, E. (1977) *Psychodrama for the Timid Clinician*, New York: Springer Publishing.

Storr, A. (1977) *Psychodrama. Rehearsal for Living*, Chicago: Nelson-Hall.

Yablonsky, L. (1976) *Psychodrama. Resolving Emotional Problems Through Role Playing*, New York: Basic Books.

Chapter three

Adolescents inside out
Intrapsychic psychodrama

Peter Pitzele

Intrapsychic psychodrama: conceptual scenery

> Roles do not emerge from the self, but the self may emerge from roles.
> (Moreno (1972) *Psychodrama Volume I*: 157)

In this compressed and gnomic sentence from J. L. Moreno (1972), I find a serviceable epigraph for the reflections that follow. There are other possible texts from which to find inspiration and technique, but this will do quite nicely to indicate a source in Moreno's writing for the ideas about personality and the methods for psychodramatic exploration this chapter will describe. The idea that roles precede the self is code and coda for some approaches to work I have done with adolescents.

I understand these words of Moreno's in a developmental sense: that each of us is first a role-playing, role-taking, role-composed being. Whatever Moreno means by 'self' it is not the Eastern or Platonic notion of a pre-existing essence, an acorn self from which all roles derive. Rather, self emerges from role playing rather than being its origin. Just how or just what this self is I shall suggest at the end of this chapter, though I have not been able to determine a definition from reading Moreno. Nor, for my purposes here, is a definition particularly relevant; rather my interest operationally is in his conception of a polyvalent identity and his emphasis on the psyche as being in some way 'a many' rather than 'a one'.

Moreno appears to be saying that, before any self emerges from our many roles, we are beings of many parts. What Moreno calls our roles are expressions of identity inseparable from contexts, reciprocities, interpersonal matrices. The old notion of an ego, an 'I', a self is challenged in his dictum. He seems to be saying that we might well regard ourselves as a collective of roles, as if we were a kind of theatre company, containing within ourselves many possible actors. In other words it might be useful to talk about the individual not as an 'I' but as a 'we'.

Though Moreno uses the word 'role' to describe the definable units of possible action that compose us, I am using the terms 'part', 'character' and 'role' synonymously. Some of these are full-blown representations in the world, others are shadowy, imagined or recurrent only in our dreams. Moreover, beyond

15

conceiving of the psyche as a collective, I do not really know what kind of spatial image to give it. Sometimes it seems levelled or layered; sometimes I think of it as a series of receding planes, sometimes fragments, sometimes holographic. Perhaps the psyche may be seen best mythologically, as a realm in which to find anything and everything.

In any event, this idea about us – that we are each a plurality of roles or parts – is a highly dynamic vision. Not only are we, at any given moment when seen in cross-section, a complex and simultaneity of parts, but through time parts or roles we play evolve, mature, wane, go dormant, die out. We are, in that sense, not just a plurality but a community, an 'Our Town', a mythological realm, in which may be found characters or beings in various stages of development, some mutually communicative, some isolated, some nascent, others moribund. There are factions, schisms, partisanships, passions and occasionally, briefly, accord. In short, to use one of his favoured images, each of us may be thought of as a group.

This way of thinking gives rise to a particular type of psychodramatic procedure that has been called intrapsychic. It may perhaps best be defined by reference to other types of psychodramatic procedure, which do not rest on a different theory of personality, but rather, focus differently through that theory.

There is a kind of psychodrama in which the protagonist sustains one principal role, part or character throughout the drama. He or she may engage in numerous role reversals, but returns to the same role. For example, if the story of the drama pertains to the relationship between a male protagonist and his parents, then the central role, the hero's part, is the role of the son. That story may move in time from present to past to future; it may move through various scenes, but the common thread will be the filial one. Such a psychodrama usually borrows the theatrical conventions belonging to narrative and realistic drama: it tells a story; it draws its materials from personal memory; it sets scenes; it calls upon actual characters (mother, father, siblings, etc.); and it often issues in the cathartic expression of feelings. Such a psychodrama may be contested by the perceptions of significant others, inasmuch as there may be different versions of the same scene as experienced by different characters within it, but unless our protagonist is delusional, his drama may be seen to refer to a verifiable social context. Such a psychodrama belongs to the world of interpersonal reality.

A second type of psychodrama is surreal, illusional (if not delusional) fantastic (as in belonging to fantasy). It is not merely the drama of dreams, though that may be its model, but is rather a psychodrama in which the laws of fantasy replace those of our everyday reality. In such a drama the protagonist may start out as the son-in-quest-of-the-father and become, for a time, a dog, a tree, a witch, and all these roles – rather than being other – are projections of the protagonist's imagination. Here, just as in psychodramatic dreamwork, the protagonist role-reverses with every part of the fantasy, and allows the fantasy to shift his shape, under the assumption that he *is* every part of the fantasy. The personal self in the dream or fantasy is fictive, and the truth to be found in this drama comes from exploring *all* the facets of imagery displayed by the imagination. The end of surreal psychodrama (whether night dream or day) is owning the whole dream. This type of psychodrama belongs to the world of what Moreno called 'surplus reality'. It may be thought of as psychodrama in the service of metaphor.

A third type of psychodrama is what has been called intrapsychic. In it there is rarely a story to be told, even a story as fragmented and strange as that of a dream. The intrapsychic psychodrama may be thought of as a kind of action sociometry exploring the individual-as-group. It seeks to discriminate roles and inner voices, inner parts and characters with their tendencies, pulls and counter-pulls as they exist at a given moment in time within the individual-as-group. Intrapsychic work aims to uncover, even as a geologist might uncover, the strata of a personality, working from surface through the layers, going down and going in. It takes as given the concept of personal complexity, plurality, groupness (the roles that precede the self) and undertakes to determine organisations and purposes within the group.

All three types of psychodrama have their appropriate occasions. I have found, however, that psychodramatic encounters of this third kind – intrapsychic psychodramas – have been most effective in working with adolescents, and the techniques and rationales for this work form the body of this chapter.

Adolescent presentations and intrapsychic warm-ups

I have already said that I have never found to my satisfaction what Moreno meant by the word self, or at what stage of personal development he imagines the self appears. I would guess that when he viewed the adolescent, he saw the personality in a pre-self stage, saw the role player in full flourish and might himself have had occasion to use an intrapsychic instrument to explore the parts of his subject.

My own experience of working with adolescents is drawn in large part from a clinical setting. In the past seven years, while I have worked in communities and schools with many kinds of young people from the gifted to the impaired, I have principally practised psychodrama in an in-patient psychiatric setting – Four Winds Hospital in Katonah, New York. Though the hospital contains many different types of patient population, there are a number of fifteen-bed units or cottages devoted to medium- and long-term adolescent care.

Young people at Four Winds come into treatment for a variety of reasons. Many come with substance-abuse problems serious enough to have taken them out of school, brought them to the attention of the courts and remanded them to our hospital for intensive, remedial therapy. Many come as identified patients from dysfunctional homes. Some carry the scars of failed adoptions; increasing numbers, the wounds of sexual abuse. All suffer from crippled self-esteem. Their relations to peers and adults are full of mistrust, denial, guardedness, and fear.

Each of these young people has a manner of presenting him/herself. I have come to think of them as wearing masks. These masks take many forms. Some appear world-weary and bored like Bert, who will yawn when telling you about his mother's suicide. Others are choleric, constantly fuming, like Willie who, on the day he left the hospital after 6 months, chose to pick a fight with his peers rather than feel other parts of himself – the sadness of departing, the fear at taking the next step. There are girls like Silvia, who, wearing her hair long over her eyes, seems like the hunted animal in the undergrowth, or Emily, who shrugs 'I don't know' in response to every question, or Paula, punk and purple, who distracts us from her scarred arms by her outlandish get-up. There is Denise – tough, intellectual, confrontive – who intimidates her peers; or Loni, street-smart, wise guy, con artist extraordinaire.

They are characters, each of them characters in a literary or theatrical sense, and if we get too much caught up in their characters, we may never get past the surface, the mask, to the group within. I present them here knowing they will call to mind counterparts in any reader's mind.

It is important, I think, to put a kind of frame around an adolescent and to consider the presented self as a creation. Furthermore, drawing on my experience within the hospital I have noticed that the more disturbed the adolescent, the more powerful the persona that faces and attempts to outface me in the psychodrama group. Call the mask resistance. Call resistance a mask.

I have found it useful to look at these faces as masks because I can then be nimble in meeting them and reaching through to what they conceal. And of course, to recognise these faces as facades, as masks, and the adolescent as a mask-maker puts me in my own world of psychodrama, a world of plays, roles, parts and instead of blocking me, gives me ideas for unmasking.

I recognise, too, from a clinical perspective, that these masks are designed to help a young person cope, and for that reason may be thought of as 'coping masks'. They have origins; they were created to serve a purpose; they have a story to tell all bound up with feelings too powerful to sustain, feelings that require the service of a mask to conceal, to freeze, to split from. Thus the mask functions as a guardian and yet also as a gateway to the complex, many-mooded, many-storied realm inside these troubled adolescents. If I can meet the mask with my spontaneity, then like some quester seeking to gain admittance to a secret world, I may pass to the interior.

In working with adolescents, my first move is to meet the mask for what it in fact is – a role. And, from the point of view of technique, I do this with two chairs, one placed behind the other. The first chair is for the mask, the second chair is for whatever might be going on behind it. These two chairs allow me to announce to the client and to the group that I know I am facing a mask and that the world behind it, under it, within it, the intrapsychic world, is the one I wish to explore psychodramatically.

Interlude one

Take Bert. At the beginning of every group Bert looks at his watch, manages a great yawn and lets me know he's 'bored'. One day I have had enough. Bert has managed to infect the group and everybody says 'I'm bored'. I place a chair in the centre of the group and ask Bert to sit in it. I give him his line: just say 'I'm bored', and I remind him to look at his watch and if he can manage a yawn, to yawn loudly.

As he comes on stage to play this role of himself-as-bored, I place behind him the second chair. As he plays the bored role, I invite any member of the group to come forward and imagine what might be going on 'behind' the mask of boredom. Always the group responds with alacrity and insight:

'I'm not bored, I'm scared.'

'I don't know how to work in this group; I feel resentful that other people get the attention.'

'I think people will laugh at me if I don't play it cool.'

'Yawning and looking at my watch help me to keep myself from feeling anything in this group.'

These kinds of statements are typical of the brainstorming 'inside' work an adolescent group is capable of, and their participation here may be thought of as a kind of group doubling. Bert sits and listens to these advocates fishing for what he may be concealing in himself, even from himself, behind his mask. Believe me, he is not bored as this goes on. I can easily move directly into action from this point with Bert as he might engage any of these auxiliaries in an encounter, now facing what he had previously hidden.

Or I may ask Bert to choose someone to play his bored role. I let him watch the interplay between first chair, mask and second chair. To do this is to make our drama about resistance itself, about masking. To shift the metaphor, we may keep the drama at the gateway to the inner world. Depending on the group and cues too context-specific to identify here, I will choose to have Bert work as protagonist, or in the mirror position where he can watch, or, of course, any of the auxiliaries may become focal points where I may use their projections as points of departure. Brief interviews with various participants extend the warm-up and help me to read the group. In any case a warm-up of this sort serves to get us started 'in'. Bert has had his mask pulled aside and glimpses the confusing world of feeling that lies behind it.

Or I remember long-haired, shy-eyed Emily with her whispered 'I don't know' every time she is asked a question. So fragile she seems, so ready to bolt, so desperate for invisibility. the same strategy may work with her.

'Choose someone to play the "I-don't-know Emily" ' I ask her.

'I don't know who to choose,' she says. But she is already smiling in spite of herself, and I say 'Perfect' to her, reframing her resistance as compliance to my request, letting her words be the lines for her role. No sooner has the mask been named than it starts to slip. Her smile tells me that. I may allow her to remain where she is and ask someone in the group to play Emily I-don't-knowing. I establish the second chair. I invite the group to imagine possible feeling states in the second chair:

'I'm too confused to know what to say.'

'I want to be left alone.'

'I want someone to notice me; this is the way I do it.'

'I'm scared to know what I know.'

'I'm so *** angry; this is the way I keep it quiet.'

Depending on the spontaneity of the group, each of these one-liners may be developed. Emily watches enthralled. How can she not? What is more interesting than seeing how accurately or inaccurately others perceive us? And of course, these doubling statements may awaken feelings in her, call forth parts in her she didn't know she had. While at the same time she is safe. She can pass it all off. She can leave the group. But she does not. And of course all this second-chair work allows the community to express in an active way its concern to draw her forth, to get to know her behind her coping mask.

I may ask Emily to put a hand on the shoulder of any of these second-chair auxiliaries and by so doing to identify any one or ones that sound like her. She may then have a chance to explore one part in depth. She may also wish not to take up the invitation. No problem. I know, she knows, and the group knows that we are in the realm behind the mask; it doesn't matter whether we are right; we are establishing the existence of this realm. We are opening up a territory. And, of course, I have six available protagonists each of whom has warmed up through Emily and whose second-chair work, whose doubling statements, may lead us inside each of them.

Often, the second-chair work that comes from members of the community derives from their masks. It will likely be the angry Willie who imagines anger in Emily, or the attention-seeking Paula who projects attention seeking onto the withdrawn Emily. A pose one patient may be stuck in may be, for another, a liberation. The anger that comes so easily to Willie may be an achievement for the wispy Emily if she is able to own the 'Willie-anger' inside her; conversely, Emily's deep sense of confusion may be an important, though difficult, 'character' for the quick-triggered Willie to feel. It would slow him down and open him up to the confusions he carries inside. As members of the community find some of the unexpressed parts of themselves expressed by others in the community, they may find legitimacy and even role modelling for their own experiments in awakening those roles. This cross-fertilisation enhances the cohesiveness of the group, and unaccepted members of the group may be found valuable.

A community may wear a mask. Everyone may be sunk in a sullen silence as thick as a fog. I cannot see inside it. I may place a chair for the silence and ask a group member to sit in it silently. Sometimes no-one will. I can. Or a staff member, if I have one, may play the role of 'the silence of the group'.

'What is this silence saying?' I wonder aloud as I place a second chair behind the first. Even then no-one may take the second chair; so I do, venturing possibilities, and after each, asking if anyone feels like playing out that role:

'Just leave us alone; we had a heavy group this morning and we need a break.'

'Nobody trusts anybody here. I am the silence of mistrust.'

'I am the anger that's just behind the silence.'

'I am the hopelessness inside the silence.'

And so it goes.

I have had one or two groups where even this did not warm up the silence to speak. So I have sat facing the silence and asked it what it needed, and again, if the group has not been forthcoming of volunteers, I have imagined my own responses:

'I need to feel safe.'

'I need a rest, a story, a guided fantasy to a warm place.'

'I need to scream.'

'I want my Mommy.'

And if even these strategies have not dislodged the mask of silence that guards and protects the group from me and from itself, I join them and sit in their silence with my second chair. I allow myself, if ever a notion comes into my head, to occupy the second chair and speak:

'There is so much deadness in me; I feel numb....I am a silence full of tears like an underground river or a dark well...I am a silence full of dreams...I am a silence that wants to get high.'

There are other masks the community can co-create: masks of wild ungovernable energy, masks of enmity and back-stabbing, masks of false solidarity, singing and joking. But I know I am facing a mask if I feel that separation, that 'shut-outness' that a mask causes me to feel. Then I know I may use the method I have been describing, in any of its many ways, and that I am then likely to get *through* or *in*. Once in, I am in touch with what is authentic, felt. I then can take my lead from the warm-up of the individual and the group in any of a hundred directions.

I said earlier that the mask is a creative act of survival designed for coping. It has its own story to tell, and there are certain contexts that bring this mask back firmly – we might even say securely – into place. It is sometimes possible to examine this aspect of the mask: its provenance, and the situations where it had in the past been, or will in the future be, required. Whom do you wear this mask to face? What challenges you to need to put it on? There are many ways a psychodramatist pays respect to the mask and the mask-maker. Once visible as an artifact of the psyche, the mask will take us back to family stories, to trauma, and to fear. As we go back to them – and back is in – we take with us the second chair. We go back to the past. We also go in to the roles the past has formed. We take with us the second chair, and a third, a fourth and more. We will take the mask, the first chair with us, so that we may seek its protection if necessary.

These new chairs we fill with the parts from within; in them what was once repressed may be expressed now. Our chairs allow us to be concrete about what could be shown and what had to be hidden, about what is protected and protecting – for whom, from whom and why.

For the adolescent, this chair-behind-the-first feels risky, surely unfamiliar. The mask covers the wound. If they can learn to show the wound, it will heal, and the roles stunted by the wounding may flourish again. If not, the mask is a prison; our resistance an iron curtain. The mask is a role we're frozen in, and its very fixity indicates how raw, unexplored and undeveloped are the parts within. All the more necessary, then, is that type of psychodrama that introduces us to these roles-before-the-self in order that a self might form.

Hamlet: intrapsychic conventions and forms

The technique or stratagem of the second chair may serve, as it does frequently in my groups, as a warm-up. It is a way of fielding the presentations of the group or of individuals within it and framing those presentations in a way that allows psychodramatic work to occur. Further and most important, the second chair establishes the world-inside-us. To recognise what kind of a world that is, what forms and procedures are appropriate to its exploration, we can hardly do better for a model than reconsider Shakespeare's *Hamlet*.

Hamlet represents as complete a theatrical version as any I know of the complex 'world-inside-us'. It may be thought of as Shakespeare's one attempt to write an intrapsychic tragedy. And a number of its conventions, and indeed its very format, provide a rough dramatic archetype for intrapsychic psychodrama. That *Hamlet* is Shakespeare's quintessential play about adolescence and role playing only reinforces my sense that this drama of the world-inside-us is especially appropriate for young people.

The Freudian, Ernest Jones, comparing Hamlet to other Shakespearean princes and heroic figures (1976), accused him of being a hero unable to act. This is almost paradoxical, given the fact that the play is so full of acting and dramatic business, but Jones meant to point out that the scenes hardly mount, as do the scenes of other Shakespearean tragedies, towards any kind of inevitable and fatal conclusion. Irresolute, partial, complex to the end, Hamlet acts decisively only through a ruse to which he must respond. Matters beyond his control or will precipitate the swift denouement of the final scenes. As a play, *Hamlet* is charac-terised by a movement of plot that constantly doubles back on itself, unwinds what it has just wound, rethinks what it has just concluded and is, like the hero, 'sicklied o'er with the pale cast of thought'. This quality of 'thought' – this image of the play as a kind of meditation on complexity – could stand as an image for adolescent intrapsychic psychodrama.

Hamlet is an intrapsychic masterpiece. In scene after scene, the protagonist tries on a dazzling array of imagined roles. Images for himself abound in the play, as Hamlet contends with the demands of many different facets of himself. Rogue, peasant slave, soldier, courtier, friend, son, prince, heir, orphan, mourner, lover, poet, statesman, scholar, voyeur, duellist, madman, comedian, player, playwright, fool, murderer, outcast and hardest of all to accept, avenger – what character in dramatic literature shows us such a plurality of parts? What play so explores the range of a protagonist's roles rather than his fate in any one? It is no wonder that a group of travelling players enter Elsinore, for they are an objective image for the acting company – the player's universe – Hamlet finds within.

The external roles Hamlet plays *out* and the internal roles he imaginatively plays *in* make up the bulk of the drama. The play is about these self-castings, these castings of Hamlet as he searches for a self, an authentic, unified place from which to act. I would argue he never finds that self, either cut off too young, or embodying too fully Shakespeare's vision of man as a theatrical being, a role-player.

Shakespeare found that for his protagonist, Hamlet, the necessary theatrical convention, appropriate to his inwardness and complexity was the soliloquy. And just so the director of intrapsychic psychodrama discovers that soliloquy becomes a dominant convention.

The soliloquy is the most direct form of verbal self-presentation. Just as Hamlet fantasises himself in soliloquy, so each member of the internal world of the protagonist in a psychodrama takes his or her time at centre stage, each needing his or her speech. Provided by the protagonist in role reversal or created from the spontaneity of the auxiliaries and corrected by the protagonist, these soliloquies are one significant aspect of the creativity of intrapsychic psychodrama.

A second is the accompanying gesture or action. Hamlet, theatrical to his fingertips, is, in every production I have seen, a striker of poses. For him it is the very posing that seems to mock authentic action. Hamlet is too acutely aware that his actions are only acts. On the other hand, our adolescents, unlike Hamlet, need to develop new ways to act. For them, acting liberates. We may capitalise on the adolescent poseur by helping him or her to open up a larger repertoire of roles. The director of adolescent psychodrama does well not to mock the poses but to develop them as the actional aspects of a role.

Unlike the more realistic interpersonal psychodrama, the quality of acting in the intrapsychic psychodrama may tend towards stylisation because many of the internal characters have not yet been defined by the personal style of the protagonist: they are, in effect, potential roles, drawn from the conserve – imaginary or derived through literature, observation, popular culture – and may take on an almost allegorical appearance. The roles – of anger, of revenge, of mercy, of tenderness; the characters of poet, fool, or outcast – may be stylised in the psychodramatic production, sometimes with a touch of costume or a representative stance.

The spontaneity of the auxiliaries is more limited in this type of work than it is in interpersonal psychodrama, for the purpose is first and foremost to establish the inner world of the protagonist. Where group spontaneity and auxiliary work come into play, however, is in helping the protagonist to discover parts he or she might not be in touch with and allowing the protagonist the opportunity to try on (or is it try *in*?) these parts. The group helps to detect where one part actually starts to modulate into another. and where we need a separate role; the group also helps to coalesce parts into one.

A particular kind of learning and skilfulness is exercised in this procedure. The protagonist, faced with leaving the hospital, let us say, is in touch with his anger and his fear, and these two internal parts are brought on stage. It takes someone in the group to suggest to the protagonist that he may also be sad. (And often it is someone who is close to the protagonist and who feels sad at his leaving that will bring that part to our attention.) Then someone else in the group will suggest the protagonist might feel regrets, regrets about things unfinished, communications left incomplete. Again the person who offers this part may him/herself be feeling incompleteness with the protagonist, or it may be a projection the protagonist rejects or is unwilling to entertain. In both these cases, a very complex kind of imagining and empathising is going on, a role reversal in which a group member asks him or herself: 'What would I feel were I leaving?' and compares his or her answer to what the protagonist is discovering. Then the group member is challenged to soliloquise the part he or she uncovers and to come up, if accepted, and join the characters assembling on stage.

There is another role for the group and that comes under the heading of role training. In this case the protagonist may have need of a part, perhaps one of assertiveness or tenderness, and may be invited to choose someone from the group to model that part. Many a drama plays out its allotted time in developing a new role for the repertoire. This endeavour will interrupt and take precedence over the inventorying of the internal world.

In such a drama, the participants use one another with remarkable intuitiveness. The person selected to play 'assertiveness' or 'tenderness' embodies for the protagonist the qualities he or she needs for expanding his or her internal cast of characters. The protagonist's choice of the person in the group to play that part for him or her is a statement about what he or she sees in that person's cast of available characters.

Participants participate with one another in a literal sense of the word, taking part by taking parts, finding parts in themselves to find reflected in the parts of others. In this way a kind of universality is dramatised in the group; a sense of shared community, within and among, is celebrated.

Throughout all of this it will be the psychodramatist's first objective to dramatise the parts, by voice and gesture, so that the internal community comes dramatically alive. Formally, then, the tendency of intrapsychic psychodrama, as with *Hamlet*, is towards elaboration rather than simplification, and it may be an elaboration that, as Dr Jones suggests (1976), clogs action. But the purpose and process of intrapsychic psychodrama is the proliferation of parts; after the second chair one discovers an orchestra pit full of voices. As parts proliferate the director may feel that he or she is creating a chaos, and that is why, after the teasing out and presentation of parts as they may be evoked in response to some external stimulus – in *Hamlet* the murder of his father – in a patient, discharge from the hospital, the visit of a parent, the news of the death of a friend – the second task is sociometric, the giving of shape and structure to this cast of characters.

Interlude two

Let us return to Bert and Emily and advance beyond the warm-up along one possible directorial gambit.

As that group opened, I worked to reframe the resistance, the guardedness, by offering a chair for the mask and a second chair for whatever feelings the mask conceals. The group accepts, as it usually does, the possibilities for doubling and offers some statements that can be used in one of two ways. The doubling statements may be used as probes that take us *in* to Bert or Emily, or as projective statements offered by members of the group ostensibly about Bert or Emily but, in fact, self-disclosing. Whatever the activity, this is the warming-up of the group in response to the director's opening move, the placing of the chairs.

Let us imagine Bert accepts the doubling; it intrigues him. I can see by changes in posture that he is warming up. I ask him to choose someone to play 'the Yawner' (he selects Loni), and I invite him to take the second chair: 'Which of the doubling statements fits for you here?' I ask him.

Suddenly he freezes again: 'I don't know,' he says.

'Choose someone who can take up these words,' I tell him. He chooses Emily. I pull him out to see the story. Yawn...followed by 'I don't know.' I place a third chair; Bert takes it. He hears the yawn and 'I don't know' and volunteers: 'I guess I'm scared.' He is scared. It is evident. He is wiping his palms on his jeans and his face is slightly flushed. Fear is quite often the first strong feeling I meet when the mask actually starts to be pulled aside.

Bert is afraid, and I define the chair he is sitting in as the place of 'Fear'. I ask Bert to choose someone to play the role of Fear. He selects Denise. As soon as Bert is out of that role, he cracks a joke. He is not in touch with the fear at that moment. On stage we have Loni 'the Yawner', Emily as 'I don't know', and Denise as Fear. Bert looks on. It is important to me to begin with this tableau; it will be something Bert remembers. We run through it a couple of times with each person in the triad playing up their roles.

We return to Fear. I invite Bert to conduct an interview. 'So whaddaya scared of?' he asks.

When invited to role-reverse, Bert flinches when he is asked the question in this tone. 'I feel like he (the interviewer) is saying: "Whaddaya scared of, dummy!" '

I redirect the interviewer to add these epithets. Bert says in response: 'I don't know.' We laugh as he goes back to Emily in the second chair.

'Choose someone to play the interviewer,' I ask. He selects Willie. Through a series of questions this figure, too, is named – Impatience. We may do it in mirror so he can begin to see the pattern: Impatience drives him back into his defences, back to feigned indifference or boredom.

I bring Bert back to Impatience. I suggest Impatience approach Fear again and see if it can find a way to speak that gives Fear a safer feeling. Impatience says it doesn't know how, and I give it permission to get impatient with me. There's some laughter. I put Bert back into the role of Fear. I ask him what he needs.

'Someone who isn't going to rag on me,' he says.

I place an empty chair beside Fear. This is a chair for 'someone who isn't going to rag on you'.

'What is the quality you need?' I ask.

'Someone who cares,' he says.

So we let this chair be named 'Caring'. I bring Denise back to play Fear.

'Bert, do you have a part of you that cares?'

'Of course, I do.'

I hear the impatience in his tone, as if he'd said to me: 'Of course I do, stupid.'

I give the line to Impatience so that Bert can hear his response: 'Of course I do, stupid.'

Bert laughs: 'Yeah', he says, his tone softening, 'I care about people. I just don't show it.'

I invite Bert to take the chair of Caring, to speak to Fear: 'Hey man, what's got you scared here in this situation? You can talk to me.'

I ask Bert to choose someone to play the role. 'Paula could play it,' he says. It becomes a role reversal and for the next phase of the session, Fear and Caring converse and the quality of affect in the group and in Bert shifts noticeably. The image of Caring is powerful, the ways it speaks, its prox-imities, give us a touching image of something each of them needs and values. A part, shy and hidden in Bert, is coaxed forth, while Paula, as if on a see-saw with Bert, experiences the parts of herself tilting back and forth from Fear to Care with the role reversals.

This is by no means the end of this session, but there is already enough for some processing. Experienced directors will note at how many different junctures I choose to keep going *in* rather than out. The object-relations school of psychology talks persuasively about introjects, and helps us to see how features of our inner world, its personnages and beliefs, are internalised from models met in childhood.

Such a conceptual framework gives the psychodramatist permission to ask a protagonist at any point (as we might have asked Bert in the face of Impatience): 'Where have you heard this voice before?' or 'Is there anyone in your family this reminds you of?'

Most often the protagonist is aware of whom he or she is mimicking. I have found, however, that the actual work of change can be conducted quite well by proceeding as I have earlier: by staying 'in' and putting pressure on the protagonist to notice his or her own operative patterns and to struggle with empowering – as in the case of Caring – demoted or marginal facets of his or her potential.

Also, this manner of working pays very close attention to the shells of resistance, how Yawn is followed by 'I don't know' and how 'I don't know' is a defensive mask to which the protagonist may at any moment return. Working 'in' is often like identifying layers of resistance. Identifying these layers respects the existing structure of a person's psyche while at the same time making it concrete. The concretising keeps bringing a kind of humour and theatre into the process: the psyche is constantly being 'staged'. This staging increasingly opens up psychodrama as a playfulness, a playing, with what we find inside.

Finally, I believe this intrapsychic work helps us to maintain a fidelity to the protagonist's warm-up as it unfolds. We do not make leaps, such as the leap offered by 'Whose voice does this remind you of?' It is much more powerful when the protagonist or members of the group say: 'Good Lord, that sounds so much like my father.' Even then I find there is value in acknowledging that and in staying with the exploration and realignment of materials in the inner world. We must sooner or later find or create the positive roles through which a person can re-establish a more functional inner community. The voice of Impatience will never be silenced; rather another internal voice needs to be heard.

Intrapsychic sociometry: staging and outcome

Just before the second Interlude, I used the image of chaos to describe the welter of parts the director evokes from the protagonist. The vignette of Bert's work, as it showed the emergence of parts, indicates how these parts make their way to the stage. There is no attempt made in the first phase of this work to give any staging or blocking to the figures as they come forth. With Bert, I preserved the layers as they were revealed, but often, as occurred with Paula when it was time for her to leave the hospital, her feelings were not as clearly nested inside one another; rather they were, as in a broken kaleidoscope, all present at once. Her feelings were a jangle of shards, her cast of characters at odds, disorganised, the stuff of a headache.

The forming of this welter into a tableau is the next stage of the work. This forming work is a considerable event, aesthetically, dramatically and psychologically. In this phase of the drama the hand of the sociometrist is evident.

Around each figure in our internal world, a sociometry develops. Each figure, coming to the centre, constellates around him or her or it, as on a target sociogram, the significant others in the internal world. When anger dominates the scene – who may be designated simply by the emotional name, Anger, or given

27

an allegorical representation, The Red Demon – Sadness, Compassion and Responsibility may be at the outer edges. Anger deserves his drama, his fantasy of revenge; anger has both a soliloquy and an act hunger, and there are times when the psychodramatist must help anger to realise his play. But it is likely after such a scene that another feeling state, another character, another point of viewing, will need its soliloquy and its time on stage, perhaps for tears.

Sociometry is a method for understanding the structure of a group. The intrapsychic psychodramatist is constantly calling on and teaching sociometric skills to find the organisation of the protagonist's internal world. The shift from the chaos of characters to their positioning, represents an advance from recognition to value. To place figures in relation to one another is an act of appraisal and judgement, and the resulting tableau – often the fruit of interview, mediation and several 'blockings' – represents a moral and aesthetic achievement. To accomplish this the protagonist moves from the role of advocate to sculptor, in the sense in which sculpting is used in the phrase 'family sculpting'.

As advocate, it is the work of the protagonist to voice and give gesture to his internal parts. As sculptor, it is his task to step back, survey his cast, and shape them into a design that organises his internal world. In this shift of role from advocate to witness, the protagonist adopts the mirror role, as Moreno defined the protagonist in his position of observer.

We cannot really overestimate the importance of this role for our protagonist, especially our adolescent protagonist. To be able to find this witnessing role inside of us – the role T.S. Eliot refers to as: 'the still point of the turning world' – has been for some religions the very end and goal of spiritual practice. Psychology values this role as 'the observing ego', while another poet, Keats, claimed that the capacity for this kind of present detachment was indispensable for poetic creation; he called it 'negative capability' and described it as the 'ability to be amid doubts, distractions, and fears without an anxious reaching after fact'.

This role, this part, of witness becomes the locus of a warm-up for the next scene, in which the protagonist becomes a sociometrist and contends with the ordering of his internal affairs. After viewing the welter, the gang, it is time to organise them. After listening to their voices, it is time to govern them.

I have used two images in the preceding paragraphs, one drawn from the plastic arts – to sculpt – and the other from politics – to govern. It may be here, where the sculptor and the governor meet, that the self is born, where self is the leader of the pack, leader by virtue of his or her awareness of the voices, needs and act hungers of the membership and able to achieve some consensual action on their behalf. The self may be in fact the psychodramatist/sociometrist, a character we must create, who is not part of the problem, not partisan, so that even the loneliest and most isolated voice among us – within us – may feel heard.

We are now in possession of a kind of intrapsychic paradigm. We may not accomplish this paradigm in any single session, but we may be able to place a part of our work within its framework. In the warm-up, the second chair opens the gateway inward to the clamour of the crowd, its chaos. Here we meet the welter, the barbarous ungoverned hoard. The protagonist has been advocate for these characters with the aid of the group. When all the characters are on stage, the director creates a frieze. 'Freeze.'

The next movement is from frieze to sculpture, in which a spirit both observing and shaping is let loose to work upon the figures of our inner world, working with co-operative gentleness, firm in discriminating, mediating, seeking the connections and relations between internal parts at war or at variance with one another, coaxing, coaching and always listening to what it is each part is saying. All the skills of the psychodramatist and sociometrist become available to this new internal figure. In our work with the mirror – in moving the protagonist back from the work in progress to observe, back into it to interact and participate – we are archetypally training up the prince or princess and future king or queen. This figure, fluent in the movement between participant and observer, is the prototype of the self. He or she is a kind of philosopher-king or queen, as Plato defined this figure in *The Republic*. The chief of our state can move from participant to observer, can be passive and active, receptive and capable of decisiveness. This figure is empowered by virtue of advocacy, empathy, concern for all.

The practice implicit in this kind of psychodramatic work trains us for more than self-understanding. The intrapsychic exercise promotes an understanding of self, group and society. It develops the skills necessary not only to function in those three arenas, but to recognise that in some essential way, these three arenas are all mirrored in one another. Ability to govern in the polity of the self is a prerequisite for the ability to lead in a group, to lead in a society. This is the classical view of leadership, derived from antiquity and passed to us through the Renaissance, which recognised the self as an image for the world. 'I am a little world made cunningly,' wrote Shakespeare's contemporary, John Donne. Hamlet could have said that.

Adolescent psychodrama: a rite of passage

Many traditional cultures mark a point of development for their young members with some occasion or ceremony. Commonly known as a rite of passage or a ritual of initiation, this occasion serves to mark a change of status for a person with regard to family and to other social groups. These rites define changes of role as well.

Initiation is derived from the Latin *in* plus *initio*, a preposition and a verb form translated as *going in* or *into*. Commonly, initiation is thought to be a leaving of childhood, a going out from the protected and careless state of innocence in the family and into the world of personal and social responsibility. This notion is partially supported by the images we have of the initiation as an encounter with gruelling ordeals, demanding tasks, which bring a young person face to face with external powers and challenges.

However, initiation rites, even in the most arduous form, are in fact inward journeys. The external ordeals are intended to summon up internal resources, to throw a person back into himself, to tap and to manifest the inner dimensions of power, clarity, faith and vision.

In many cultures the initiatory rite takes the form of a vision quest, which dramatises the shift from seeing with the physical eye to seeing with the inner eye. But more than a new way of seeing outwardly, it helps initiate a person to a new way of seeing in.

In this way the vision quest, apparently a dangerous encounter for survival between a young person and the rigorous external world, is the first solo venture of a person into the interior world of dream, vision, ancestor, guide and totem. In Jung's terms, the young person draws upon roles or parts or images that are part of a collective, rather than a personal, unconscious. This rich, interior world breached in the initiation rite becomes a resource for the rest of a person's life. In this sense, the initiation rite is spiritual; the door that it opens swings inward.

In the ancient and traditional cultures, the internal states were well defined and named. The gods, the totem figures, the animal guides, the heroes from the spirit world had their dominions within the soul of each man as well as a habitation in the village or the polis. We moderns are by comparison impoverished. With the disappearance of that polytheistic world, which had its mirror image within each of us, with the loss of our sense of ourselves as *selves*, with the advent of the mono-God and the almighty single ego, we leave ourselves with no myth except a pathological one – multiple personality disorder – to account for that inner diversity each of us may actually experience. Without a complex model for our human nature, we will falsify, simplify, and enforce a singleness where we are, in fact, a plurality. We try to fashion a mask to control what we fear is the madness of our many-sidedness. For no-one is the threat of this madness more real than for the adolescent, and for no age group is the validation of a pluralistic internal world more liberating.

For the adolescent feels acutely the power of many lords. Their internal world, as we have seen it revealed through intrapsychic psychodrama, is feudal; civil war is often the usual state of affairs. Before coherent or responsible action can take place in the world – action which is not in the next breath revised or contradicted – the adolescent must meet the urges of action within. He or she must look inside and there discover the complex, many-headed world of his or her inner life. This inward looking, this exploration of the interior, fulfils the ancient purpose of initiation and may, as this chapter has suggested, be carried out in our time by the experience of psychodrama.

Psychodrama, used as I have indicated here, pays tribute to the emerging roles and characters in the adolescent soul. Through it they may explore new possibilities for personal expression and group experience. By means of psychodrama's diverse agencies, a young person can make friends with the roles that precede the self and may then see a self emerge, flexible and spontaneous, that can create a world.

References

Jones, E. (1976) *Hamlet and Oedipus*, New York: W.W. Norton.
Moreno, J.L. (1972) *Psychodrama Vol. I*, Beacon, NY, Beacon House.

Chapter four

Everybody's a somebody

Action methods for young people with severe learning difficulties

Ken Sprague

What does the chapter aim to do?

This chapter sets out to do the following:

1. To show how young people with severe learning difficulties were introduced and helped by action methods.
2. To explain how a psychodramatist working as an art teacher can become an agent for change.
3. To explain the delights and difficulties of working psychodramatically with two on-going groups of young people all of whom have severe learning difficulties, and to explore the tools and the technique used for releasing human spontaneity and creativity.
4. To compare what happened in two similar groups under different conditions: one group primarily Down's syndrome, the other autistic.

Dr. Jacob Levi Moreno's claim that 'a truly therapeutic procedure cannot have less an objective than the whole of mankind' is not a modest aim. It clearly comes from a man who believed that the development of psychodrama was much more than the building of a specialist tool for use in clinic or classroom. Important as such daily use of the method is, Moreno knew that he was creating something bigger – a philosophy for life – a life method, in fact. It is a method based upon the realisation that humankind is a social and organic unity. Tendencies continually emerge between the different parts of this unity that at times bring them together and at other times drive them apart. The idea of studying and intervening creatively in this global relationship of attraction and repulsion seems to me to be particularly relevant in the age of nuclear weapons and star-wars mentality. The concept of star wars involving, as it does, the export of earthly nuclear madness out into the cosmos must surely represent the ultimate blasphemy. In such a time, Moreno's ideas of men and women, not only as social beings or individual beings, but as cosmic beings has, I believe, a special importance. I have found ready acceptance of Moreno's 'life method' among young people with severe learning problems. They accept the creative spontaneous potential of us all and repeatedly say to me, 'That's a sensible idea,' or 'What a good way – why haven't we done that before?' They are speaking of the simple Morenian concept: 'Don't tell me, show me'. Important people in our lives need to be brought into the action by having other group members enact their roles. This allows us to see what happens in the relationships and to learn by reversing roles.

These are basically simple, creative ideas. It must be admitted, however, that they are not so simple, usually, to put into practice. That's what this chapter is about.

What is the history?

The histories and 'her-stories' behind the groups discussed in this chapter go back a long way. During the 1930s in Britain, physically and mentally disabled people were usually shut away in institutions well apart from what was regarded as normal society. These establishments were often housed in, or were extensions of, the workhouses or asylums of earlier times. Most towns of any size had their quaintly named institution. 'Fairmile' was a favourite title, denoting that it was at least a fair mile from the residential and work areas of the more fortunate.

Since those days, there have been considerable political and social changes that have promoted greater community responsibility and caring attitudes towards those in need. Smaller units are replacing the old 'battleship' institutions. The aim is to introduce greater normality into the lives of those with disabilities.

What changed in 1981?

The changing social climate has helped to bring about a major change in Government thinking. The Conservative Government introduced the Education Act 1981 which calls for special educational provision to be made for young people with special educational needs. While it was a positive move that the law was passed, it seems, unfortunately, to have been carried out more for political motive than to offer support for life education. The scheme has never received the resources needed to be fully implemented in the community. It is underpublicised and is staffed largely by untrained personnel. Neither the implementation nor the training needed was thought through from the beginning. In particular, the workshops and adult centres to cater for the young people at the end of their schooling are still woefully inadequate. In spite of all these difficulties, considerable progress has been made due mainly to the heart of care attitude and enormous dedication of the teachers, unit heads and therapists involved, and the loving support of the young people themselves.

How it all began for me

I had been working in a psychiatric hospital running psychodrama sessions with long-stay patients. The work was hard and rewarding but I had become increasingly interested in working with people who were not sick. Before training in psychodrama, I had worked for many years in local politics, trade union organisations and journalism. I had also been active in the peace movement and ecological affairs. It was clear to me that patients in mental hospitals do not make and threaten one another with H-bombs or cut down rain forests. In fact, hospital inmates spend a good deal of their time caring deeply for one another. Many institutions could not function without such loving input from those in care. Even a cursory look at the way 'normal' people and governments behave toward one another suggests that they need help. It seems that they may even suffer, from time to time, with some sort of hateful disease – let us call it 'normosis'. Such thoughts had led me to work with two English colleagues, Peter Haworth and Susie Combes, conducting public sessions on issues of social concern. I had also been attending sociodrama workshops with Claire Danielson in the United States of America and running action-method courses for shop stewards of the British Transport and General Workers Union.

Continuing to broaden my experience and test the method's relevance, I had taken a job teaching print-making and drawing at an art school attached to a technical college. In both the print and drawing classes I was using action-method warm-ups to stimulate the imagination of the young artists for their practical art work.

How did involvement occur?

Involvement occurred by being open to a creative situation. One cold winter's morning a barrage of faces appeared at the windows of the college art class, gesticulating and happily demanding to come into the art room. It was a group from the special unit of students with severe learning difficulties. They were out with their supervisors for a brisk walk. The college had a system for allowing students interested in other disciplines to be shown around but, in practice, few students from one department showed interest in the others. The learning-difficulty students with their disabilities and wheelchairs knew nothing of all this, and cared even less: their spontaneity was boundless, their interest high and, looking into the art room, with all its colour and activity, they simply wanted in.

As the art teacher, I was delighted by their enthusiasm, and invited them to join us – artists need spontaneity. The result was a chaotic and successful meeting of a group of learning-difficulty students with a class of art students. This led to once-weekly mixed classes and the beginning of greater integration of the students with severe learning difficulties with the general college activities. These students will now be referred to as 'the Down's Group' because of the large number of Down's syndrome people involved and to differentiate them from the autistic group that will be mentioned later.

What were the immediate results?

The Down's Group began sketching alongside the art students whom they regarded as 'proper' students and 'professional' workers. They felt good about attending classes within the actual college buildings instead of their prefabricated huts 'out the back'. The adventure of leaving their own territory was instrumental in producing more creative behaviour.

The art students quickly overcame their initial embarrassment and, with help, their fear of mental problems. They found they had willing models to pose for them. Soon the models wanted to reverse roles and become the artists. Mutual exchange promoted new relationships between both sets of students. The art students were deeply moved by the tremendous efforts they saw being made to overcome disability. The general creativity improved all round and the Down's Group were responsible for bringing a refreshing spontaneity and naivety into the lessons and the resulting art work. Art students becoming tight in their professionalism were helped by the naivety they saw. Friendships were made that continued outside of classes and in the longer term helped to influence the social atmosphere of acceptance within the college. A closer tie-up between departments was made and I was asked to join the staff of the Down's Group unit to conduct twice-weekly creative drama sessions.

Was there an early specific success?

Only a small number were invited to attend the art student classes at first and therefore the Down's students worked hard to be included. The fact that students had to earn a place led to an interesting and delightful situation where some students promoted others. 'Tom deserves to be included', for example. Something quite magical took place in the third lesson. No art room was available on this occasion so the class was held in the college gallery – not ideal but adequate. It proved that the surroundings are of less importance if the motivation is high. Four Down's students joined the class – Peter, Jack, Carol and Tom. The art students were told to use the visitors as models – to draw exactly what they saw and pull no punches in their visual statements. I wanted the Down's Group to see themselves as others saw them but asked that they, in turn, should draw their drawers as accurately as possible, warts and all. The exercise produced some emotional contact between the two groups; there were a few tears and comforting on both sides. The lesson was not easy. Each of the four visitors reacted differently to the lesson's stimulation.

What were the differences?

Peter, a big and very powerful lad, was aggressive, alternating with disinterest in the whole thing. Nevertheless, he made a simple drawing of the art student drawing him and was particularly taken with the boy's earrings. These he observed and drew well. He then lost interest, became disruptive and was sent back to the unit hut. The rest of the class was going well so I walked back with him, on the way establishing a better relationship and dispelling all hint of punishment. Peter was pleased to have me to himself.

Meanwhile, Jack had formed a friendship with one of the mature art students and made two big pictures full of faces of his new friend. They had cried together at the accuracy of their drawings. Jack was badly disfigured. Carol worked away diligently, occasionally mothering others and displaying a good sense of colour.

Tom, the smallest and most withdrawn, said he felt that his companion was staring at him. Since he was being drawn, this was true. I left him with his problem but once or twice called encouragement from across the room, keeping my distance. Tom had chosen to sit at the only desk in the room but refused to pull his chair up to the desk. He hung his head and tried to hide himself. I indicated that Tom's companion should keep drawing him, forcing him into some reaction other than hiding, and at the same time pushing the desk up to Tom's chair and laying out large coloured pens and two big sheets of paper.

Tom grabbed a pen and drew a tiny square right at the bottom of the paper. He drew savagely and with such energy that his pen tore through the paper in several places. As one square was finished he took anther sheet and attacked it with another square. I kept an eye on him but made rounds of the other students, maintaining my distance from Tom.

His behaviour slowly changed. He began to look around at those drawing him. They were all concentrating, working hard and intrigued by what was happening. Tom moved away from his chair and desk, placed a sheet of paper on the floor, arranged his pens with almost military formation, sat cross-legged, looked at his companion intently and drew a figure half as big as himself in bright green. The student next to him was wearing a bright green jumper. Everyone was amazed and voiced their congratulations. Tom reacted with pride, took the pen and carefully wrote 'TM' alongside the head of his figure. I asked quietly, 'Anything missing Tom?' Taking the pen again and with deliberation, Tom proudly inserted the letter 'O'.

What were my thoughts?

Driving home afterwards, I thought of the obstetrician who insists that women in labour lie on a table so that he can see better and, in doing so, perhaps inhibits their natural birthing position.

Similarly, and perhaps particularly, with learning-difficulty people, they should be encouraged to find their own comfortable creative position, as Tom had done in moving from his desk. In a lesson lasting no more than half an hour, Tom had moved from a situation of isolation and discomfort to a position of creativity, sitting on the floor: he had found his own 'active' position. He had personalised the action of the artist. Tom's drawings were somewhat infantile, the work equivalent of a struggling four-year-old, not of a young Rembrandt, but the leap from isolation to one of creation was Rembrandtian in proportion.

At this point I decided to use group action methods in a more therapeutic way; a way that would be tailored to the needs of the Down's Group. As a new member of staff I also planned to use drawing as an integral part of the action. I have a love and enthusiasm for drawing and accordingly use it as an important contribution to teaching. The more general application of the idea is that teachers should take their enthusiasms into the classroom. Like laughter, enthusiasm is contagious.

What were the next steps?

I looked through relevant medical notes of students who needed particular care. Claire, for example, had a serious heart condition and could not climb stairs or take strenuous exercise. Clearly it was important that I be aware of such problems. However, at this stage, I did not get too immersed in the medical notes, I preferred to discover the difficulties by direct exchange with the students and to check my findings against the notes later. This direct exchange involved warm-ups in which students mimed their own and others' disablements. The performances that followed were light-hearted and sometimes very funny. There was a humorous shopping expedition arising from speech difficulty, problems of impaired vision leading to wet floors in the toilets and severe shaking that made any mealtime a disaster area.

> The warm-ups developed into an enjoyable game and Arthur, a rather tough 18-year-old, began to mime actor John Cleese's silly walk. The whole group caught the mood and stomped around the room trying to out-do each other in ludicrous walking styles. Suddenly, Annie, who had taken some stick from Robert, got her own back by saying, 'Robert walks like that anyway'. He looked a little hurt but braved it out and began to exaggerate his own walking difficulty. The mood changed and he demonstrated the frustration of being imprisoned in his own disability. I asked him to add sound to his movement and with his great difficulty in speaking at all he gave vent to an anguished squalling. He had become the personification of all the group's difficulties. In group-action terms he had become the protagonist in a protagonist-centred sociodrama.

How much was planned?

The warm-up had been planned beforehand and began with me showing my own difficulty with a bad headache and some clowning of what happened when I was recovering from knee operations. This touch of showmanship and over-acting the roles encouraged the group members to show themselves, each taking a turn and trying in some cases to out-do the others. The suddenly more serious response to the actions and to Robert's protagonist position arose spontaneously. It should be understood, however, that while it had not been *planned*, the conditions for the spontaneity had been *created*. If we take a parallel example from art, some art consists of happy accident. The truth, of course, is that the artist constantly creates the conditions in which accidents can be creative. The artist chooses the conditions and trusts his or her method. So does the psychodramatist or socio-dramatist. Robert's impact on the group allowed several group members to unburden themselves of anguish and others to show their empathy. It was at this moment that a second happy accident took place, which again emphasised the importance of being open to creative possibilities.

> We had been moved into the college theatre. It was free and we had earned a right to use it. A technician walked through the theatre carrying a spot light and electric lead. I asked him to connect it, set it on the floor and beam it toward a large end wall. All the other lights were extinguished. By having each group member now show their difficulties within the beam and close to the light, huge shadows were projected on to the wall and theatre ceilings. The attention was taken from the individual to the shadow, which allowed us all to see the problems of the whole group rather than concentrating on the individual burdens. The 'action period' ended with everyone's playfulness and enthusiasm 'on high'. The session had overrun its time but the feeling of 'groupness' was strong. Walking back to the unit hut for the next class, sharing took the form of mutual helping and encour-agement in negotiating stairs, swing doors and a rain-swept playground area, while talking happily about the shadow drama we had all been involved in.

What were my conclusions?

From these experiences I concluded that sessions should be planned beforehand but that preconceived ideas should be readily abandoned in favour of what was happening in the moment. The director must continually watch both the group and what is happening around the group, and be responsive to the creative potential as it emerges. I also resolved to keep a closer eye on the timing of each session so that an adequate period for sharing was built in and not squeezed out at the end. In the particular lesson, good sharing had taken place more by luck than design. I further resolved to walk the students to their next classroom after every session to allow for a rounding-off of relationships that had grown in the session and to help my own closure. This has become standard practice. The group began to look forward to the sessions and many would watch my arrival in the car park from the unit hut windows. I began to take boxes of props and other paraphernalia in the car boot and calling on the students to help carry the gear into the hut or theatre. Sometimes the gear was used in the ensuing action and sometimes not, but the jostling and the fun of carrying allowed time for me to ask

'What have you been doing?' or 'What has happened since last week?' This procedure nearly always produced a warm-up and occasionally the subject of the action, as in the case of 'I fell off the bus,' which is written about later. I believe that sessions begin in the car park!

How did the ripples spread?

The local grapevine soon carried news of these developments to an enthusiastic supervisor of autistic children in a residential school. The school is run by a voluntary society of parents and supporters who asked me to start weekly, afternoon and evening creativity sessions. The understanding was that these sessions would be based on action methods and would involve twelve autistic young people aged 17–19 years.

Within a few weeks I began working with the second group, 'the Autistic Group'. The circumstances were very different. All the Down's Group lived in residential centres, institutions or private homes and went into the technical college each day by bus or taxi. The members of the Autistic group lived in a residential school and journeyed to my home in a minibus driven by a school supervisor. I live in a small hill farm, which has been converted to a teaching centre for Dr Moreno's ideas and methods. It has a theatre built from the old granary and workshops for my printing and drawing enthusiasm.

Learning from the car-park, warm-up idea, I met the young people as their bus arrived, and walked them to the theatre, establishing tentative contacts. All but two were friendly and happy with what they regarded as a day outing: Sam and Jason were the exceptions, both being very withdrawn into themselves. After some initial cushion-throwing games in which they called out their names, I repeated the idea of showing my headache suffering (from the Down's Group) and asked the autistic youngsters to show their own difficulties. The idea fell completely flat and after another cushion game we retired to the kitchen for tea and biscuits. This began to interest all of them, and exploration of the kettle, biscuit tin, kitchen contents, toilets and the whole house, ensued. Everyone had a good time, even Sam and Jason. We walked back to their minibus and they went off happily.

What were my feelings?

I walked back to the house knowing that the group had been successful due to the young people's spontaneity, not my planning. An idea successful in the Down's Group had been unsuited to this new group. It was too early to expect the young people to show their difficulties before trust had been established. Added to this, each member's difficulty was similar to the others'; they were all autistic. There was not enough room for expansion and mimicry. I had made a foolish mistake.

In the following weeks and in the light of subsequent events, I had to consider the fact that mistakes can have very different natures and effects. A mistake in clearing furniture from a stage or action area can lead to injury of group members. Other, less physical mistakes, can open the door to a more creative process. It depends on how the director handles it.

To use parallels from art again, an engraver who misuses or abuses his cutting tools will do himself an injury and cover it by calling it an accident. Many print makers will admit to being open to the creative potential of accidents in the process. A mistake in cutting a block or even a split in a block may result in simplified and bolder presentation. A few artists will even acknowledge consciously setting up the conditions for such happy accidents to take place. All artists learn by making mistakes. So do people using action methods. In their case, however, they must see to it that their mistakes and accidents are not the kind that damage their clients.

I had failed to see that for the Autistic Group the visit to my centre had been experienced as an outing – a break in the routine of their residential school. Trust was built, not by the exercises planned, but by the young people's spontaneous enjoyment of my home, the expedition and their own togetherness. At the next session, when they were all seated round the big kitchen table, I admitted making a mistake the week before in using exercises not tailored to them. Their own enjoyment of the place and time was more important. The young people may or may not have understood my honesty but they certainly liked it!

Teacher can be wrong!

What was happening?

The group process was now rooted very much in the here and now. The group interest was high and one member, Jessie, said 'Let's draw it,' by which she meant draw the difficulties of being autistic. Jessie is 18 years old, intelligent, withdrawn, rarely speaking, but very gifted as an artist. A box of coloured pencils and some paper were quickly produced and Jessie immediately became totally absorbed in drawing a head without a mouth. It was a large, colourful and complex series of drawings, one imposed upon another.

I moved around the table, encouraging each person to draw some visual symbol of their difficulty and then act it out individually with me by leaving their seats and taking some space alongside the table. The others watched for a few moments but quickly returned to their own drawings. It was one-to-one therapy within the group work. When there was a problem of understanding and getting it out on paper, we acted it out first and then made a drawing or an attempt at drawing. Sometimes it worked and sometimes it didn't, but every person remained involved. Isolation, hiding away, mannerisms and being unable to speak were all presented, each with individuality, but when one young man began to act out a friend's mannerism of lurching about, the whole group responded and cohered into joint action.

A truly sociodramatic action sequence developed in which group members acted out their own or another's mannerisms. It differed from the more psycho-dramatically based approach used with the Down's Group in the sense that we were looking not at individual difficulties, disablements, mannerisms or feelings, but at the universal struggle of the disabled. Each became an advocate for the others. The sharing flowed naturally out of the action and took the form of touching, laughing or giggling together; there was little verbal exchange.

If drawing led to action, could action lead to drawing?

My antics (action) in the first session had led Jessie to put her feeling on paper in the form of drawings. But as a gifted artist she probably would have drawn anyway. She remembered the idea of a week earlier of expressing autism. Her imaginative drawing (action) encouraged other group members to follow her example and enjoy using lines and colours. Half the drawings produced by the group would have appeared to an untrained observer as meaningless scribbles. In fact each drawing was full of meaning: they meant involvement and enjoyment. They also meant a shared experience. The question I now asked myself was how could a system of teaching this group be developed by alternating shared experience with shared expression.

> When the group next arrived in their minibus, I walked them across the fields, looking at sheep, trees and fish in a pond.
> In the theatre each was encouraged to take on the roles of the animals and the movement of the trees. Of the group of twelve, about half responded. No attempt was made to push the others who were too shy to take part. They stood waiting quietly while some watched with varying degrees of interest. Three remained isolated within themselves. After ten minutes of action, everyone went to the kitchen where coloured pens and paper were already laid out on the big table. For 45 minutes everyone drew excitedly the trees and animals they had enacted and a few human figures were introduced. The drawings were much more expressive than previously. Everyone took part and, given some help, even the most withdrawn res-ponded to some degree. The session ended around the table sharing by exchanging and appraising each other's drawings and passing around tea and biscuits.

Was there a qualitative leap?

After several weeks the group's progress continued to be steady, more members being involved creatively for longer periods. Sometimes the amount of involvement was quite large and sometimes smaller: sometimes enactments just flowed and other times needed a good deal of encouragement, even prodding. Progress could be described as quantitative.

A visit was now arranged to a neighbouring farm. The farmer and his wife were nearing retirement and were burdened by the recent death of a son. They were only too pleased to have children around the place again. They put on a display of sheep shearing and had the young people help carry the fleece and tie the bundles. The visit ended around the stove with specially baked chocolate flapjacks.

It was during the next session that acting-out of farm life and reversing roles with the farmer and his wife just took off and every group member became an active participant. The farm visit marked a turning point where quality was added to quantity. The qualitative leap made during that outing set new conditions for promoting greater involvement and release of spontaneity. The group has not yet reached a position where full psychodrama sessions are possible, although role play and role training are used regularly and successfully.

Did cross-fertilisation occur?

An unexpected result of the Autistic Group's progress was a cross-fertilisation with the Down's Group. It is interesting that it was the more inhibited group that sparked the less inhibited. Over several weeks so many expressive drawings were made in the Autistic Group sessions that I photographed them and had them made up into colour slides. I then arranged for a showing to the next Down's Group session.

The excitement of the big screen, grouped seating on the floor mats, a chance to work the projector and a darkened theatre set the scene for an enjoyable session. The drawings, including those by the more withdrawn autistic members showed remarkable examples of observation (e.g. the ridges left on shorn sheep by the electric cutters). As young people who had also grown up in rural surroundings, the Down's Group responded to the drawings of animals and country landscapes. They were delighted to recreate within the college theatre their own enactments of farmyards and episodes from their lives or their family lives. All was acted out excitedly. The warm-ups in which they vied with each other for a chance to 'show' developed into full-scale psychodrama. I began to see the pressures and encouragements they received outside of college life and was able to plan individual help more sensitively and consider intervention with families or the staff of the young people's residences. Sharing became more intimate and some even took turns at directing scene-setting.

How did it happen?

Of the many classical psychodrama/sociodrama sessions that flowed from weeks of this cross-fertilisation, the following example from the Down's Group encapsulates the process.

Humphrey wanted to show his room in the family farm home. Time was short and he had to wait a full week for a chance. His enthusiasm was undiminished. The room, its colour, contents and atmosphere was built in the stage area using group members to play wardrobe, wash basins and record player. There was a great deal of noise from banging doors, running taps and 'pop' cassettes. Everybody took part and Humphrey enjoyed having staff members play toilets and derogatory items. The warm-up was good-natured and at times very funny. I encouraged the 'peopling' of the scene and the developing of the relationships. Humphrey got into bed. His mother, played by the staff helper whom he had previously had play a toilet, knocked quietly on the door and, on his invitation, came in. A tender scene followed, with some tears. The scene changed. Humphrey was still in bed but this time his father barged into the room without knocking and ordered him to round up some bullocks that had broken out during the night.

Several incidents with brothers and father entering the room were explored, going back in time. On each occasion the person entering the room did so without knocking and in the role state of an intruder. It emerged that all the sons received wages or pocket money, depending on age, for helping around the farm. Humphrey, however, was regarded by his father and brothers as the family 'dummy', although it was admitted that he was competent at jobs like round-up or even driving the tractor. He had never received payment. The session now erupted into participation with group members urging him to negotiate with his father. The whole group was on fire, their own life frustrations suddenly finding expression. Humphrey was allowed to explode his anger at father and brothers, and sat exhausted but triumphant while the sharing poured forth.

This remarkable session was followed by a role-training lesson in which Humphrey conducted wage talks with his father. That session became sociodramatic with every person taking part, fired with supportive feelings for Humphrey's previous week's work. Group members criticised Humphrey, calling out 'You are too nice a person to say that to your Dad' and then reversing roles with him to demonstrate what they considered to be a more persuasive approach or more within his capability. At one point the whole group spent a brain-storming period working out a pay scale and estimating back payments. A level of mathematical abilities emerged that had not been seen during maths lessons! The session was protagonist-centred sociodrama whereas in the first session with Humphrey, classical psychodrama took place. Role training became role testing and at one point

Joseph, from his wheelchair, took over as director while I became his supervisor. (It transpired in the sharing that Joseph had been through an almost identical episode with his stepfather.)

What followed in real life?

Humphrey did talk with his father. He was not successful in winning backpay and only marginally so in his bid for 'wages'. It did not matter to him, however. He had made his point, and when I next met the father at parents' day, there was clearly a greater respect for the boy and the beginning of pride in his son's growth.

Humphrey's self-esteem has continued to develop. He regularly takes over sessions as director for short periods and criticises his own and other's work more readily. He takes greater pride in himself and dresses with sharp style. His behaviour is more 'manly' and he is consequently more relaxed with the young women in the class.

What happened in the session with Humphrey is a good example of Alice Miller's (1986) observation that 'true satiation of old need is no longer possible since the right time for that lies irrevocably in the past', a statement that seems to me to justify psychodrama. In psychodrama the past *can* be re-entered. Humphrey was able to experience again the different time periods and encounter father at different stages of mounting repression. He found advocates to speak for him and, in turn, learned to speak for himself. He became, at each step of the relationship, what he had been unable to be in real life. Instead of being punished, as he would have been in reality, he received respect from those playing supporting family roles and applause from the audience.

He came out of it all with new-found confidence and a hesitant but growing belief that he can effect change in his life.

What was the effect on the group?

Humphrey's sessions stimulated the Down's Group and staff, not least because everyone had taken part and thereby felt that they had contributed to his growth. Their belief in their own effectiveness as friends and helpers was enhanced and pride in belonging to the group accelerated.

Annie, a rather fat girl, who rarely spoke and had very low self-esteem, was clearly moved by what she perceived as Humphrey's courage in 'showing' his difficulties. She asked to show her own room, at home, to the group.

The room was unimportant but she latched on to it, having seen Humphrey's beginning, and it provided a starting point and allowed the scene to be set. It was a case of it didn't matter where the action started but *that* it started. Annie's grandmother had spoken up for her and been a good listener. She had died some weeks before. Annie was not at the funeral because her guardians had a misplaced sense of protection and also admitted to being fearful of what might happen.

Annie hid her disappointment but grieved inwardly. She was asked if she would like to say goodbye to Grandma and where the parting should take place. Annie responded with energy and clear recall of detail. She now created on stage, the scene that was important. It was her grandmother's kitchen and she delighted in the placing of saucepans, cups, curtains and colour.

To play her beloved Grandma she chose a wheelchair-bound boy of her own age, accepting, without even thinking, psychodrama's lack of barriers, man, woman, child, able or disabled. Annie positioned her grandmother at the kitchen table, spoke quietly, almost whispering, her love and farewell. She then arranged the other group members at the graveside for the burial. The normal procedure was gone through and clearly had little importance for Annie. She regarded it all as simply a build-up to the high point which, for her, was the placing of the flowers upon the grave. Paper and coloured pens were always waiting ready among a pile of possible props. Flowers of all shapes, sizes and colours were drawn. Even the most spastic arms can draw a flower head. Granny's grave was piled with colour and joyfulness. 'What do we do now?' I asked, and Annie said, firmly, 'We go home to cups of tea and ham sandwiches.'

She sat among the imaginary, yet very real, sandwich-munching and cried uncontrollably for many minutes. She was visibly tired and listened to the sharing, unhearing but at peace. Her catharsis had come not at the high point of the action but at the sound of her own voice encapsulating the essentials of British working-class funeral behaviour – tea and ham sandwiches.

What is the importance of drawings?

Each member of the group drew a flower, or flower head, and arranged it upon Grandma's stage grave. It was all done with seriousness and the greatest respect for Annie's loved one whom no-one had ever met but who came alive and died again before their eyes. They felt the old woman's living and passing and knew, in the full sense of knowing, their friend's affection for her Grandma. Some cried; all were moved emotionally. The drawing was another form of 'acting out' but its importance lay in being an integral part of the action, not a separate drawing lesson.

I realised that my enthusiasm for drawing or the introduction of other forms of expression into a session, whether artistry or science, must be integral to the overall action. The design objective of each session should be to create a river of activity in which all the spontaneous creative and essential truths flow together. Separate lessons were now ousted in favour of 'life flow'. Students and staff were encouraged to think of the sessions and the lessons in terms of continuing normal life patterns. Paying for goods in a shopping trip is not a separate arithmetic activity. On the same shopping expedition, acknowledging someone's garden or an exciting piece of architecture is not a compartmentalised aesthetic experience. The physical activity of walking around the shop or jumping on a bus to take us there are all respective parts of the whole shopping event. Geography, history, maths, modelling, domestic chores, and even physics, are woven into sessions alongside drama and therapy. I introduce this philosophy into all my groups. I also have students and staff become interchangeable participants. Even visitors or technicians and maintenance people passing through the theatre are encouraged to contribute something to the sessions. The use of the electric lamp mentioned earlier is an example. Observers are discouraged, except in the case of new, shy students, or excessively withdrawn ones needing to acclimatise slowly.

How are failures perceived?

As the work has developed and the two groups have become more coherent and proud of their achievements, so the concept of failure has become less important. It took three terms, each of twelve to thirteen lessons, to reach this point. Failure is not only allowable but seen as a step toward something else. Even the words 'good' and 'bad' are heard less, being replaced by positive attitudes in a less judgemental group culture.

As staff and helpers become more experienced and less inhibited themselves, the policing attitudes and 'Don't do that' responses are increasingly abandoned. They are seen and understood to be redundant methods. Staff and helpers are still largely untrained and changing this must be an urgent next step.

The contribution of every student is valued, however seemingly bizarre or contrary it appears to be.

Disabled and autistic Frank was caught masturbating in front of some girl students from a nearby hairdressing school. The moralists had a field day. A session was held on sexual behaviour, including a lesson in human development. The intention was to explain that the moral uproar was a waste of time since about a million years of development drive people to sexual satisfaction. The hard truths of being disabled and perhaps not so attractive to the opposite sex were not avoided. Action and discussion were intermingled: there was, of course, much humour. Frank was not singled out; he took part as everyone else – a group member.

A second session, psychodramatic in form, was held within a few hours, in which Frank became the protagonist and the contract was that he have a lesson in geography, namely how places relate to activities. Walking together as a group through the town in scene-setting on the stage, Frank and others learned that there are places to do things and places not to do things. Loving situations and relationships, or lonely bedrooms, even toilets, can be places for masturbation. Public places, before an audience of hairdressers, should not be.

The sadness and isolation that a lonely bedroom can represent in such a situation was not avoided but faced squarely. This brought forth deeply compassionate sharing and intimate revelation. I had rarely seen such empathy in these two groups. They were seeing themselves. The message was simple, spelt out with clarity, compassion and humour. Frank found himself not only amongst friends but also amongst champions. There has been no recurrence of the problem.

What kind of struggles are there?

Robert is the very opposite of withdrawn. He walks about with a lunging motion, talking in long sentences that are very difficult to understand, or singing loudly. He is usually cheerful although it's often hard to see why, and he sings the first verse of a hymn over and over again. The singing can get under people's skin, and consequently he hears 'Stop that!' more than any other phrase in the English language.

He repeatedly puts himself forward as a protagonist or proudly claims 'It's my turn'. His sessions are unintelligible to most but happy-making for him since they consist mainly of solo performances of his vocal delight. They have to be kept short or the whole group loses interest and disintegrates.

A breakthrough came, quite unexpectedly, one winter's morning. Walking from the car park, helping to carry the prop boxes, Robert announced 'I fell off the bus'. A bus of chairs and tables was quickly built in the classroom and students chose to be passengers and conductor. Three young men started to fight for the driver's seat. It was clear that big Peter would win, so I made little Tom into the bus inspector who had to check on Peter's driving. Joe, the third angry male, was appointed bus company owner and all three were satisfied and ready to be supportive of Robert. He, meanwhile, lunged about delighted at 'his scene' but taking no part other than that of an active observer.

Fares were exchanged, tickets issued, together with monetary calculations and arguing over prices. A moralistic exchange developed between several passengers about a 'free-rider' who got off the bus without paying his fare. It was all taken very seriously except by Robert who continued to circle the room clapping with delight at 'his scene'.

With some difficulty he was persuaded to fall from the platform and with even greater difficulty to lie reasonably still in the street. Someone phoned for an ambulance and students took turns at the phone to find a short, clear sentence that would convey the urgent need to the hospital telephonist. Doctors arrived and Robert was attended with considerable skill, all the students having had plenty of experiences of doctors' ways!

Robert still remained reluctant on the floor and hospital bed, keeping his observer role. Group members were then encouraged to make a hospital visit to their friend. They arrived with magnificent gifts, competing with each other in their inventiveness. Robert, now deeply moved, cried with some of his visitors, and broke free of his observer isolation. A circle was formed with Robert in the centre: the group was asked to keep him in this circle prison. It was important that his pent-up energy be released. He fought hard to free himself and found he could do so by tickling one of his jailers. It was a breakout and a breakthrough. Robert quickly reverted to his singing observer role but he now knew, as did the rest of the group, that he could leave it when he wanted. In the following months, increasingly, he did so.

Is the method democratic?

Built into the psychodramatic/sociodramatic method is the real potential for democracy. Can it become actuality? I believe that it can but it is difficult to achieve in practice. There are several needed ingredients.

The first is a high degree of active participation on the part of all members to the best of their abilities. This is always going to be difficult in an educational system where authoritarian methods are still entrenched, often encouraged, and, therefore, become a model. These methods, in turn, are re-enforced by a larger society in which money represents power and power does not favour democracy. Such a situation encourages conformity and the abdication of personal responsibility to teachers, administrators, bureaucrats and political leaders.

An added difficulty is that active participation means hard work and it is much easier to hand over to someone who wants the job or says that they want the job. With people who have low self-esteem due to disability, the willing worker, the self-promoting do-gooder and the charismatic group leader can represent take-over danger. Charismatic people need controls. This century has given us many examples of that truth. Dr Moreno's methods, properly used, offer some necessary controls. The first is his method of experiential group action releasing individual and collective spontaneity, creativity and responsibility. The second is the idea and continuous practice of role reversal.

A group working together in a practical, caring way can be intensely creative but pressure within a group can become tyrannical for some members. Disagreement and differences must not be just tolerated – which in itself can be arrogant in the extreme – but they must be encouraged as part of group health.

These are some of the most difficult obstacles to group democracy, which cannot happen because the group leader or members say it is desirable, however eloquent the plea may be. It has to be built into the system by the participants. A big responsibility for this rests with teachers, group leaders and sessions directors.

We have all been to lectures where the speaker begins by saying 'Please interrupt me if you have a question or disagreement.' In practice, few people dare interrupt because, although the speaker has vocalised permission, the 'idea' of entering in on a lecture is not built into the situation. The listeners have not had a part in promoting or accepting the idea and therefore do not respond. Building such acceptance and active participation into the two groups discussed took three terms of working together and often received setbacks from newcomers. Even now, after four years, time and effort has to be expended on renewing the group commitment to the democratic process. The results, however, in terms of group pride and individual growth, justify the time and the effort.

Are there guidelines?

I am wary of rules or set answers. Different criteria produce different results. What is suitable today may not be tomorrow. The following six points were helpful in establishing the two cohesive and democratic groups in this chapter:

1. Every single day, life reminds people with disabilities of the things they *can't do*. It is therefore important to encourage and promote a belief and a pride in the things they *can do*. Einstein spoke directly to and for young people with severe learning difficulties when he said, 'Imagination is more important than knowledge'.
2. A properly trained and experienced director committed to the ongoing process of learning.
3. A supportive and loving environment where trust is established and group members can make deep personal disclosures without feeling judged or punished.
4. A determination to face the unpleasant and the ugly in how we treat ourselves and are treated by others.
5. An equal determination to have fun together and value the sense of humour that maintains health.
6. Careful time management of each session and ample sharing that allows people to be reintroduced to the realities of the outside world.
7. I have also found it most helpful to write up sessions, firstly the outline plan with a commitment to dropping it in favour of here-and-now action, then, what actually happened and, third, conclusions (to be incorporated in further work).

Is it worth it?

A session took place towards the end of term. It was particularly intensive and all the members had been involved, worked together or agreed to differ, looked at the dark side as well as the sunshine, and shared long and strong. As the group dispersed, a young girl with Down's syndrome came to me and said, with energy and affection, 'That was just great, Ken; like everybody's a somebody.'

Reference

Miller, A. (1986) *Pictures of a Childhood*, New York: Farrar, Strauss & Giroux.

Further reading

Crum, T. F. (1987) *The Magic of Conflict*, New York: Simon & Schuster.
Fox, J. (1981) in G. Schattner and R. Courteney (eds) *Drama in Therapy*, New York: Drama Book Specialists.
Gray, N. (1979) 'I'll Take You to Mrs Cole', private publication, communicated in correspondence.
Pearson, D. (1989) 'The Drama', paper presented to the Australia New Zealand Psychodrama Association.

Chapter five

Time, space, reality, and the family

Psychodrama with a blended (reconstituted) family

Zerka T. Moreno

Introduction

This chapter deals with a fairly rare set of circumstances in that an entire family made the decision to enter residential treatment and to spend a week – the only week available in their various summertime schedules – having an evaluation and some guidelines for further conduct. As they live far away, we cannot be in continuous contact. The report of our psychodramatic explorations has to be less detailed than might normally be the case, due to lack of space and because of the fairly large number of participants. Therefore, the sessions are given in somewhat skeletal form.

This is the second marriage for both parents. The father has five children; he divorced their mother three years earlier. The mother was widowed and brought one child with her. (See Figure 5.1.)

The main focus seems to be to find a solution to some of the daily irritating interactions and to see where and what changes appear to be indicated.

If need be, the parents are willing to have the family continue in treatment when back at home with other therapists; alternatively, we may have to go to them to re-evaluate and guide further developments.

We decide to proceed as systematically as possible, examining together the facts, the individuals and their various needs, the structure of the family in terms of overall system and subsystems, the boundaries, the levels of intimacy and communication, generational and intergenerational conflict, role interactions, ethical considerations, the pushes and pulls, past history and what some family therapists indicate as obligations and entitlements (Karpel and Strauss 1983). 'We' means J. L. Moreno and myself, working as a team of co-therapists.

First contact

The long-distance telephone call from across the continent is our first contact. The family has searched for a residential treatment setting in which the entire family can be accommodated. The parents know about our work and the psychodrama process is one of the reasons they chose to contact us. The family

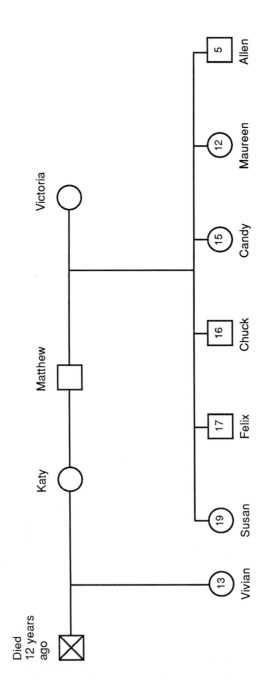

Figure 5.1 Structure of the family

is setting aside two weeks for this project from their summer vacation. One half of that time has to be for travel by family bus.

'Is it possible for you to admit all of us?'
'Yes, of course, be glad to have you. how many of you are there?'
'Eight, two adults and six young folks.'
'What ages are the young people?'
'Ranging from 12 to 19.' (See Figure 5.1.)
'What do you see as the most pressing problems?'
'Increasingly violent conflict between the two boys. The other children are girls.'
'Do you feel one boy is the main instigator, or are they about equally responsible?'
'We have observed it is the older one.'

We have the presenting problem and one identified patient. We know this is but the beginning.

Mutually satisfactory dates are determined and suitable housing preparations made. We already know not to place the two boys in a double room and beyond that, that the four remaining youngsters are girls. We are also told that five of the offspring belong to the father, the only child of the mother being the 13-year-old.

Matthew	Felix
(Father, Driver)	(17 years)
Katy	Susan
(Mother, Stepmother)	(19 years)
Chuck	Candy
(16 years)	(15 years)
Maureen	Vivian
(12 years)	(13 years)

Figure 5.2 Seating in the family bus

First meeting and opening session

Soon after arrival, when they have settled in their rooms, we enter into the theatre. Its uses are explained and how we proceed outlined. Clearly, the play aspect appeals to them; they are open and seem eager to start.

As they came in a rather large vehicle and the journey took several days, much time was spent in its enclosure. We decided to start there, going from the so-called periphery to the centre, but being aware that this may reveal some of the essential features of family members' interaction.

The director begins the session:

'Please step on the top level of the stage and set up seating arrangements in your bus.' Soon done (see Figure 5.2).

Now we have a visible seating sociogram. The arrangement is how they chose to be together.

'Did the seating arrangement change at all during the trip?'

'No, but that, too, was the cause for arguments between the two boys, the only arguments.'

Matthew is largely the spokesman, with Katy chipping in at times to give details; they have an harmonious interaction.

'Please proceed and let us see the essence of the interaction during your trip.'

The argument is a fairly low key one, but it demonstrates the tug-of-war between the two sons, both vying for Matthew's attention and proximity. Matthew uses a light-handed approach, tries not to interfere too much, but when he does it is to pour oil on troubled waters.

Felix, the oldest of the father's sons, and Chuck are each other's absolute opposites. Felix is domineering, determined not to give way, aware of his position as the oldest son and using it with a good deal of machismo. His attitude of superiority reminds us of the Alpha animal. It is his major route in dealing with the siblings, but is especially in evidence towards Chuck.

Chuck, on the other hand, is a rather shy, delicate looking boy, somewhat undersized in appearance. He wheedles and tries to negotiate to exchange seats with Felix, but to no avail. Matthew evidently is aware that rearranging the seating will lead to a good deal of upheaval among all the others as they tend to be afraid of Felix.

As the argument between them develops, Susan begins to stiffen in her seat; she appears to become growingly disturbed. As she remains silent and is seated next to a protective figure, her stepmother, and all the others show no such external behaviour, a double is assigned to her, and her function explained. It is intended to search and feel out the reason for Susan's obvious discomfort. The double's task is to bring to light the inner, silent processes in Susan. She notes that Candy's right foot is placed on Susan's back and seems to be pressing her. Feeling herself into Susan, the tension, the anger, the double suddenly turns around to Candy and explodes at her:

'Who do you think you are, pushing your foot into my back? Do you want me out of the way? It's not fair. I'm getting tired of it. Stop it.'

The tension in the group shifts from what appeared to be a central problem of interaction to a new area, to everyone's amazement. Candy is dumbfounded and silent. The reason for the amazement comes out later in the post-action sharing.

Susan's face is flushed as she softly explains to Candy: 'That's right. I've never been able to tell you, but I've felt your anger at me for quite a while. I don't understand it. I don't know what I've done to you to cause it.'

Candy is unable to speak.

We recognise that this is a second area that needs further examination. The action is ended here, sharing and dialoguing commences. The amazement at the Susan–Candy interaction comes through: 'The double did just the right thing. Candy is another bossy character in the family and Susan has difficulty with such people. But we did not notice what happened between them on the ride.' Some of the not-so-visible conflicts are beginning to emerge.

Second session – divorce and after-effects

It is time to look into what the families were like before the divorce.

> The interview reveals first Matthew's story, which, as he is the father of the large brood he brought into the marriage, is more complex than that of the mother–stepmother. Her only child is Vivian.
>
> Matthew is 50 years of age, a successful professional. Lately he has begun to search for a new career, one which he feels will give him both greater satisfaction and be more useful. Financially, with his wife working, such a change might be arranged. Katy is 38; she is also a professional, but her career is of more recent date. Since her first husband's death when Vivian was a baby, she has been her child's only parent and sole support. Upon marrying the first time she gave up graduate studies. Her husband's insurance helped to sustain her and the child while she worked part-time, but her second marriage made her present career possible after completing her degree. Matthew wholeheartedly endorsed her achievement. They have been married for two years.
>
> Katy's marriage was not of sufficient duration for anything remarkable to have occurred in the way of problems, except for her husband's illness and death at a young age. She has managed her life extremely well and is a warm, stable person.

It is time to explore the relationship between Matthew and his first wife, the mother of his children. We discover that there is yet another child, Allen, a 5-year-old boy, still living with his mother.

The auxiliary ego for the first wife is the stepmother (second wife). She knows Victoria and all agree that she will be a fair representative; the director asks Katy if she will allow corrections from the family members, with possible doubling for Victoria as they see fit. Katy agrees. The rest of the family is now well warmed up and becoming more and more available for the psychodrama process. In fact, we are rather taken by surprise at the negligible amount of resistance we have thus far encountered with them. Clearly, they are eager to find peaceful resolution of some of their interactional irritations. In spite of their youth, the children seem to be aware of the psychological impact of their history and the game-playing aspect of psychodrama appeals to them. They are also learning a great many new things about themselves and each other.

Matthew confronts 'Victoria' with his decision to leave her and the children and start living alone. This scene took place four years earlier. There is no other woman in his life, but the conflicts with Victoria have become too hard and his work suffers under the strain.

One of the essential elements in the dissolution of the relationship is that Victoria is reputed to be a seriously ill depressive who refuses to undergo treatment. She is not merely withdrawn, but also suspicious and hostile. She is especially hard on Candy, whom she accuses of all kinds of apparently unfounded misdeeds. Matthew tells 'Victoria' that the main reason she rejects Candy is that she is a healthy version of herself, fortunately without the depression. The more accusing 'Victoria' becomes, he explains, the more he tends to protect Candy and thus the fire gets fanned.

Although taking himself out of the field of action seems to be both callous and lacking in courage, he finds it absolutely necessary, if only for economic reasons. He must at least be able to earn a decent living for such a large family. When asked to turn his head and soliloquise he reveals how stupid he feels, not having recognised Victoria's illness earlier so that suitable decisions could have been made. But now it is too late and he must do what he can to salvage the family. He sees this as his only way out.

All of this is a true revelation to the children, who have, as is usually the case, never been let into the reasons for the family difficulties. At the same time, Matthew is not accusing 'Victoria', but makes clear that he sees his own part in all this.

Katy, in the role of Victoria, accuses him of desertion, of being unfaithful, a bad husband, father and a poor example for the children. We are aware that this is also a way of purging Katy from the feelings she has absorbed from the reports given her about Victoria by Matthew and the young people in the last few years.

Her enactment meets with recognition by the others, who feel very little need to add, except for some of them to state that they have heard these kinds of remarks directly, especially since Matthew remarried.

It is often noteworthy that the various family members have different perceptions about some of the others, but that, given the evidence here described, the absent mother and ex-wife represents for them an insoluble source of conflicts. We derole Katy and thank her for her good work.

Because of this and her own subsequent decision to leave her mother's home, Susan requests to be allowed to confront her mother as she has not been able to in reality, due to her mother's emotional state.

Now it is Susan who, tearfully and remorsefully, explains to her 'mother' in the empty chair why she had to leave. She reports she can no longer tolerate the divisions in the family, the mother's attempt to get Susan on her side against Matthew, whom Susan loves, and her relationship with Felix, using him as her standby and agent in disciplining the younger children. Susan especially accuses Victoria of her rejection of Chuck and Candy, which she feels to be dreadfully unfair and unrelated to their behaviour. It is true that Candy tries to fight back, but Chuck is completely subdued and frightened, as is the youngest boy, Allen, who becomes confused by the turmoil.

Here we are beginning to understand some of the behaviour Felix has thus far displayed. He has been trained since the divorce to be the male head of the family and this behaviour puts him now, in the new family, in opposition to Matthew, the true head of the family. He also maintains his stance towards Chuck, as earlier fed by Victoria.

> Susan ends the scene by informing her mother that, for the sake of her own sanity, she must leave, she can no longer be of help.

In reality this scene never took place, it is an interaction in 'surplus reality', but it should be recalled that in psychodrama, scenes, relationships, events which never took place are frequently the source of the deepest catharsis for the protagonist who needs them for healing. Essential to psychodrama is to remember its prosopopoeia which is certainly a central idea in surplus reality as it means personification, as of inanimate things, representation of an imaginary, absent or deceased person as speaking or acting.

> There is much sharing and discussing and the members feel they are beginning to do a lot of clearing up as to the various steps taken by each of them, with some relief of guilts expressed as they see that their actions were not made in bad faith, but had rational soil.

It becomes clear that the only one present not involved in conflict with Victoria is Maureen. She was still too little, though like her younger brother, bewildered by the troubles; but she has learned to be everyone's pet, as compensation, fairly successfully. This innocuous behaviour has stood her in good stead, but also weakens her emotional ties to the rest of the family. In a benign way, she is also an isolate, as much as little Allen. We store it away for future reference, if needed.

The striking contrasts of images of masculinity represented by the older boys is another aspect we need to deal with.

We are seeing some of the substructures in this family: Matthew–Katy (mutual attraction); Felix–Chuck (mutual rejection); Susan–Candy (ambivalent); Vivian–Maureen (not yet clarified, but they seem to be together a good deal); Chuck–Candy (mutually supportive, very close in age, but with some ambivalence); Katy–Susan (mutually supportive); Katy–Vivian (mildly conflicted since the additional members have come); Matthew–Felix (ambivalent). No doubt further cliques will be revealed as we continue, possibly some triangles, for instance, as well as other pairs.

Third session – How did you meet?

The third session deals with the newly reconstructed family.

> Katy and Matthew met at the house of friends after he moved out. The romance flourishes rapidly. To show what the early period of the marriage was like, Matthew, Katy and Vivian, sitting at the dining table, complete with wine and candlelight, represent an unreal-seeming trio, with Vivian being warmed by their new-found happiness. She has no memory of her own father and gets along well with Matthew. He, in turn, has no trouble relating to a single, younger child, and shows himself in general to be a nurturing parent, also to his own troubled brood. Here the vivid contrast between the old and the new are sharply brought to our attention.
>
> We are made aware that Vivian, once the little princess in the second marriage, is about to be displaced by the emergence of her stepfather's children and we need to gauge what this means to her. We have unveiled some of the strands that tie the past with the present.
>
> The director ends this scene and asks: 'How does this change? When do your children come to stay, Matthew?'

After a brief discussion the next scene is set.

> The time is a day or two before Christmas of the previous year. School holidays have just begun. Matthew, Katy and Vivian are decorating their tree. The honeymoon stage has not yet ended and the joy in their being together is evident. Matthew's children have been coming for vacations and weekends on and off, but they return home in time for school. The new family has moved from the earlier home to a larger house, to accommodate the regular influx.
>
> The procession starts: there is an unexpected visitor, Susan. She arrives loaded down with suitcases, on vacation from college. As soon as she enters she starts to cry. The three of them stand around her, Katy shelters her until she quiets down. In a still-tight, small voice, Susan announces that she has permanently departed from her mother's house. After her first semester at college, she finds life at that very troubled place unbearable. She does not plan ever to return there.

We think we need to hear everyone's soliloquy. This is a very dramatic development that is going to create some juxtapositioning in the family.

> 'How do you feel about what is happening? Matthew, please start. You already know how to do that. We need to hear your reflections and feelings. Do not talk to the others. This is not dialogue, this is talk with the self that normally others do not hear. But here we do it out loud.'
>
> Matthew (looking very worried, frowns at first): 'Good Lord, how will Victoria take this? I'm glad to see Susan here, but it is bound to have other consequences. Will Victoria put still more pressure on the others? I see

Katy being helpful to Susan. I'd better go soon and see how the rest of the gang is doing.'

Katy (not in the least perplexed, concerned for Susan): 'This was inevitable. Anyway, Matthew knows I was prepared for something like this happening. I did not know it would be so soon, though. Wonder how Vivian will take this!' (Looks at her daughter who is standing by and watching with much interest.) 'It may be complicated, but we must be ready to stand by. I think I can manage it well enough. It's good to know Susan feels secure enough to come.'

Director: 'You, too, Vivian, let's hear from you.'

Vivian: 'Wow, wonder what it'll be like, having an older sister? I rather like Susan; anyway, she's in college most of the time. Guess I can take it. Wait and see.'

Susan (at a nod in her direction by director): 'It went better than I thought. Hope the others are not going to be too upset, but I just can't stand it any more.'

We end the dramatic exploration here and find out that there was a hiatus of several months before the balance of the young people joined their father and Katy. It is decided to leave that for the next session. We ask the children to think about their own entrance into the new household, not to discuss it yet, but to go out and relax somewhere. There has been enough dealing with upheaval for one day.

We now see some more complex substructures, triangles have developed as well as a quadrangle: Matthew–Katy–Vivian, Matthew–Katy–Susan, Matthew–Katy–Vivian–Susan. We are looking forward to learning about the migration of the rest, but, like Matthew, feel for Victoria, who seems to be becoming more and more isolated.

Fourth session – the others follow

Felix is the second arrival and becomes our protagonist.

We see him alone in his room at his mother's house, fretful, brooding. He does not talk to anyone about his feelings so we ask that he, too, soliloquise. Felix is an athletic boy, of average height. While Susan has always been a good student, he manages to get by, preferring sports to studying. However, he has never failed any courses. Possibly he is more affected by the various distractions at home, which Susan has managed to overcome. In fact, she gives evidence of having delved into her studies to shut out the turmoil. Matthew has kept Felix at an acceptable level by insisting he makes an effort in order for him to be allowed the athletic activities.

Felix (note how often we resort to soliloquy in order to give the protagonists a chance to open up without having their revelations discussed or opposed, accepting them as they occur, since it is rare for family members

61

to be sufficiently open with one another and such openness leaves them vulnerable):

'Since Susan's gone, Mother depends still more on me. I miss Dad. I can't take his place. Besides, Mum is so demanding, I feel strangled (puts his hands around his throat here). Nothing I do is right. Wish I could do better. Mum is so unhappy.'

(He goes outside, starts pacing up and down in the yard of his mother's house, playing with an imaginary basket ball, tosses it into the area indicated as the basket. The movement and this activity seem to be easing him.)

'Wish Dad and Mum could've gotten along better and hadn't split up. Dad has a much better thing with Katy. And Katy really is trying hard to be a friend. I think I'll go and talk with them.'

(He takes his bike and leaves.)

Director: 'Let's hear what you're feeling as you cycle, or what you're thinking about.'

Felix (on his bike, pedals while sitting on chair): 'I'm worried about Allen. I like him a lot. He's still small and I'm too young to take care of him. I'm going to ask Dad what to do about Allen.'

(Note that he seems to overlook his two younger siblings nearest to him in age; there is a year between himself and Chuck, two years between himself and Candy. We record this and later find out more about this triad.)

Felix stops: 'That's about it.'

Director: 'Who's at home at your Dad's and Katy's house?'

Felix: 'Both and Vivian. Susan's at school.'

Director: 'Go ahead and talk with Matthew and Katy. Is Vivian there as well?'

Felix: 'I don't think so.' (They step up on the stage.)

Director: 'Let's just go into the meeting between you three.'

Matthew: 'Hi, Felix, come in. What brings you here? Is there anything wrong?'

(Matthew is always aware that the old family situation has a very tenuous base and that there are frequent problems.)

Katy looks apprehensive, different from when Susan arrived; clearly she feels her relationship with Felix is more complicated. Later exploration reveals some of Katy's emotional history related to this difficulty.

Felix tells them pretty much the same things as we have already heard in the soliloquy, but he suddenly bursts out: 'I don't think I can take living with Mum any more. Can I move in with you?'

Here we ask each of the parents to soliloquise their reactions.

Matthew: 'Here we go again. It's just the way we have talked about it, Katy and I. Sooner or later this was probably bound to happen. When Susan came, Victoria was very bitter. This is going to hit even harder. Felix is her best support. Lord, this is becoming heavier all the time. She's very unhappy and we just don't seem to be able to help her.'

The children are keenly listening; all these revelations are eye-openers for them and they are becoming more sensitive to their elders and their concerns about everyone involved.

Katy: 'I've never had a son before. Matthew and I are going to have to work together on this. Well, the youngsters do need help. Victoria is really not able to manage them. It's a large family and would be complicated under the best of circumstances.'

Director: 'Vivian, do you remember what you feel when this happens?'

Vivian (takes a moment before responding): 'This may be interesting but I'm not sure how I feel about it. I've never had sisters and brothers; I feel a bit swamped at times. It's harder for Mum and me to be close like we used to be.'

Now Felix confronts his father and asks what should be done about Allen. Matthew points out that he still needs his mother and conversely, she needs to keep him. Furthermore, he reminds him that, because of the age discrepancies, whenever Allen comes and visits, Katy is the one who has to take care of him, as they all have their own friends and do not give up their various activities. It would be grossly unfair all around to take such a drastic step as to remove him from the only home he knows and would totally deprive his mother, besides.

In the course of sharing and discussing we find out that Felix is the only child who still goes and visits his mother and Allen from time to time.

The director asks Felix to show him how such visits go and Felix chooses Katy to be his mother, Maureen to represent Allen. It is clear from his role reversals with Victoria that she does feel very deprived by his departure and accuses him much as she did Matthew of disloyalty. Felix has a good deal of residual guilt, but his need for emotional stability helps him fend off some of her accusations. A touching scene takes place when he role-reverses with Allen who asks him what divorce means and, in that role, says to Felix, 'I did not divorce my Daddy.'

This appears to be one of the most unsettling and unresolved areas for the family to face. The smallest child has put his finger on one of the most disturbing aspects of a family's breaking up.

We have unearthed another triangle, Felix–Victoria–Allen, and the absent dyad, Victoria–Allen. The family talks about how Allen defends his mother whenever he comes for a visit with them; clearly the little boy is very early made aware of some of the substrata of conflict and has become his mother's protector.

Fifth session – Chuck and Candy's turn

The two next eldest children, Matthew informs us, being so close in age, were brought up like triplets with Felix. He believes it was at this point that Victoria felt her burdens to become too great and the marriage began to unravel. This is what Matthew referred to earlier, blaming himself for not having understood how and when it occurred. It also throws new light upon the conflict between the two boys. As Felix was the much preferred child, emotional neglect of the next born was almost inevitable and when Candy appeared, an energetic, feisty girl, the dissolution became even more obvious. Furthermore, Felix displays characteristics somewhat resembling his mother, perhaps learned, while Chuck is completely different. Having his younger sister as his best friend, and Susan as a protectress, his idea of how not to be a male is embodied by his taking a position at the opposite end of the pole from Felix.

It may be said that Felix was his mother's 'psychodramatic baby', her ideal child. Evidently, she did not desire or need any others. But they came and here they are, little nestlings in need of care.

We next turn our attention to Chuck and Candy as we understand that they came to their father's home together. They step up on the stage and show us what happened. It is about 1.00a.m. during Easter vacation. We find out that Chuck goes to a private school, having some minor learning difficulties. His vacation date differs by a day or so from Candy's, so she waited for his to start. They have talked about leaving and plan to do it now. They hastily pack a few clothes and run for it.

There's not much new information about their reason except that Victoria has become still more harsh with the two of them and they often have to be each other's helpers. Thus far all the young people display intact self-protective mechanisms, although Chuck is least well endowed. Their arrival, although in the wee small hours, has been more-or-less expected and by now the transfers are becoming routine. Katy and Matthew were aware it was only a matter of time.

Technically, their mother has custody, but in their state, at a certain age, the children are permitted to choose with which parent they wish to reside.

The assumption is that Victoria is fairly relieved to be free of the two children she least wanted and with whom the relationship is most troubling to her. There are now only Maureen and Allen living with her; the consensus is that she can manage that rather better.

It is decided to let Chuck have his session now and we are again struck by the wondrous diversity in the family.

Chuck goes about, in monodramatic form, taking all the roles himself, to show how he spends his time as a junior counsellor during summer vacation, at a camp for disabled children. He is a tender, nurturing counsellor and it is clear that here he shines. At home, the evaluation is that he is a little bit of a misfit, but now, with everyone able to see him in a different setting, some of his true nature is revealed. It is evident that this is new information for the rest of the family; although his parents receive positive reports about his work, they have not witnessed him in action.

The awareness that the adolescent has many roles and that these potentials are not always activated in the family fold, is helping the others to see him differently.

> One highly significant aspect of family structure is its role structure – that is, the roles which are assigned to and assumed by individuals in the family and the relationships between or among those roles. This discussion does not refer to family roles in the functional sense, i.e. the role of the mother or father, etc. but to roles in the sense of interlocking identities, such as the 'little angel' or the 'peacemaker'. The term 'role' is often used to describe those presentations of self that we all assume in social or work situations. These roles are usually fairly temporary and limited, and are consciously and deliberately assumed. In other words, there is actually very little overlap between who we feel we really are and whom we may act like with the corner grocer or a neighbour down the block.
>
> When we speak of roles in the family, however, we are discussing a very different phenomenon. The roles we are given and assume in our families are more permanent, less flexible, and usually less conscious. In these cases, there is a great deal of overlap between who we are in our families and who we feel we really are. We can move in and out of the roles we play with our neighbour as easily as we may put on and take off a coat, but trying to change our roles in our families is more often like trying to struggle out of a straightjacket.
>
> (Karpel and Strauss 1983: 26)

The fact that Chuck has been seen in a position of strength helps us to decide to go into the actuality of the present problem, namely, the fights between him and Felix. We keep this plan in mind for the next session.

Sixth session – the boys and their conflict

As the layout of the family's living quarters is unknown to us, Katy and Matthew drew a schema of the house and its residents (see Figure 5.3). As in most families, there are sexual considerations in placing the young people together. But the difficulties between the boys make such proximity rather undesirable and may increase the problem between them. In the next scene we see how the 'territorial imperative' works here (Z. Moreno 1966: 235).

We are informed that the worst scenes take place during evenings, at weekends and during holidays, periods when sharing time and space are particularly in evidence. Sociometrically, sharing time and space are dynamic living categories, opportunities for interpersonal contact of both positive and negative impact.

TOP FLOOR

Bedroom	*Bathroom*	*Bedroom*
Felix		Chuck

SECOND FLOOR

Bedroom		*Bedroom*
Matthew and Katy		Susan
Bathroom		Bathroom
Bedroom		*Bedroom*
Vivian and Maureen		Candy
Bathroom		

GROUND FLOOR

Living Room	*Kitchen*	*Dining Room*
Family Room		*Half Bathroom*

ENTRANCE

Figure 5.3 Living area inside the house

It is evening. The boys are upstairs in their rooms, doing homework or whatever needs to be done, each away from the other. They have separate television sets, a provision for reducing clashes. There are visitors downstairs in the living room, which makes the parents particularly eager to have some peace and quiet, another aspect of sharing time and space. The rest of the young people watch as this scene develops. At home, they are not only spectators but also involved actors. We decide to focus at the essential interactors.

Suddenly the fight erupts. Felix goes into the bathroom, comes out and shouts at Chuck, because he has left the bathroom messy, has not hung up the towels, scrubbed out the tub, mopped the floor, as he should have done, it being his turn. They have been alternatively assigned these chores and Felix feels he does them well, while accusing Chuck of being neglectful and sloppy. Chuck tries to defend himself but Felix now becomes physically aggressive and starts to hit him. This is the pattern he learned at his first home, this being the only way their mother was able to handle what she saw as unruly behaviour of the children. Katy dashes upstairs, tries to calm them down and to shield Chuck, but now Felix turns against her and takes a physically threatening stance towards her; while he has not actually hit her, it is clear that he comes very close. Katy appears frozen, unable to handle her response to this, calls for Matthew to come and help, and this is how the scene ends, with father becoming the mediator.

By now the entire household has been aroused and the mood is one ranging from irritation to controlled anger.

According to the post-enactment sharing, this is rather a frequent series of events and very little impact has been effected by talking about it. What to do?

Reorganisation of the living space

We return to the schema of the house and note that Susan is not home a great deal of the time, being away at college. What about trying the following: since proximity is such a difficult arrangement, why not move Chuck downstairs to her room and have Susan move into his? Susan is asked how she would feel about that and after thinking it over she agrees, noting that if that will bring greater peace in the house, she is willing.

Felix agrees to this, while we point out that now the care of the bathroom will be largely his very own responsibility. But as he and Susan seem to be more compatible and she is away a good deal of the time anyway, he feels relieved. He will have more living space for himself and can determine his own obligations.

The greatest relief is evidenced by Chuck, who is clearly intimidated by the conflict with Felix. He, too, is now assigned to take his part in being responsible for the chores in the bathroom shared with Candy. They accept this and Candy makes it clear to him that she, too, will expect him to carry his part. Because of the better relationship between these two, this assignment appears to be a more positive one. It remains to be carried out at home and tested out.

There is a good deal of discussion and sharing at the end. We have noted Katy's fright at the fighting and decide to have a talk with the parents alone, so they can ventilate some of their own angers and concerns, before the next session.

Seventh session – interview with Katy and Matthew alone

We review together what we have thus far experienced together and the various dynamic underpinnings. We turn our attention to Katy to ask how she feels about the boys' conflict of which the bathroom and bedroom proximity are merely a part, and particularly her response to the suggestion of separating them. She admits that this is likely to reduce at least that particular difficulty, but states that Felix's aggression is very hard for her and frightening. He is getting taller and stronger and she fears that this type of behaviour may lead to further difficulties if not corrected, not only at home.

While not in any way mitigating the threat as such, we enquire whether Felix's wild behaviour reminds her of anyone in her past. She admits that her father was an alcoholic, physically abusive to her mother and herself. He died of the consequences of his illness while she was an adolescent, but the fear remained.

Katy is given an opportunity to address the empty chair and releases a lot of feelings in her own role. When asked what she needs from him now, she states that he ought to ask her forgiveness. We suggest a role reversal with him and she takes time to get into his role. What comes out instead is how much he regrets not having been a good father and how proud he is of the way she has developed and lived her life. Also, that he realises that her own mothering of this enlarged family is partly due to her own experiences, lacking such care. He further suggests she should not mix Felix up with himself.

It is not uncommon to learn in role reversal what protagonists really need to receive from an absent other, and that it is not quite what they thought they needed. The role reversal was actually a more complete encounter than mere asking for forgiveness.

We purposely do not ask Matthew to undertake the father's role for Katy in order not to confuse the relationship. It is hoped that Katy's empty-chair completion will ease her interaction with Felix.

At this point Matthew remarks that he senses Felix is confused by his physical attraction to Katy. Katy is younger than his mother, energetic and pretty. Matthew adds how eager Felix is to show off his athletic accomplishments and disappointed if Katy cannot always be there to see his success. The classic father–son, daughter–father conflicts come to the surface as well as the father–mother–son triangle. Katy agrees that all these factors may play a part in her inability to be more receptive to the boy.

Further clarification comes when Matthew states that there are traces of character in Felix he sees in Victoria as well and they are not the ones that he finds most endearing. There is the situation with Allen already reported. Matthew feels that Felix is here in parental competition with him and wants to show him up as a failing parent. Triangle father–eldest son–youngest son, but also quadrangle father–eldest son–youngest son–mother are in evidence.

When role-reversed as Felix, he is asked what about Matthew he finds difficult; he says he'll never be able to equal his father's professional achievement. He feels the need to break free of the family. He wants very much to go to a local private school, in which there is more stress placed upon athletics than in his present, public school. Back in his own role we ask Matthew what changes fulfilling Felix's desire would entail. Matthew says that financially it would mean that Chuck would have to go to a local school rather than the private one he now attends.

We point out that maybe Felix feels he should have a chance to attend a school of his own choosing and that this, too, may be another source of his rejection of Chuck. Could it be that he interprets Chuck's schooling as a preferment to which he is also entitled? This is discussed as a distinct possibility which did not occur to them since there appeared to be a good reason for that decision. We ask, is it conceivable that Chuck's current level of achievement may be good enough so that he can meet the local school's standards?

It is agreed that they will look into this. We talk about how such a change may decrease Felix's demands, give him a needed sense of accomplishment and support his need for individuation. In any event, the change gives the parents an opportunity to set limits in order for Felix to attain his goal.

Matthew ends the interview by taking Katy's hand and telling her, in an emotion-filled voice, how deeply he appreciates their marriage and her devotion to his children. He believes the children may never fully comprehend the adjustments and sacrifices she has made and continues to make to ensure their healthy development. We applaud this and add that it was nothing short of heroic, and how central her role is in the family. Katy is touched and a bit embarrassed by these accolades. For us, Matthew's love for Katy, his appreciation of her and his relief that she is his partner, are clear.

Eighth session – the last newcomer

Maureen is the youngest of the girls, the final immigrant.

Her soliloquy prior to her departure from her mother's house shows her unhappiness. She has been spending weekends and holidays at her father's new home, but the school weekdays are not happy ones for her. She is particularly attracted to the new family because of her relationship with Vivian and this is one of the big pulls in her case. She has never had such a close agemate in her family before. Vivian is by now quite used to the additions and good-naturedly takes to Maureen's presence, with minor reservations.

When she has completed her scene of decision, which is timed before a long holiday weekend, we ask Maureen and Vivian to present us with a typical interaction between them.

Although they are fairly convivial, there are some irritations between them because Vivian, being older and more mature, has trouble dealing with Maureen's tendency to adulate and imitate her, clinging more than she is able to bear. There are some altercations between them about clothing and borrowing things. Role reversals are suggested, which help clarify the feelings on both sides.

It is fairly remarkable that Vivian has been able to emerge in her own right without being altogether overcome. Possibly it is the piecemeal pace at which the father's children entered the family fold, or the particular way in which the parents have managed to steer the ship, as well as the fact that Katy sensed well before it happened that the family would some day be much enlarged and prepared Vivian for that eventuality.

Maureen, on the other hand, has avoided conflict in the past, as already indicated, by being generally well accepted and has managed to stay afloat in the formerly troubled waters. In the main, it is clear that what strikes us as a problematic earlier family life has not made as negative an impact as might be expected. Therapists may tend to see these difficulties too darkly; there may be more health than we assume. When Maureen was left alone with her mother and younger brother, however, she felt the impact of her mother's depression too much and, like the others, felt unequal to the task of helping lift her out of it. Besides, she was lonely for her siblings.

There is another sister pair that needs further work, Susan and Candy.

We now focus on their interaction and ask them to have a good talk, such as they were never able to have before.

A very touching confrontation ensues in which Candy explains to Susan what she feels to be the source of her anger, brought to light in the bus scene. Susan protected her and Chuck against the severe attacks on them by Victoria and her departure made life especially untenable at home. Their protectress had left them still more vulnerable. Susan and Candy both weep and Susan asks Candy's pardon and tells her how much she admires her fighting spirit. She, Susan, sees Candy as stronger than herself in this respect and therefore unaware of how much her withdrawal from the scene of battle meant to the younger girl. Role reversal at this point reinforces the interchange. When back in their own roles they hug, admit that they love each other and are glad to be reunited.

Sharing and further discussion lead to the statement that parents have power over their children and that is fine, as long as they do not abuse it.

As we have had a good deal of emotional revelation, it is decided that the next session will be dedicated to the 'Magic Shop', it being the final one. This allows for a more cognitive way of looking at their needs and is often filled with laughter.

Ninth session – the magic shop

The magic shop is a place where people can come and express a wish for something they want to attain, nothing of a material nature, but goals or feelings or attributes they feel they want or need. In exchange, the shopkeeper will ask for something to be given as the shop must never be depleted; it must retain a certain inventory so all those who enter there may find something they require.

Everyone steps up and some find resolution of their wishes. Exceptionally notable is that all enter into the spirit of the game, as is demonstrated when Matthew expresses his desire for new skills that will enable him to build a new career. When the shopkeeper asks him to yield in exchange the very skills that have made him successful because they are valuable and needed by others, he is willing, shakes hands with the auxiliary ego and declares it to be an acceptable bargain.

The element of what seemed to be pure play helped to make the closure a more lighthearted one than might otherwise have been achieved as there was a good deal of laughter in the course of this session.

Follow-up

Contact three months later informs us that the changes for the rooms and schooling have indeed been made; in general, the atmosphere has greatly improved and the interactions are less charged with negative feelings. Matthew has begun to look into his special needs for training in order to be prepared for the eventual career change, which is, however, some years in the future.

During a meeting with the parents a decade later, we are told that the young people are pursuing careers, some of them abroad, and are doing well in their chosen path. Matthew has reached his goal of the career change he aspired to and is more fulfilled in it.

Summary

We tried to proceed in a manner consistent with sociometric and psychodramatic principles, not imposing our own ideas, but allowing information to guide us from step to step. Soliloquy was used as a form of 'surplus reality', largely because the kind of communication and information it highlights is rarely brought out in complex and intimate relations. It is also useful as an educational tool, to help family members become aware of what may not be communicated, but may have to be searched out. Other psychodramatic techniques were used sparingly; we were not training these people to become each other's therapists, but tried to sensitise them to their own needs and those of others. Full role reversal was used only twice, between the two sister pairs, to cement the relationship or to ease it. It was not used where it might be interpreted as a weapon to hurt another person through new insights of vulnerability or a misplaced sense of power or authority over another. Mostly, we used self-presentation to affirm, support and clarify.

We proceeded from a model of health, not of pathology. Where there is pathology that diminishes the ability of healthy aspects to come through, the best any therapy can contribute is to reach the autonomous healing centre of the individuals concerned. This approach meant that, while the presenting problem was not to be overlooked, we wanted more background information before assuming that it is the most important problem. Therefore, we did not start there, but entered into the family organisation with the most recent and common experience. The family members guided us and, hand in hand, allowed us to guide them.

The time and space interaction explorations had been used by us earlier in family guidance. Based upon the children's expressed choice for partners at the dining-room table, which was in discord with their assignment by their parents, we changed the seating positions around the table and thus eliminated the presenting problem: the throwing of food at one another of two siblings, across the table. In a residential centre for neurologically impaired children such seating arrangements, too, were changed according to the children's sociometric choices, altering the assignments made by the staff. The staff reported that accidents, spillages, temper tantrums, breaking of dishes, arguments and noise level were all greatly reduced in number. But, after one month of this sociometrically fertilised emotional soil, the most startling finding was made by the nursing and medical staff, namely a general, overall improvement in the physical condition of the entire school population, an improvement shown on the health charts several times greater than the previous curve for this particular item (Z. Moreno 1966: 231–42).

The idea that runaways often come in strings, not as separate occurrences, was clarified by sociometric investigation of relationships in a residential community of adolescent girls. These did not have to be, as was the case in our family described above, face-to-face relationships, but were an aspect of the network effect. Our family of protagonists were, therefore, at far greater intensity of interaction and influencing one another directly (J. L. Moreno 1953: 441–5).

The question remains: would this family have done equally well without our guidance? What might have happened if they had not been ready to ask for help? It cannot be answered except to say that we truly do not know. It is conceivable, though not likely, that some felicitous and welcome changes could have occurred by themselves, or that other forms of therapy could have been effective. The fact is that changes were achieved in fairly short order where previously they had not, and that certain patterns related to both past and present appeared to make change difficult without some external intervention.

Roles and role interactions often become fixed and enmesh family members in ways hard to overcome without some outside help. Certainly, the illness of an absent family member hovered pervasively over various developments and that person remained outside of treatment and guidance.

One may consider some of the changes due to both cognitive awareness as well as emotional satisfactions, catharsis and integration, or to 'reframing'. Perhaps one thing that was learned is that in order to *act* differently, one must first learn to *see* the world differently.

> The problems we want to change are not problems related to the properties of objects or of situations – to the *reality of the first order*, as I have proposed to call it – but are related to the meaning, the sense, and the value that we have come to attribute to these objects or situations (their *second-order reality*). 'It is not the things themselves that worry us, but the opinions that we have about those things,' said Epictetus some 1900 years ago.
>
> (Watzlawick 1987: 140–2)

Therefore, if we were helpful it may well be because we were able to change some of the ways they viewed and experienced one another. This, in turn, led to changing their interactions, leading to achievement of better intrapersonal and interpersonal integration. Not only their inner world changed, but also their outer world, as well as their various fields of interaction.

Is this an artistic approach or a scientific one? Can we really make this distinction in psychotherapy? Is it not, essentially, a mixture or a synthesis? Here is what Otto Rank said about play, which is after all what psychodrama is, playing with life but also playing with serious intent:

> For play, after all, differs not only conceptually, but factually, from art. It has in common with art the combination of the real and the apparent; yet it is not merely fancy objectivized, but fancy translated into reality, acted and lived. It shares with art the double consciousness of appearance and reality, yet it has more of reality, while art is content with the appearance.
>
> (Rank 1968: 356)

General comments

Family therapists differ somewhat as to their various approaches. Some will deal only with the total family when all are together and refuse to see any of the members individually; others will combine these two forms of intervention. We leave ourselves the option to see one or another person individually or in subgroups, as the occasion may demand. We state this clearly at the outset, contracting for secrecy of what emerges there, as indicated by the person or persons involved. The enmeshment of family members and their fear of retaliation outside of therapy may make constant openness difficult to achieve at times. The adults in the family, moreover, bring into the marriage their former life experiences, which may have no bearing upon the current situation, yet manage to colour it deeply and may distort it. Such findings force us to take a look at these experiences without the constraints of the presence of all the others.

Secrets are generally not supported in family therapy, there being a belief that openness makes for better relationship; we have found that this much vaunted openness may, in fact, be dangerous and inflict wounds that are lasting and hard to heal. Evaluating this openness with the family is part of the therapeutic alliance and needs careful handling.

Because psychodrama is largely done in groups to maximise its effectiveness, does not mean that we eliminate individual intervention when indicated. We resorted twice to leaving out some members, once having the parents by themselves and once the younger generation. We sensed there was a need for separating them and the resulting interactions were very fruitful. Would they have been the same with all persons present? Of course not; every participant makes for different interactions. Would these have been more productive? We do not know; we only know that some barriers seemed to be lifted.

What are the differences between the psychodramatic approach to families and other forms? Psychodrama actually fits very well into family-therapy theories. What it offers is a set of instruments that are useful in deepening the learning process. One of the most intense is that of role reversal. But the way we deal with time and space in our format is another contribution. Family therapists describe themselves as action oriented. Psychodramatists go further in that interactions are explored not as reported, but as re-enacted, embodied in time and space, in the spaces in which the events took place; within a play context the drama soon becomes deadly earnest as the warming-up process proceeds.

A rather good plea for psychodrama may be extracted out of the following statement:

> When there is conflict within the family, family members try to figure out who is right and who is wrong. The harder they try to prove rightness and wrongness, the more the conflict accelerates. Very few people have been trained to become aware of process. One way to understand the use of conflict or the attempt to prove right and wrong is to see it as a way of defining process and how people position themselves in relation to the other. One of the most helpful procedures for working with families in therapy is to stay tuned in to the process and not get caught up in the content that people present.
>
> (Howells 1979: 12)

References

Howells, J. G. (ed.) (1979) *Advances in Family Psychiatry*, vol. I, New York: International University Press.

Karpel, M. A. and Strauss, E. S. (1983) *Family Evaluation*, New York and London: Gardner Press.

Moreno, J. L. (1953) *Who Shall Survive? The Foundations of Sociometry, Group Psychotherapy and Psychodrama*, Beacon, NY: Beacon House.

Moreno, Z. T. (1966) 'Sociogenesis of individuals and groups' in J. L. Moreno (ed.) *The International Handbook of Group Psychotherapy*, New York: Philosophical Library Inc.

Rank, O. (1968) *Art and Artist*, New York: A. A. Knopf.

Watzlawick, P. (1987) 'If You Desire to See, Learn How to Act', in J. Zeig (ed.) *The Evolution of Psychotherapy*, New York: Brunner Mazel.

Further reading

Ardrey, R. (1966) *The Territorial Imperative*, New York: Atheneum.

Moreno, J. L. (1972) *Psychodrama Vol. I*, Beacon, NY: Beacon House.

Moreno, J. L. (1987) *The Essential Moreno*, Beacon, NY: Springer.

Moreno, Z. T. (1987) 'Psychodrama, role theory and the concept of the social atom', in J. Zeig (ed.) *The Evolution of Psychotherapy*, New York: Brunner Mazel.

Moreno, J. L. and Moreno, Z. T. (1969) *Psychodrama Vol. III*, Beacon, NY: Beacon House.

Moreno, J. L. and Moreno, Z. T. (1975) *Psychodrama Vol. II*, Beacon, NY: Beacon House.

Moreno, J. L., Moreno, Z. T. and Jonathan, D. (1964) *The First Psychodramatic Family*, Beacon, NY: Beacon House.

Satir, V. M. (1966) 'Family therapy: an approach to the treatment of mental and emotional disorder', in J. L. Moreno (ed.) *The International Handbook of Group Psychotherapy*, New York: Philosophical Library Inc.

FAMILY FRIEND

Chapter six

Learning to live again

Psychodramatic techniques with sexually abused young people

Anne Bannister

'I learned to trust in our psychodrama group. I can't remember the last time I trusted anyone'. Debbie had been intimately fondled by a family friend for years, from the age of eleven. Her parents were emotionally cold and the family friend, together with his wife and baby, had seemed to offer warmth and affection. The fondling progressed to mutual masturbation and the abuser used Debbie's strictly religious upbringing to terrify her with threats of eternal damnation if she told. He also capitalised on her feelings of guilt so that she truly believed herself to be a wicked person. Learning to trust was also about trusting herself, trusting her feelings, her judgement and in the quality of her own worth.

Caroline and Rita had both been abused within the family. Caroline's father had been fondling her and digitally penetrating her from the age of 4 until she told someone who believed her, two years later. Rita's stepbrother raped her when she was 12. 'I desperately needed someone to confide in', she said. 'In psychodrama I did what I couldn't do in life – I told my grandmother and she comforted me. She told me it wasn't my fault, and I believed her.'

Between the ages of 4 and 6 Caroline expressed her anger in the only way she knew how, symbolically, through severe and violent temper tantrums. In psychodrama this behaviour was 'allowed' and was controllable and safe. Through the use of puppets Caroline brought together the 'loving' part of her father and what she termed 'the monster'. The nightmare world of monsters and powerful giants was real for this child. Moreno, the founder of psychodrama, encouraged his patients to act out their fears and fantasies in a controlled setting so that these fears could be incorporated into the patients' understanding of themselves and their world (Moreno 1977). Caroline, at the age of 6, was able to destroy the 'monster' part of her father without destroying the affectionate part, and so she began to deal with her ambivalent feelings.

Sam's stepfather demanded that Sam, aged 4 and his brother, aged 2, should sexually stimulate him by sucking his penis. Already, at 4, Sam resented his victimisation. He was able to talk about his brother more easily than himself. Eventually, using psychodramatic techniques, he was able to talk about and 'own' his experience and thus express his anger, pain and grief. Sam had already been assaulting other little boys in his nursery class, perhaps in order to control the situation. This behaviour ceased soon after treatment commenced.

What is child sexual abuse?

These case histories (with names and details changed) are introduced to show that child sexual abuse takes many forms, from fondling to rape and the damage is caused by the betrayal of trust and the abuse of power, rather than by the nature of the sexual act. Abusers will choose a child who is most available so most abuse occurs within the family, or within a circle of extended family and friends. Boys as well as girls are abused, although current studies show that approximately twice as many girls are abused as boys. The abuse of boys is being revealed more as research progresses and it may be that boys find it even more difficult to tell than girls do (Finkelhor 1986). This may be because of the homosexual implications, since most abusers are male (over 90 per cent in studies). The stigmatisation, however, clings to victims of both sexes and is a reason why the incidence of child sexual abuse is likely to be under-reported in the population.

How often does it occur?

The incidence of abuse has been studied in the USA since 1929 and in Britain within the last ten years. Incidence figures have increased as research has become more accurate and researchers have improved their interviewing techniques (Herman 1981; Baker and Duncan 1985). Retrospective surveys are the usual way that research can be done realistically and the figures show that between 10 per cent and 50 per cent of the child population is likely to have been sexually abused before the age of 18. The higher figures generally include non-touching abuse ('flashing') and are also for females rather than mixed population samples (Russell 1984).

Figures based on reported cases are likely to be an even more severe underestimate than figures based on retrospective studies. In the USA these figures are based on the American Humane Society's clearing house but only 31 states and territories submit information (MacFarlane and Waterman 1986). In Britain there is no central register but the NSPCC collect figures from those areas where they administer the child-abuse registers. From these they estimate that 5 in every 1,000 children may come to professional notice because of sexual abuse, but they admit that this is likely to be a severe underestimate of the true incidence. Although physical child abuse has been registered in Britain since 1974, after the Maria Colwell case, there had been no nationwide agreement on the registration of child sexual abuse, but this tended to change in the wake of the Cleveland crisis in 1987. Police figures are unlikely to be helpful since abuse within the family is less likely to be reported than abuse by a stranger.

As the subject is being more widely understood, the realisation is dawning that children are abused from a very young age. Again, studies have put the age at which abuse usually begins somewhere between the age of 7 and 11, but recent reports show that this average age is falling alarmingly. In Los Angeles the average age is now 4 years old (MacFarlane and Waterman 1986). In Britain this impression is certainly borne out by those working in this area. Whereas ten years ago young adolescents would most commonly reveal their abuse, now it is not at all uncommon for under-5s to tell someone about their abuse, and, most importantly, to be believed.

The question of whether children lie about sexual abuse has been addressed by several studies (Goodwin 1982; Jones and McGraw 1987). There is no evidence to show that children usually lie about such matters, nor is there evidence to show that they are less reliable witnesses except for very young children who may need prompting to recall all the details that they have remembered (Davies 1987).

Is it always damaging?

Not all children who have been sexually abused need professional treatment and many children are able to deal with the trauma effectively with the help of family and friends. If a child is believed and supported immediately and is assured that he or she is not to blame, then the damage need not be lasting (Gelinas 1983). Abuse that has continued for many years, where the abuser is a trusted family member, and that has progressed from fondling to other forms of abuse may be most damaging.

Some of the effects of abuse have already been mentioned in the case histories. These are feelings of guilt, loss of control, feelings of worthlessness, anger, depression, fear and the loss of trust and feelings of betrayal. These effects may lead, in adulthood, to an inability to make relationships other than purely sexual ones. Relationships between survivors of abuse and their own children may be affected but this is not to say that survivors of sexual abuse frequently become abusers. If this were so, the majority of abusers would be female. Some survivors of abuse may find it difficult to show affection to a child in case this should become sexual, and some survivors may express their anger against their own children when they are reminded, uncomfortably, of their own childhood. It is true, however, that many abusers reveal that they have been abused, but this is likely to have been physical and emotional abuse even more than sexual abuse (Groth and Birnbaum 1979).

The effects of child sexual abuse, listed previously, are the most common ones, and therefore they are the treatment areas towards which one should be working. There are others and many of them are listed by Suzanne Sgroi (*Handbook of Clinical Intervention in Child Sexual Abuse*). The book includes several sections on treatment and is essential reading for those working with abused children (Sgroi 1982).

Studies in populations of drug abusers, alcohol abusers, prostitutes and runaways (Benward and Gerber 1975; James and Meyerding 1977) have also shown a very high percentage who have been sexually abused in childhood.

Sexually abused children have been forced to suppress or repress their most intense feelings in order to survive. They may seek to regain this lost intensity of feeling with the help of drugs or alcohol. Alice Miller (1986) has noted this amongst her patients, but it has also been noted amongst those who work with people who have been neglected or emotionally or physically abused. It was described by one social worker as 'a searching for something missing; they may not know what they have missed but they surely know that they have missed it, and that they needed it'.

How can psychodrama help?

Adam Blatner (1973) tells us that 'psychodrama makes explicit the unconscious acting-out that we use as a psychological defence mechanism to discharge internal impulses through symbolic or actual enactment'. So psychodrama harnesses the natural healing methods that are used by children and adults after they have suffered trauma. Some of our natural defence mechanisms are unacceptable in society and, in children in particular, these mechanisms are ignored and suppressed by controlling adults. Hence children who run away from home are taken back without adequate investigation by the police force, children who abuse others are dismissed as bullies or sexually promiscuous by their teachers, depressed children are urged to cheer up and angry children told to calm down by their parents. Adam Blatner also points out that our civilisation has relegated many things to childhood, such as spontaneity, creativity and play itself, and urges us to preserve the spirit of childhood in our adult lives. Psychodrama with children can foster and respect that spirit. Children understand symbolism very well. They use it in play to enact many roles, to 'try them on for size' whilst they learn to integrate their experiences into their personalities. Explaining metaphor to most children is superfluous. They will use it in their drawings, in their storytelling and in their games. Psychodrama makes this acceptable, it makes their behaviour acceptable, and, by extension, it makes the children themselves feel accepted and valued.

Children understand that most adults have lost the ability to play and the ability to understand symbolism. Tania, who had been raped at the age of 9 by her father's friend, confided to a schoolfriend that 'the "group-lady" (the psychodramatist) really plays – doesn't just watch us'. Tom, whose father had buggered him for as long as he could remember, told the psychodramatist after a long symbolic re-enactment of the abuse, that he was now going to tell the 'really real truth' and he proceeded to state, quite simply, the exact details of the abuse that he had never been able to reveal before. He had shown it very clearly using animal puppets in a symbolic way, but he wasn't sure that the psychodramatist would understand, since she was an adult. Tom was 9 years old.

A psychodrama session usually takes place in three stages, often termed warm-up, action and sharing. Using psychodramatic techniques with sexually abused children one can divide the sessions into three parts. These may be termed 'the three Rs'. They are reassurance, re-enactment and rehearsal. These phases correspond roughly to the three parts of a group psychodrama session although these techniques can be used with children and young people individually as well as in groups. They can be used also in sessions that are primarily for 'disclosure' of sexual abuse as well as later sessions that are primarily therapeutic.

Reassurance

This is the first stage of any session with a young person or group of children who may have been abused. It corresponds with the first stage of a psychodrama session in that it warms up the group or individual, and the director or therapist to the action, which is the main part of the session. With abused children it is very much more than this, however. Because of the nature of the abuse, it is unlikely that the child will be able to trust anyone and in psychodrama, as in any group psychotherapy, the relationship between the therapist and client is crucial (Yalom 1985). Moreno called this relationship and the transference and counter-transference it engenders tele and establishing tele with an abused child can be painful indeed. Alice Miller (1987) reminds us that a child can only express his feelings when there is somebody there who accepts him fully and understands and supports him. The therapist must establish this relationship, must be aware of the tele, before there can be any really productive work.

Adults often impose themselves on children without explaining who they are, or why they are asking questions. Abused children, more than most, are used to being ignored and disregarded. They may not be very verbal and so they are used to being misunderstood. They may expect to be exploited. One anxious 4-year-old boy, abused by both parents, asked the therapist rhetorically, 'You don't take your knickers off, do you?' Small children will often grab at the genitals and breasts of the therapist, checking anxiously for reactions. They seem relieved when the therapist firmly but gently tells them that this is not allowed and no-one may touch another's 'private bits' without permission. Control is established, a framework is set up and some of the child's worries about the therapist are relieved.

Loss of control and powerlessness are invariably very important factors to an abused child. Children are told by the abuser that the abuse happens because of the way the child looks, or because of something the child does, but when the child tries to change this, the abuse does not stop. Examples of this can be seen in children who start to be wet or dirty after previously being toilet trained, or in children who become obese (especially girls) and girls who ignore personal hygiene. Despite their efforts to be 'unattractive', the abuse continues. How plaintive the cry of one abused girl: 'He said I liked it, I told him I didn't, I told him to stop. But he didn't hear me.' Children often tell another relative or a teacher and are told not to be so rude, not to say such dirty things and that they are liars. No wonder that their powerlessness and loss of control is increased and emphasised.

In psychodrama the client (the protagonist) controls the action and the therapist (director) uses skill and creativity to facilitate the action. The method itself then increases the control felt by the young person and gives them some power. The director is not another 'controller' who may abuse his or her power and it is very important that the abused child is able to understand this. Consequently, commensurate with the age and understanding of the child, an explanation must be given as to who the therapist is, and what the sessions are for. The young person must feel supported and there must be no ambiguity about the therapist's statement that a child cannot be responsible for its own abuse. As the psychodrama progresses, the child will be the author of his or her own story, the actor (actress) in his or her own drama and will gain power, self-esteem and confirmation of his or her own feelings through this, but even in the early stage of reassurance, it is important to work at the child's pace and thus to respect his or her feelings.

Sometimes a whole session and even more than one session, can be spent in reassurance. For older children and young people, working in a group, there can be reassurance that others, too, have been abused. Many are amazed that this has happened to anyone else. There can even be reassurance to know that other abusers are apparently normal fathers and grandfathers, brothers and uncles, and that they are not part of an abnormal family that contains monsters. There is reassurance as warm-up games are introduced that exaggerate feelings of power and powerlessness. Abused youngsters can understand how power can be misused and can appreciate their own vulnerability.

For example, the group can be asked to form pairs with someone roughly their own height and weight. The couples join both hands, facing, and move their weight between the pair, pushing and yielding as they feel the power passing between them. More verbally, the pairs can feel power as they play the 'yes/no' game. One member of the couple (A) may think of something he or she desires and may imagine that the other person (B) can provide it. A then says 'Yes, yes, yes' constantly and B says 'No, no, no' constantly, neither being allowed to say anything else. After several minutes, the couple share with the group what this exercise uncovered in themselves. Young people often remember lost incidents of powerlessness and of power. The exercise is then reversed and participants can share how comfortable and uncomfortable they felt from each position.

Younger children especially will need reassurance about the use of 'rude words'. These can be introduced by using anatomically correct dolls, by drawings and diagrams, and especially by the therapist calmly repeating the words the child uses, without correction to 'proper words' so that the child does not feel rebuked for using swearwords. In a group it is reassuring for a child who has no words to describe what has happened, to see another child demonstrate their own experience and perhaps provide some vocabulary that the child can comfortably use then to demonstrate its own abuse.

Confirming to a young person that it is all right to express feelings is another form of reassurance. Many sexually abused children, like those who have been physically abused, are 'watchful' of adults and try their best to please. 'I was trying to be a really good daughter,' said one 9-year-old who had been abused by her father since the age of 5. Many such children will be unable to express anger, fear, pain or any intense feeling, because this caused discomfort to the abuser. Some children become completely cut-off from feeling as a defence mechanism against severe pain and acute fear. Such children will state that they don't care or that it doesn't hurt, and in adult life state that the abuse 'never did me any harm'. Other judgemental adults may state that the abused person is shallow or lacking in emotion.

Reassurance for such children can be a long and painful process. 'Is it all right to kick the cushion?' asked one anxious 5-year-old boy in a therapy session. The therapist confirmed that it was and even helped him to thump the cushions harder. 'Why are we angry?' she asked, breathlessly as she thumped away. 'Because of my dad and all that', replied the boy, later going on to talk about 'all that' for the first time. 'Underneath the anger lies the tears. Beneath the tears lies the anger,' says Claudia Jewitt (1982). Tears have been unacceptable for many children. They have not brought sympathy or understanding. They have brought ridicule and sometimes even further abuse.

Most children and adults who have been sexually abused need to rediscover the healing power of tears and to regress into a childhood where babies and children are allowed to cry. This can be facilitated in a psychodrama session by playing games at a slightly younger age level than the young person expects. Soon these games are played with gusto and relief and even younger games are suggested, usually by the child. Many abused people regress to babyhood and like to suck a bottle or curl up in a foetal position where they feel safe. It is only then, after they have been allowed to find their own safe place, that they are able to re-enact the abuse and learn to live again, from the beginning.

It is important to discuss the sessions with the child's mother or foster mother so that she can understand if there is regressive behaviour at home. The confidentiality of the child can be maintained, but the carer needs to be warned that such behaviour as bedwetting or temper tantrums could temporarily reappear during the therapy. These symptoms are usually short-lived.

Re-enactment

Moreno (1977) tells us: 'Enactment comes first, retraining comes later. We must give (the protagonist) the satisfaction of act completion first, before considering retraining for behaviour changes.'

83

Freud, in one of his final essays, also noted that one of the common ways of dealing with the after-effects of a painful trauma is to arrange one's life in such a way that one 'happens' to get into situations that repeat or re-enact the original event. The individual does this in order to gain a sense of control over whatever it was that once left one so injured and conflicted or totally defeated.

Repetition, says Miller (1986), is the language used by a child who has remained dumb, his only means of expressing himself. A dumb child needs a particularly emphatic partner if he or she is to be understood at all.

By assisting the abused person to re-enact the circumstances of the abuse in a controlled setting, the person is able to regain control and will not remain vulnerable. Unfortunately, experience shows that children who have been abused may become the victims of further sexual abuse. Girls who were sexually abused sometimes become the victims of physically violent husbands. Children who have been abused by one member of the family frequently become abused by other members or, occasionally, by foster parents or other professional carers.

Most children when they start to re-enact like to take the part of the abuser, the one with most power.

> Sam, aged 4, did it with puppets. He enjoyed being the 'wicked wolf' who stole the little dog and little cat and threw them in the prison, while he terrorised them and threatened to eat them. The therapist played the dog and cat (one on each hand). She showed fear, indeed terror, and called someone to help.
>
> Sam picked up an angel puppet and flew into the 'prison': 'We will have to be very strong,' he said, reversing roles with the angel. 'We will have to do this together.'
>
> He ordered the therapist to reverse roles: 'You be the bad wolf', he said. Somehow, Sam managed to play the angel, the dog and the cat (who had now become a magic dog and magic cat who were the angel's assistants).
>
> After a great struggle (literally), the three managed to vanquish the wicked wolf who was buried under a large cushion in the therapy room. 'Sit on it', Sam ordered the therapist and handed her the angel puppet (reversing roles again).
>
> 'Now the magic dog and the magic cat will tell the angel all about the wolf.' Sam picked up the puppets. 'It's really my dad', he said. 'He's doing rude things to me and my brother.'

This was a way of using psychodrama techniques on an individual basis with a small child. Teenage girls gain a great deal from a group setting.

> Rita was able to be the protagonist several times in a psychodrama group. Using the 'surplus reality' technique, Rita was able to do what she could not do in real life. She was comforted and supported by a 'psychodramatic grandmother' after her stepbrother had raped her. Rita had tried to commit suicide more than once and had mutilated her body, which she hated, which

she felt was the 'cause' of her abuse. In psychodrama she talked to her body, especially the mutilated parts and was able to accept it and to absolve it from guilt. Rita's outward appearance changed dramatically from that point. She wore clothes with confidence and ceased to hide behind her hair. Debbie was also able to act out her abuse within the psychodrama group. There was frequent role reversal, Debbie obviously feeling more comfortable when playing the role with power. She had never been able to accept that at 11 years old she had not 'tempted' her abuser, a middle-aged married man. Gradually she was able to accept her own role and feel her complete vulnerability. This was totally terrifying for her and there was a catharsis followed by a request to act out other situations in which she had been vulnerable.

Debbie was torn with feelings of disloyalty to a very strictly religious father. She found enormous relief after 'splitting off' those parts of her father that she hated, and burying them, after making sure that the parts of her father that she loved were quite safe. The group assisted at the 'funeral' of the judgmental, critical parts of father and the symbolically religious ceremony comforted Debbie and offered relief and support.

Six-year-old Caroline enacted a similar scene, as described at the beginning of this chapter, when she destroyed the 'monster' abusing father, and saved the 'loving' part. Like many children of this age she accomplished this with very little direction from the therapist.

Once again, this seems to show that young children are able to use psychodramatic techniques quite naturally, with the director acting as facilitator and supporter and as an auxiliary (the player of roles). In group psychodrama the director does not usually play auxiliary roles but children demand that the director takes part. It may be possible to work with small groups of young children, (two to four only) but confidentiality is difficult to maintain and peer-group pressure with young children is not always helpful. The most satisfactory work appears to be with individual children or with sibling groups for children up to 11 years old, and with groups of six to eight adolescents.

Children who have been sexually abused may protect themselves by declaring that the abuse happened to someone other than themselves. Occasionally a child will say that a sibling has been abused but that he or she has not. Sometimes, of course, the sibling has been abused and the child tells this before speaking of his or her own abuse. (For example, Sam, mentioned already in this chapter p.76). But often the child is projecting the unbearable truth onto someone who may be a fantasy person, another little boy or girl.

James, aged 3, showed oral sex in detail, using anatomically correct dolls. He shook with terror whilst demonstrating with 'the daddy' and 'the little boy'. 'He's doing it to the little boy', he cried, 'not me, not me.' James worked then for a long time, using first puppets, then dolls, before he and the therapist were able to re-enact the roles and eventually, James was able to re-enact his own abuse.

Tania, at 10, was able to use fairy stories to project her abuse outwards and re-enact it safely. She was full of fear, so the therapist asked her to place herself where she felt safe. This psychodrama was enacted using supportive family members. Tania placed herself in her mother's arms with mother reading a bedtime story. She reversed roles with mother and told the story of the 'naughty witch who had ridden too hard and her broomstick had broken'. (The sexual symbolism is fairly obvious.)

Tania was guilt ridden about her rape at the age of 9 by father's friend and obsessed by fears of being 'broken' or damaged. Playing her own mother, she comforted herself (played by her real mother) and assured Tania that she was not to blame and that she was undamaged and 'quite beautiful'. Roles were reversed again; the real mother (whose own sexual abuse as a child was inhibiting her from supporting Tania) was able to reassure Tania. The child then went on to do more explicit re-enactment and to rehearse future behaviour with men and boys.

Working with sexually abused children is stressful and difficult for the therapist. Whilst a child is re-enacting abuse the therapist's own horror and outrage can be overwhelming. In a group setting the psychodramatist can use those angry feeling positively to support the protagonist. Working with an individual child, the therapist has to decide whether it is helpful to the child to express those feelings or not.

Caroline was playing her abusing father 'the monster' whilst the therapist played Caroline.

The child had set the scene well: 'There is no-one to help you', she boomed in a 'monster' voice. 'Mummy can't hear and your brothers can't hear either.' She then added, for good measure, 'Teddy and dolly are dead and dog and cat are dead and you are all alone.'

At first the therapist whimpered helplessly but then the outrage of the situation overwhelmed her and she jumped up shouting: 'I'm not having this, I'll get someone to help me.' Immediately, Caroline froze. This was not how it had been.

Suddenly, she climbed onto the couch and said: 'I'll be the little girl' (reversing roles). She thrust the therapist into the abuser role. 'I'll get someone to help me', Caroline cried (as herself), repeating the last line spoken before the role reversal in classical psychodramatic fashion. 'I'll get . . .' (naming the therapist).

This role modelling, although born out of the therapist's need, helped Caroline to move from endless enactment to more positive rehearsal for the future.

A more difficult feeling for the therapist to cope with is possible arousal if the child is re-enacting a specific sexual act in an explicit way. This must be totally repressed during the session and the therapist must be responsible for ensuring that there is a consultant to act as support for herself after the session.

A useful part of re-enactment, and of the final stage, rehearsal, is the opportunity for the child to act out feelings. Many children find it difficult to identify feelings and to know how they are expressed. Simple games like 'in the manner of the word' can be used to express this. The child thinks of a word to express a feeling, e.g. happy, sad, proud, angry, afraid, disappointed. The other group members ask the child to complete an action, e.g. walk, put clothes on 'in the manner of the word' and the group guesses the feeling. This works best with older children, but young ones can also be asked to walk round the room happily, angrily, etc. so that they can experience the feelings and, especially, watch others as they experience them.

Young children like to draw circles to represent faces. The therapist completes a few, showing sadness, happiness, etc. The child completes a few more, often using great imagination to express anger, puzzlement, and so on.

Another purpose of re-enactment is desensitisation, which is a technique often used in psychodrama, and, of course, in behaviour therapy. Some of the initial effects of child sexual abuse are very closely related to the type of abuse. A child abused in bed at night may suffer from nightmares, problems with sleeping or going to bed, fear of the dark, bedwetting, etc. A child upon whom oral sex has been forced may have difficulty in eating or swallowing and children who have been abused in particular places such as a swimming pool will feel fearful of entering such a building again.

In psychodramatic terms the swimming pool can be built up, using cushions or furniture and the child can practise entering, pretending to undress and diving in 'the water'. An orally abused child can set out the toy teaset and practise preparing and eating a meal just as night fears can be overcome as the child prepares the setting of a darkened bedroom, using cushions again, until confidence returns.

Rehearsal

The opportunity to practise future roles and not to be punished for making mistakes is an important part of psychodrama. Young people, in particular, need practice at assuming roles they have never experienced. Adam Blatner (1973) describes using the 'symbolic distance' technique with two children from broken and inadequate homes. The children were afraid to return to a 'family' situation because of their own experience but were able to portray different family situations and test their own behaviour. Eventually, they felt confident enough to state the kind of family with which they might feel comfortable.

Judith had already left home but had been unable to tell her mother why she had left. Her stepfather had been abusing her for many years. She talked to her mother using the 'empty chair' technique and then played her mother's role until she felt able actually to meet her mother. The meeting was successful and mother was supportive.

Debbie found 'future projection' helpful when she wanted to look at her possible future relationships with men and with a child of her own. The terrifying unknown becomes a possibility, to be accepted or rejected and again the protagonist realises how she can control her future by being more assertive.

Assertiveness seemed like aggression to Rita. Aggression was unacceptable, except for others. She had moved from sexual abuse by her stepbrother to an early marriage where her husband 'battered' her. Through practising more assertive behaviour, she learned not to accept her husband's behaviour and he realised he had to change if he wanted to keep her. The relationship improved greatly and Rita says she is no longer afraid of men.

Small children can be helped to recognise 'good touching' and 'bad touching'. Children know automatically what feels good and what feels bad, but abusers tell children that their abusive touching is enjoyable and that it is part of a 'loving relationship'. Children soon doubt their own feelings. They are in a process of learning about emotions and they gain that knowledge from adults. If the most powerful adult gives them false information, the child becomes confused but, depending on the child's age and upon other powerful adults, the child will tend to accept the information given.

A helpful analogy may be that of a starving child who is offered bread. The bread contains a bitter substance, say heroin, that could be harmful. The child queries the taste, the adult says all bread tastes like that. The child is hungry so eats the bread. This is the kind of package that is offered to abused children, especially where the abuse is within the home.

Abused children frequently wish to confront their abusers, usually at a stage in therapy after they have done some re-enactment and discharge of feelings. It is helpful for them to overcome their fear by role playing, either in a one-to-one situation or in a group.

It took 6-year-old Caroline several weeks before she wished to see her father. First of all she suggested she should talk to him on the telephone and she picked up a toy phone and asked the therapist to 'be dad' and to pick up the other end. There was a short conversation and Caroline said, rather shakily, 'Don't do those things again.' Later she asked the therapist if she could speak into a tape recorder for the tape to be given to her father. This was done and soon Caroline asked to see father face to face. All these suggestions came from the child. When she was in control of the situation, she felt better. She did not wish to see her father alone though. She was able to recognise her vulnerability and to understand that since the abuse was not her fault it could still happen again unless her father changed.

Rehearsal for the future should include, if possible, direct work with mother and child, especially where small children are concerned. Just as Tania was able to obtain direct comfort from her mother after a re-enactment, so mother and child need to rebuild their relationship, which may have been shattered by the revelation of sexual abuse. Most therapeutic work with young sexually abused children needs to be on an individual basis, except perhaps for groups of siblings, but the mother must not be ignored, since she is likely to be carrying on the therapeutic work long after the therapist has left the scene.

The birth mother or foster mother should be invited, with the child's agreement, to some sessions, which will be specified as 'rehearsals for the future'. These sessions will usually be after the therapist feels that first, the whole of the abuse has been disclosed, second, the child has been able to express some strong feelings about both parents and third, the child is expressing strong needs to be mothered. The need for mothering may have been expressed through attachment to the therapist or in a psychodramatic situation, particularly when a child plays a mother herself and demonstrates 'loving care'.

It can be particularly helpful using the 'future projection' technique to ask the child to set up a scene in his or her family in the future.

Sam set up a tea party for himself and his brother. Dolls played the parts of 'new mummy' and 'new daddy'. These were his foster parents. The therapist asked if his birth parents could come to the party. He considered the question, then picking up the puppets that represented them he took them to a far corner of the room and sat them on a cushion: 'They are in prison', he said, 'they are better off there'.

Previously, this child had 'thrown his mother on the fire' in a session and 'chopped up' his father. Now, quite calmly, at 4 years old, he had decided upon his future.

With groups of adolescents, several sessions should be spent on rehearsals for the future. After a warm-up discussion on the type of situation that was most threatening a sociodrama can take place, enacting the fears and fantasies. Most common choices are: (1) coping with bullying teachers in school; (2) how to behave at the disco; (3) what will we do in court (where children are appearing as witnesses); (4) how to cope when other children make taunts and gibes.

With adolescent groups, sociodrama, which clarifies group themes instead of focusing on personal problems, may be more appropriate, but the director needs to judge the 'feel' of the group and often a sociodrama can lead on to a personal psychodrama that is helpful to the whole group.

The final part of a psychodrama session is the sharing. This is not an advice-giving session, but is to enable the group to share with the protagonist the emotions aroused in them during the enactment. Sharing can be done in a formal way in a group setting, and is extremely valuable for those children who feel isolated and alone in their abuse. The sharing can also be part of individual sessions, as the therapist shares some of his or her own anger and grief. With young children, however, the therapist's own feelings must be carefully controlled since it is lack of control that is so frightening for youngsters. In rehearsal sessions, however, it is in order to share one's own uncertainties about behaviour in particular situations and to learn with the child as the child decides what feels right. There should be no attempt to impose the therapist's suggestions upon an already impressionable child.

Discussion

It is important for the therapist to understand a child's developmental level. This needs to be assessed in the first session, when working with an individual child. Youngsters brought into the group setting should be developmentally assessed prior to the first group meeting. If in doubt, at an initial interview, only simple toys and equipment should be introduced. Otherwise children can become frustrated trying to use toys that are too difficult or advanced and this can add to their feelings of failure and uselessness. Use care in groups about playing writing games. Some children may feel inhibited about this. Many children will draw happily though, or sculpt with clay, and these techniques can be used both in reassuring warm-up and in re-enactment. How satisfying it can be to throw clay at portraits of the abuser drawn by the child and fastened to the wall.

The extent of a child's concentration must be considered also. Most children under 11 years of age can cope with a session of up to an hour. All children need 'time out' during the sessions and children will take this automatically. One child may stare out of the window periodically or return to the same pile of building blocks at intervals during the session. Another may even curl up on a cushion and rest or sleep for a few minutes. Others demand a drink or the use of the toilet as another way of taking time out. Simple rules should be made about drinks and visits to the toilet, however. This is easily done with school-age children who accept 'break time' and the need to visit the toilet before and after sessions. Under-5s have more difficulty but it is still important to provide boundaries for a child who may be confused and lacking control. Adolescents are quite happy with refreshments being provided before or after a session and peer-group pressure can prevent too many disruptive visits to the toilet.

Adolescent groups need to go on longer than an hour. Two hours, including refreshment time is long enough. Although adult psychodrama sessions commonly last up to three hours, most youngsters will find that length of concentration impossible. Weekly or fortnightly sessions can usually keep their momentum for adolescents but for younger children, a week is a long time and twice-weekly sessions may be more productive.

Where abuse has occurred outside the family circle, or where the abuse has been revealed soon after it commenced, a child may benefit from only one or two therapeutic sessions, followed up by a supportive ally, preferably the mother. If a mother has been abused herself, she will find it more difficult to be supportive because of her own needs and the child may need therapy for several weeks or even months. Each child should be carefully assessed to see whether therapy can be terminated and termination should be well prepared.

It must be accepted that according to the child's maturational level, he or she can only deal with so much 're-learning' at any one time. If the relationship between therapist and child is satisfactory, if the tele is complete, both child and therapist will know when they have come to the end of that particular piece of work. The child will have disclosed what he or she is able to recall, he or she will have expressed feelings of grief, anger, fear, sadness and confusion, he or she will have been able to place the responsibility for the abuse upon the abuser. Behaviour will have been rehearsed for the future and the child will be confident that he or she has an ally to call upon if help is needed.

This is not to say, however, that the trauma has been fully integrated and that no more work needs to be done in the future. As children face other life situations (puberty, death or separation of a parent or an older sibling leaves home), they may be reminded of their earlier pain and may need further therapy. Even into adulthood there can be more difficulties. especially upon marriage or becoming a parent. But the early work may be a foundation, enabling any future difficulties to be more easily resolved.

In addition to understanding a child's developmental level a therapist with children would do well to study the works of Virginia Axline (1969; 1971) and Violet Oaklander (1978). Personal work on the 'child within ourselves' also helps the therapist to enter the child's world and look at events from a childlike point of view. Psychodrama, dramatherapy, gestalt and transactional analysis can all help the would-be child therapist to uncover his or her own unmet needs and to understand the overwhelming need for love that is within every child. It is easy to understand that the starving child must not be given adulterated bread that will harm him or her; it is not so easy to realise that 'love' that includes abuse is not love at all, because it is given only for the gratification of the abuser.

A worker with child sexual abuse should aim to keep a balance and work sometimes with adult members of the abused child's family and also, sometimes, with abusers. It is not therapeutic for one worker to be supporting the child and his or her abuser. There can be no trust for the child in this situation except, perhaps, at a later stage after individual work has been done. A therapist who has not worked with abusers, however, will find it difficult to understand the powerful rationalisation that abusers use, and may even underestimate the power relationship between the two. It is easy to get 'sucked in' also to a child's helplessness and it is easier to keep a balance if family dynamics are thoroughly understood.

Suzanne Long in her chapter 'Sexual abuse of young children' (MacFarlane and Waterman 1986) recommends a thorough knowledge of systems theory and quotes Giarretto and Giarretto (1982) for an understanding of the mother – child dyad, which is so important if therapy with the child is to be successful.

Most important, though, is to look at the child through the child's own eyes. 'Walking in another's moccasins' is how the American Indian describes this state.

> A meeting of two: eye to eye, face to face. And when you are near I will tear your eyes out and place them instead of mine, and you will tear my eyes out and will place them instead of yours, and then I will look at you with your eyes and you will look at me with mine.
>
> [Moreno (1977)]

This is Moreno's description of tele, but with a child and an adult it requires a tremendous act of faith. We have to believe in the child, to believe that what he or she is saying is real to that child.

The problem is described by Miller (1986) when she first read that Henry Moore used to massage his mother's back with oil to sooth her rheumatism when he was a child. Suddenly, Miller said, Moore's sculpture was understandable. Those great reclining women with tiny heads and huge backs. Exactly the perspective of a child.

In psychodrama, the protagonist will choose someone to play an auxiliary part in his or her drama because some aspect of that person reminds him or her of the parent or partner or whoever is to be portrayed. It is not at all uncommon for the auxiliary to share with the group afterwards that there was something in the character of this person that really touched his or her own personal problems and with which he or she could identify. Similarly, a child may choose a puppet to play him/herself in the drama. One boy chose a dog. He was obedient and faithful to his master (his father), but if he did not respond immediately, he would be beaten. (This boy was literally beaten by his father.) He looked up at his master for a long time trying to understand what was required so that he would not offend. Eventually, the master asked him to crouch on all fours and turn his back while he 'poked a stick up him'. The small boy was describing exactly what his father had done to him and this was proved later upon medical examination, but how easy it would have been to dismiss this as fantasy.

During psychodrama training, one is urged to 'trust the method'. The protagonist may be resistant, the drama may seem to be going nowhere, but the director needs to trust Moreno's methods and believe that they will succeed. In work with sexually abused children, we must also trust the child. Only the child and the abuser know what happened. Only the child knows how he or she perceived what happened and how it affected him or her. Only the child knows what he or she needs. Psychodramatic techniques can facilitate the fulfilment of those needs and assist the child to learn to live again.

This is a short quotation from a poem by Rita, one of the young women who attended a psychodrama group and whose experiences have been quoted:

The time I thought would never come
When my life meant something to me.
But when you spent your time with me
My life had meaning once again.

References

Axline, V. (1969) *Play Therapy*, New York: Ballantine Books.

Axline, V. (1971) *Dibs in Search of Self*, Harmondsworth: Penguin.

Baker, A.W. and Duncan, S.P. (1985) 'Child sexual abuse: a study of prevalence in Great Britain', *Child Abuse and Neglect* 9: 457–67.

Benward, J. and Gerber, J.D. (1975) 'Incest as a causative factor in anti-social behaviour' *Contemporary Drug Problems* 4.

Blatner, A. (1973) *Acting-In: Practical Applications of Psychodramatic Methods*, New York: Springer Publishing.

Davies, G. (1987) 'Is the Child a Reliable Witness?', paper presented to National Children's Bureau Conference.

Finkelhor, D. (1986) *A Sourcebook on Child Sexual Abuse*, Beverly Hills, London and New Delhi: Sage Publications.

Gelinas, D. (1983) 'The Persisting Negative Effects of Incest', in *Psychiatry* 46.

Giarretto, H. and Giarretto, A. (1982) *Integrated Treatment of Child Sexual Abuse*, Palo Alto, California: Science & Behaviour Books Inc.

Goodwin, J. (1982) *Sexual Abuse – Incest Victims and Their Families*, Boston, Bristol and London: John Wright Publishers.

Groth, A. N. and Birnbaum, H.J. (1979) *Men Who Rape – the Psychology of the Offender*, New York: Plenum Press.

Herman, J.L. (1981) *Father–Daughter Incest*, Cambridge, Massachusetts and London: Harvard University Press.

James, J. and Meyerding, J. (1977) 'Early sexual experiences as a factor in prostitution', *Archives of Sexual Behaviour* 7: 31–42.

Jewitt, C. (1982) *Helping Children Cope with Separation and Loss*, Cambridge, Massachusetts: Harvard Common Press.

Jones, D.P. and McGraw, J.M. (1987) 'Reliable and fictitious accounts of sexual abuse to children', *Journal of Interpersonal Violence* 2 (1) 27–45.

MacFarlane, K. and Waterman, J. (eds) (1986) *Sexual Abuse of Young Children*, London and Sydney: Holt Rinehart & Winston.

Miller, A. (1986) *The Drama of Being a Child*, London: Virago.

Miller, A. (1987) *For Your Own Good*, London: Virago.

Moreno, J.L. (1977) *Psychodrama, vol. I*, Beacon, NY: Beacon Press.

Oaklander, V. (1978) *Windows to Our Children*, Moab, Utah, USA: Real People Press.

Russell, D. (1984) *Sexual Exploitation*, Beverly Hills, London and New Delhi: Sage Publications.

Sgroi, S. (1982) *Handbook of Clinical Intervention in Child Sexual Abuse*, Lexington, Massachusetts: Lexington Books.

Yalom, I.D. (1985) *The Theory and Practice of Group Psychotherapy*, New York: Basic Books.

Chapter seven

Psychodrama and piccalilli

Residential treatment of a sexually abused adult

Marcia Karp

I want to be remembered as the man who brought joy and laughter into psychiatry.

(Dedication from the urn of J.L. Moreno)

It was the worst example of sexual abuse I had ever treated. Anne, the client, was repeatedly raped by her grandfather, her uncle and her father throughout her childhood. She found it impossible to escape. After several months of severe abuse she had told her mother and her mother had refused to listen. For the following years she was alone to witness her own guilt, fear and torment. She wanted to die.

Anne had come to work on some of her personal difficulties in our psychodrama theatre. I had only known her for two and a half weeks prior to that. She was brought to me by a local social worker. We had arranged for six individual sessions. Anne was a plain speaker. She was a 42-year-old, down-to-earth Devonshire woman.

They arrived in the morning when I was heavily immersed in making piccalilli. I was stirring a much-too-liquid concoction when the two arrived at the door. I invited them in and asked if they knew anything about piccalilli. 'I'm in the middle of a disaster', I said. 'Come and look at this.' The three of us gathered around our coal-fired stove. Staring at us was a 20-pound caldron full to the brim of bright, mustard-coloured lumps of piccalilli. I looked at them both. 'I've done something massively wrong, haven't I?' The social worker winced, wondering to what had she brought her client. Anne smiled and stared into the yellow vat. I sensed that she was quietly relieved not to be met with questions about her life, her sexual abuse and her unhappiness. 'I hate mustard' were her first words to me. 'My grandmother used to make piccalilli. You've definitely got too much liquid in there. It doesn't look like my grandma's.' I noticed an air of satisfaction in Anne's voice. She was able to tell me about something she hated and also to tell me that I had done something wrong. She'd only met me one minute before but I suspected that both the medical and social services had conditioned her to be critical. It was an unconventional meeting and I liked it. It gave Anne immediate responsibility. I genuinely needed her help, or the social worker's or anyone else's. I didn't want to fail at the piccalilli.

The recipe, the best piccalilli I'd ever tasted, was given to me by my daughter, Maureen, and I wanted faithfully to repeat it. I handed Anne a big wooden spoon given to Ken, my husband, by a Finnish minister and writer. The spoon had been used to mix many old recipes by the minister's mother in Finland. It was now our big wooden spoon. 'Could you stir' I said to Anne, 'while I add some cornflour?'

The social worker looked on inquisitively and was resigned to take a support-ive but doubtful back seat to the proceedings. I could see she had the same response to me that I had had to the founder of psychodrama, J.L. Moreno, when I first met him. 'He's either a genius or he's stark raving mad.' I could hear her saying the same thing to herself. The social worker was reserving her judgement.

'Why don't you pour off some of the liquid?' said Anne, now caught in the dilemma and finally offering some help rather than criticism. 'Pour off some liquid?' I parried her query as if in a well-matched fencing tournament. Her first challenge to me wouldn't go unmet. I said, 'Why don't we add some cornflour first and then see where we get to? You stir.'

Anne held the big spoon and carefully mixed in the flour and water mixture from the cup. It made no difference. 'This definitely does not look like my grandma's.' Anne repeated the most devastating piccalilli criticism she could muster! 'My grandma's was very thick and all the lumps were sticky.'

I glanced at the social worker. she looked at me as if to say 'That's 10-minutes gone of her session.' 'Oh well, come on, Anne', I said, 'Let's go into my office and talk.'

Anne moved easily with me. She trusted me. We'd already been in trouble together and I needed her help. She also realised that I was a person with a life outside that of being a therapist. There was a new perspective to her all-encompassing massive sexual abuse. Life goes on and the piccalilli had to be dealt with, despite her sexual abuse. She liked me and I could feel that that was no small accomplishment in ten minutes. We had established a contact between the three of us, but it was clear that the major interaction was to take place between Anne and I.

The social worker had told me previously that Anne wanted her support in the session. She was afraid of meeting me. This piccalilli party was a conscious desensitisation process of therapist and client. It made separating with the social worker a natural and easy process. 'Make yourself a coffee,' I said to the social worker. Anne smiled rather coyly. She was okay and the three of us knew it.

She followed me up the stairs to my consulting room. It smelled of new carpeting and fresh flowers from the opening ceremony several days before. Anne was my first client in the new room. Though there had been hundreds before her, the contact felt fresh and new like the flowers and carpet. We liked each other and we were keen to get going.

Anne settled into her chair. She pushed back her glasses, ran her hand quickly through her hair and said, 'I suppose you know how all this started, with my kids getting into trouble and all that?' She was so certain I knew all the details, as if I was a doctor with intricate case notes piled high in front of me. I knew briefly that her children were the original cause of concern, which brought the social worker into the case. I didn't remember much more than that. Anne was dismissive and obviously not wanting to talk about the details. 'Yes, I know about it', I said confidently and reassured her that she didn't have to tell me then.

I later heard that her 17-year-old son was accused of sexually abusing her daughter. Anne had repeatedly told them never to get into bed together, never to touch each other nor to let anyone touch them against their will. The statement: 'Don't ever get into bed with each other,' is what therapist Petrūska Clarkson (Conway and Clarkson 1987) calls a hypnotic induction. It can produce an unconscious command. They got into bed with each other because it was what they were most warned against doing. Because of their mother's denial and failure to deal with her own sexual experiences as a child, the unconscious command became part of her own pattern of repetition. 'That which you deny and fear the most', say the believers in hypnotic induction, 'is what is most likely to occur in the present.'

A classic hypnotic induction occurs in an argument when a person says, 'Don't hit me!' The person saying 'Don't hit me' may be inviting the other to hit him or her. 'Don't betray me' is another hypnotic induction. People, in most instances, are not aware of what they are constructing. To compound the error, Anne also repeatedly told them that, 'You are only children, not adults.' The one thing teenagers want most to be is an adult. Consequently, the daughter, aged 13, dressed like a 16-year-old and the son, aged 17, had begun his career and wanted desperately to have a girlfriend. Because of their mother's own negativity towards sexual intimacy, both children were denied sexual acknowledgement. The mother's own fear of sexuality created a distance between her and her teenagers.

There is an interesting passage from Moreno's book (1953) *Who Shall Survive?*, which relates to Anne's negativity about sex. Moreno writes about original Freudian psychoanalytic theory. The historical background to the writing is that Moreno and Freud were contemporaries, both living in Vienna in the 1900s. Moreno was a medical student when Freud was becoming well known for his work. Though modern post-Freudian analysis has become more sophisticated, and more encompassing of the human condition, it is important to note the significant differences in the thinking of the two men during the 1900s. Freud had gathered his data on neurotic patients only and therefore developed a framework of pathology. Moreno wanted to promote a methodology based on a framework of health rather than pathology. He based psychodrama on the 'here and now', rather than the 'there and then'. The great human resources of spontaneity and creativity formed the basis of his action methods. Moreno felt that 'Freud was a greater scientist than those who criticised him'. He also thought that Freud's hypotheses 'were based on partial evidence and perhaps at times on as little as ten per cent probability, but he knew it'. Moreno goes on: 'He was always willing to change his hypotheses with new evidence and he changed them several times during his lifetime. My critique', continues Moreno, 'goes against the psycho-analytic system in its entirety and the unconscious motivations underlying it.' (Moreno 1953) Moreno felt that the psychoanalytic situation permitted analysis but excluded natural action or that which is expressed in bodily movement. Moreno writes:

> The patient was placed on a couch in a passive, reclining position. The analyst placed himself in back of the patient so as not to see him and avoid interaction. The situation was hermetically closed; no other person was permitted to enter it and the thoughts which emerged on the couch were to remain the secret of the chamber. It was to omit the positive and the direct in the relationship to the patient. The technique of free association is not natural talk. The patient reports what is going through his mind. The transference of the patient upon the analyst was not permitted to extend and become a real two-way encounter. Life itself was banned from the chamber.
>
> (Moreno 1953: Liii Preludes)

Moreno felt that the subject of the session or the protagonist should speak directly to whomsoever was being addressed. If the person wanted to speak to his mother or to his father, then those primary people, played by group members, should be brought into the therapy room. They should not be spoken to via the therapist. These members are called auxiliary egos. Moreno described them as:

> a staff of auxiliary egos to become extensions of the director and subject and to portray the actual or imagined personae of the life drama. The functions of the auxiliary ego are threefold: the function of the actor, portraying roles required by the subject's world, the function of the counsellor, guiding the subject, and the function of the social investigator.
>
> (Moreno 1953: 83)

Moreno felt analysis was built on a 'negative bias', that is on a framework of pathology. Here is where the original psychoanalytic theory has a similar neg-ative set to our subject, Anne. Moreno writes:

> The psychoanalytic system has in common with other analytic systems which followed its steps, the tendency to associate the origins of life with calamity. The key concept of the Freudian system is the libido. But Freud, instead of associating sex with 'spontaneity' associated it with anxiety, insecurity, abreaction, frustration and substitution.
>
> (Moreno 1953: ii)

Analysis has moved on from there. However, in Freud's original framework,

Anne would have been a perfect example of a patient with traumatic sexual history causing the present neurotic behaviour. This concept was the very pre-miss of Freud's early work.

Anne's negative sexual history created an overprotectiveness in her role as mother. Both children felt cloistered and trapped. They were rebellious and wanted sexual experimentation. Rather than telling her mother, the daughter had reported the sexual exploratory encounters to her teacher. She was afraid to tell her mother because she feared she wouldn't be believed and would either be thrown out of the house or her brother would be sent away.

That is exactly what happened. One day the daughter arrived home at midday with her teacher. Together they talked to Anne. From the accusation and admis-sion of sexual activity, the social services machinery took over the case. A local psychiatrist became concerned. Social services decided that the 15-year-old boy was a sexual offender. He was removed from the home and put into care with relatives for five months 'to protect his sister'. He no longer slept at home.

This was devastating to Anne, who now believed that she had produced a sexual abuser as a son. It brought her past traumatic experiences to the fore-ground. She demonstrated symptoms of sleep disturbance, extreme irritability and general inability to cope with her family. She wanted to leave them, and in her own words said, 'I wished the children were dead. If it wasn't for them I wouldn't be in this mess. I can't get on with my life.' She sought help for herself.

A year later, the children were back in school, living together within the family and relating well. It was Anne who was left with the problem. Her husband, Jon, a loving, long-suffering and loyal man became the attentive, loving father. He often put her on his lap to comfort her. He supported her like this for many years. She slept cuddled up to Jon and had to be continually reassured in the night that she was safe.

I was not to know all that in the first interview. Basically, what I heard was that Anne was very angry at her mother for not protecting her and angry at her father, grandfather and uncle for damaging her. Psychologist Andrew Feldmar (1989) said that: 'the moment a parent sexually abuses a child, that child becomes an orphan. The child loses the security of the abusing parent and loses the protection and trust of the parent who didn't stop it from happening.' It felt like Anne was, indeed, an orphan. The only solace she found was in attending boarding school. It was there that she was safe from sexual interference. She dreaded the school holidays when she had to return home.

Anne's love of books and her enthusiasm for learning struck me on our first meeting. She had been to the local library and took out books on psychotherapy and psychodrama. The latter she had seen several times on television. The BBC2 programmes were called 'The Session'. Six psychodrama programmes were presented on Saturday nights at peak viewing time. They were directed by a graduate student who trained at Holwell, Jinnie Jefferies, a London-based psychotherapist.

Anne had studiously watched these programmes and was impressed with 'people showing real emotion, able to say what they really felt'. She had 'wanted to be part of the group'.

With her obvious inquisitive nature and love of books I asked: 'Anne, why didn't you go on to school and find a profession you could study and learn well?' Anne was utterly resigned:

> When boarding school ended I was so eager to get out of my family that I took the first job I could find away from home. I worked solidly until I met my husband and got married. I loved books. They were an escape for me. I read all the time, all kinds of books. For example, about the love affair between King Edward and Mrs. Simpson, Catherine Cookson stories and books on psychotherapy.

I looked directly at Anne:

> 'I think you're going to be wasting your time coming here for six individual sessions. You need to come to a group session that meets everyday. We could start with a week. You'd need to live here. You say you have a lot of anger. I think that would be better expressed with the support of a psychodrama group.'

I thought to myself that she needed to enact what didn't happen in the original scenes that had occurred. She needed to vent the powerful emotions of fear and anger that she didn't express to the appropriate people at the time. Until she got in touch with her rage and pent-up emotion, she would remain emotionally blocked and locked in conflict.

Freud said, 'What happened? Tell me.' Moreno said, 'How did it happen? Show me.'

In individual sessions we could talk about what happened, and eventually release some emotion. However, the intensity of the original traumatic dramas needed an equally dramatic format. What better way to do this than a well-guided psychodrama, focusing on that which didn't occur in life. It would give her the opportunity to express the emotions that life hadn't given her the chance to express. She was held prisoner in her own childhood. As Alice Miller, the Swiss psychoanalyst, points out in her thesis the abused child needs an enlightened witness, someone to absorb the child's pain, to stand up for him or her and to stop the abuse. To use Alice Miller's terminology, Anne had no 'advocate', that is to say, no-one to speak for her. Our job in the ensuing psychodramas, was not to help her understand the action of her perpetrators or to forgive them; our job was to unleash the blocked wells of emotions that were choking her, causing an early emotional death and aborting her ability to face life with spontaneity and creativity. To obtain a vibrant and buoyant life, spontaneity and creativity are the greatest human resources.

'Can you come for the week, Anne?' I asked determinedly. She looked at me with hope. 'I don't know if I can stick it but I'll come.' 'Okay', I said, 'now we have to transfer the money from your six individual sessions into a week's residential session. There is a place available in two and a half weeks. It would be helpful for you.' Anne became equally motivated. 'We'll pay the difference in the money. I'm coming!' Before she left, we discussed some of the concepts in Alice Miller's books. I gave her the book *The Drama of Being a Child*. After the session, the social worker talked with 'the powers that be'. She rang me back that afternoon to say that the money had been arranged. The six sessions would pay for one half of the week, and Anne would pay for the other half.

That night I had a telephone call from Anne's husband. 'Do you want cash or a cheque?' Jon asked me. He was direct and sounded committed to the idea. 'Either is fine,' I said. 'Can you give it to Anne when she sees me next week?' I wanted to make Anne's next appointment as concrete and purposeful as possible. The money would serve that purpose. 'There's a slight hitch,' I said apologetically. 'I may have to see her on Wednesday or Thursday instead of on Friday. I shall be going on holiday to Portugal with my daughter Mandy on Friday. I have been trying to contact her social worker.' 'Would you like to speak to Anne? She's right here', said Jon. 'I'd love to', I said reassuringly. Things were working quickly and well since the afternoon session and I was pleased to make contact with Anne again. She spoke into the telephone:

'I don't know what happened this afternoon but everything seems different now. Even Jon noticed a difference. I think I'm going to make it. I think I can get better. I must get myself sorted out. I'll come any day to see you'.

The meeting was set for Thursday. When she arrived I had hoped to be in the same place with another load of piccalilli but the salt layering of the vegetables was incomplete. When they arrived I invited Anne and her social worker, Louise, into our larder which was built in the 1800s and originally had a stream running through it to cool the food.

'Would you like to taste the piccalilli?' This was our second meeting. The unconventional beginning to our sessions was now becoming normalized. I gave them two teaspoons and opened one of the bright yellow jars. 'Now that looks like my grandma's piccalilli!' said Anne.

'This is good! Delicious!' exclaimed both client and social worker. She was saying 'well done', and I felt immensely proud.

Duly satisfied, I then escalated her thoughts a bit further. 'Look at this.' I was talking to them both. Yesterday, my husband, Ken, went to Routledge, the London/New York publishers of our book *Psychodrama: Inspiration and Technique* with the design for the book cover and the illustrations for each of the chapters. They loved them. While he was there, he was handed a complimentary copy of the book, *On Becoming a Psychotherapist*. I showed it to Anne. 'It says, "Ten eminent psychotherapists write about their profession and their careers, exploring how and why they became psychotherapists." What a brilliant idea, eh?' I said to the social worker. 'And look', I pointed proudly to my name and the chapter I had written. Anne looked delighted. Her trust in me was confirmed and she had that I've-chosen-the-right-therapist look about her.

I handed it to Louise. 'Would you like to have a read?' Anne was as excited as I was. 'I haven't even had time to read it, Anne', I said, as we walked to my therapy room. 'I only received it at midnight last night. I wrote it over two years ago so I'm interested in how it reads now. The whole book looks fascinating, I'm going to read it on the beach in Portugal.'

Anne's interest in books was again obvious. 'I'd love to read it.' Her eyes got bigger. 'I'm going to get a copy when it comes out.' 'How did you get on with the Alice Miller book?' I asked. She said:

'Marcia, it's just about the best book I've ever read. I've read it twice since last week. It seems as though she is talking directly to me. She really understands. It's the first time I've ever read anything that make so much personal sense. But now I'm trying to get her other books, *For Your Own Good* and *Thou Shalt Not Be Aware*'.

For nearly half an hour, Anne and I scanned the Holwell library to find the books. We looked on shelves, in boxes and in the outbuildings. When we were in one of the barns looking for the books, she complained to me about her social worker. 'She never touches me, never holds my hand, never hugs me when I'm crying. Sometimes I think she doesn't care.' I said, 'It seems to me you're expecting your social worker to be the mother you never had. She can only give you what she is prepared to give you. Let's see what the week will bring.' Anything I said or did seemed secondary in her quest to find more of Alice Miller's words. She said to me: 'All I want is to find those books.' In full support, I took her into my office and phoned the local library. I modelled for Anne who was afraid to ask anyone for anything, how to get what she needed. 'We need the books immediately.' I said to the librarian: 'How soon can you get them in?' It was arranged that within a few days she could pick the books up from the library. 'Thanks', Anne said, 'I can't wait to read them.' We parted company after less than an hour.

I arrived back from Portugal late Saturday night. Anne was due to arrive at our house on Sunday night. A message was waiting for me to ring Anne.

I rang her on Sunday morning. 'Can I go home every night instead of staying over at your place? I need Jon and I've started sleep walking again. I'm so anxious.' 'The anxiety about coming here is normal', I said. 'Of course you can go home at night. You are not a child. You are an adult with needs. You must do what feels right for you. I will support you.' I heard in her voice a fear that I might make her stay. She was sensitive to being manipulated both by her parents and by the boarding school. I reassured her: 'Anne, you can't stay here tonight even if you change your mind. Another night is okay but tonight tell Jon to pick you up at ten o'clock.' 'I needed to hear that, Marcia,' she said. 'I'll see you tonight at seven o'clock. Thanks again.'

She arrived fearful and quiet. She sat in the living room reading her books as the other thirteen participants arrived. Most of the others were either therapists in training or individuals who, like herself, were seeking personal help. We have always mixed the two needs, knowing that the personal and the professional can complement one another. Each person comes as a human being first.

Moreno felt that equality of status was crucial in establishing group interaction. People should be raised to their highest common denominator.

'How many people are here for the first time?' I asked after people had gathered in the lounge. Four people raised their hands besides Anne. Dinner conversation in twos and threes had made talking together somewhat easier for most but still difficult for some. 'What does it feel like to be here?' There were varying responses. 'My anxiety is that I won't be able to come off the Portuguese beach and calm down enough to be able to listen to people,' I said, hoping other people would share their anxiety. 'My anxiety is that I won't be able to reveal my personal problems because it's too sensitive an issue,' said another.

'I'm having trouble at work. I don't want to get up in the morning.' 'I'm in a job that I've been trying to leave for years.' said others. 'I don't know if it's my loneliness generally or if I just don't like my job.' 'I spend three hours on the M25 each day going back and forth to work. Sometimes I feel like I'm going mad. When I get to work I spend three-quarters of my time staring into a computer screen, I don't get to talk to people at all. Then I go home to an empty flat.' There was a pause, the speaker had tears in his eyes. 'The only time I feel human is when I write poetry and now I've even stopped doing that. I'm in a mess.' He shook his head and stared at the floor.

Anne watched and had raised her hand with the others when I'd asked who had some anxiety. She looked around at the other people and had companions. 'Are you also afraid that your problems are too personal?' I spoke towards Anne, she nodded her head. Colour was coming back into her face. She looked less alone amongst the strangers. A Danish girl spoke up, 'I am afraid that my English won't be good enough. Not that I can't speak it but I'm afraid my mind won't think quickly enough.' She had travelled from Denmark to be with us for the week. 'I always have the same problem too,' said a man from Norway, 'particularly when I'm directing a psychodrama session here. Other people understand me but I get panicked about the language.' A psychiatrist from Yugoslavia agreed, 'Zis is za problem,' she reiterated. 'Say me the words and I understand zem. But my English, oh God.' She laughed and others laughed with her. She was glad that there were other people struggling with the English language.

I said, 'My teacher Zerka Moreno always says, "Your English is better than my Danish or my Serbo-Croat or my Norwegian"'. They smiled. Anne may have had other problems but I could see she was thinking that at least she spoke English. 'For now, it is not important how much you know about psychodrama or psychotherapy. It is more important that you, alone, are the greatest expert on your own life.'

More comfort set in as we arranged the week ahead. We spoke about the schedule and deviations from the schedule. We might have a Devonshire cream tea, see the countryside or watch tapes from our video collection. I had wanted to show Anne a TV programme I'd made with film director Midge MacKenzie in

May 1989 on Alice Miller's work. There were four programmes. The one I wanted her to see was a documentary made with ten actors and two script writers. In it, we psychodramatically enacted the actors' early childhood experiences. These experiences served as part of the base material for the three subsequent scripted plays about emotional and physical child abuse. I was waiting for her to have group support before she saw them. I'd also wanted her to see a sequence from an R.D. Laing interview, where he talks about child abuse. It would all happen in time.

The session ended and people were invited into the kitchen for tea, coffee or hot chocolate. Anne said quietly, 'Jon likes hot chocolate. Would anyone mind if my husband has a cup when he picks me up?' Several people said they'd like to meet him. 'He won't want to come in. He'll be embarrassed.' 'It might be important for him to see that we're regular people,' I spoke to Anne, as we moved to the fireplace in our farmhouse kitchen. The kitchen has huge, blue slate slabs on the floor. These were laid down at least three hundred years before the present conversation took place. That floor always gives perspective.

Jon came in and sat by the fire with Anne on his lap. 'She did very well tonight,' I assured Jon. Anne beamed. 'It's good here,' Anne said to her husband. 'I'm looking forward to tomorrow. Goodnight everyone,' They left and went into the dark night and started on their 35 minute drive home.

Jon dropped her off at 6.30 the next morning on his way to work. 'I almost didn't come back,' Anne said as she entered. 'I'm scared, Marcia, but I'm going to do it. Two good things happened to me last night.' Anne was excited to tell me. 'First of all I like the fact that they wanted Jon to come in and have hot chocolate; that meant a lot to me and, second, Phil gave me a hug by the stove.'

Phil had mentioned in the group the previous evening that he worked with sexually abused women up North. Anne had winked at me in approval. She looked as if to say, 'Where has he been all my life? I didn't even know people like that existed.' It was important for Anne to see that sexual abuse was containable and treatable. The fact that someone in the group dealt with abuse professionally made her feel more hopeful. 'When he gave me a hug, he said, "We've all been there. It's okay." That's the first time anyone but Jon has hugged me.' Anne looked relieved that the stranger, who dealt with sexual abuse, could touch her. It made her aware that she is not untouchable, either physically or emotionally.

At 6.30 a.m. the first morning, a group participant named George was already at the kitchen table. We three had a cup of tea and I showed them my shells from Portugal. I left George and Anne discussing the shells while I got dressed. Anne began to see that sleeping, washing, dressing, making breakfast and tea were all part of our household too. I could tell she liked George. He was the computer expert/poet who had the ghastly drive on the M25 every day. He was also a plain speaker. He was anxious himself and was looking for a life direction.

Unthreatened in his company, Anne, with George, laid the breakfast table.

Because of the past, relating to men was difficult for her. Her husband had told me the night before that the one thing she needed most was to be cuddled by people other than him. 'I'm the only person she talks to and the only person who touches her.' He looked at me directly, almost pleading to have someone else to share his load. I hoped we could fulfil his desire to reduce the pain of his beloved Anne. They were like two devoted swans, together for life. One swan, however, had a broken wing. How could he, Jon, help his stranded partner without tools or knowledge? He had love and dedication to offer but sometimes that is not enough when a whole wing is broken.

On the first morning the group assembled in our theatre, which is a converted granary. It has oak beams, patterned carpets, white walls and a raised balcony. One part of the room is designated as a stage area. Here, scenes from everyday life are enacted. The balcony is used for authority roles; gods, teachers, parents and aspects of the self that need to be more assertive. Often people find it easier to be angry if they are physically higher.

I put an empty chair in front of the group. 'Imagine yourself sitting in the chair. Talk to yourself about your expectations for this week, what you want to accomplish, what you hope will happen. Tell yourself these things.' One by one, participants got up and spoke to the empty chair. This was one of hundreds of warm-ups used to increase the group's creativity and to set out the areas to be worked on in the week ahead of us.

Anne bravely faced the empty chair. 'You have been sexually abused.' I was proud of her already. She had raw nerve to tackle the truth so soon. I could see she was summoning up immense courage to speak. She spoke again, 'How much longer can you live with this? You have to get rid of what you feel. These people here will listen to you.' She looked tearful, and sat down. She knows when to quit, I thought to myself. She knows how not to overstep her own boundaries. I can trust her to know what she will need from me. I felt encouraged by her first emotive statement in the group.

After everyone, including Ken and myself, had faced the empty chair, we shared points of identity. Those who had trouble in the work sphere commiserated over their uninspiring jobs. Those who had relationship problems shared their fear that it may never get better. Those who had been sexually abused, (there were three) spoke of the devastation and anguish it produced. Another participant spoke about her mother who was dying. She wanted to ventilate her negative feelings towards her mother so it would leave her free to express positive feelings during the death process. Her mother was dying of a degenerative lung disease. Each time she saw her, there was less breath and less life. She wanted to say goodbye to her mother in the best way possible. In this case, psychodrama could serve a preparatory function, disentangling the past from the future. This last point was understandable to Anne. Her mother-in-law had just died and her father had a heart attack only a few months earlier. What did it all mean? Could she let go when the time came? It all ran through her head. A perspective began to fall into place. 'I'm glad I'm here,' Anne said over lunch. 'This is where I need to be.' More than anyone else's advice, she accepted her own assurance. She knew her own mind and saw that I respected it too.

The first protagonist, or subject of the session was a man who had difficulty making relationships. Moreno used to say: 'Psychodrama is a therapy of relationships. Perhaps the psyche doesn't exist here' (pointing to his head), 'but it exists *between* people. The relationship I have with you (pointing to someone in the group), is different to the relationship he has with you.' (Personal communication.) Moreno was always immediate, using the here and now as his friend, the medium in which he always worked. Once, when working with a young lady who had difficulty with her boyfriend Moreno suggested, 'Phone him now. We'll wait. Tell him what you told us. See if he agrees.' He gave us the feeling that he had all the time in the world and was interested in each of us. Genuine interest and curiosity are crucial in the psychotheraputic process.

Anne enjoyed the first day and felt safe. At 10.00 p.m. her husband, Jon, came to pick her up. He looked relieved that she was still alive. There must have been many moments like that when he had worried about her. They went off happily and glad to be rejoined. It seemed right for her to leave us. In fifteen years of running the Holwell Centre for Psychodrama and Sociodrama, we had only seen three other people who left to stay somewhere else. It never worked. The participants always regretted it. So did we, but this time it was right. Anne needed the safety of her bed and her husband. 'Throw away the script,' Moreno said, 'You cannot judge one moment based on the last moment.'

On Tuesday, Anne came back saying it was the best night's sleep she'd had in a long time. She had had a bath, was too tired to dry herself so her husband helped. He made her a cup of tea but before she could drink it she was asleep until morning. 'I never even cuddled him!' Anne said proudly. 'And when he told me that he'd drive me down your long lane this morning, I told him to "Piss off!" I walked down in the dark. I bet he'll think about that all day.'

She looked a little agitated. 'What's wrong?' I asked. 'I think I have to do my session today, I can't wait any longer.' Several of us were sitting together outside. One held her hand, some listened. 'I think you could work today', I assured Anne, 'but the longer you have to watch other people's lives, the more prepared you'll be to look at your own life.' I tried to hold her off. It was too early to plunge her into what was going to be deep emotion. Maybe I wasn't ready myself. 'I'd like you to continue to listen to other people and play some roles in their dramas so you can get used to the stage and the process.' I wanted to desensitise her to the depths of emotional expression and for her to feel the support of the group. She winced. 'I don't know if I can wait.' She was like a little girl waiting to go to the toilet. 'I think you can wait. I've had twenty years of experience. I'm not telling you this without some wisdom.' She reluctantly agreed.

The next protagonist was relevant to Anne. It was a woman, Claire, who wanted to look at men's violence towards herself. She felt the violence in 'men's loud voices and hairy bodies'. It had affected both her emotional and sexual expressions. She wondered if she had been sexually interfered with as a child. She had a memory of being on a black-and-white tiled floor, under a railing at school, and a memory of heavy men's boots coming at her and of being very frightened. We explored her Catholic school convent education and her relationship with her father. There was a lot of violence between her parents. In the session she shouted out her fear, terror and anger. Anne cried pitifully into the arms of two group members. She was supported by a man in the group whom she said: 'was the first man I've ever felt safe with besides my husband.'

We were on the second day and she was crying in public, something she'd never done before, feeling frightened and being comforted by strangers, which had never happened before and being hugged by a man who wasn't her husband, which had also never happened before. We seemed to be making progress. In the content of the sessions, she was seeing her own traumas mirrored in the life experiences of others. It allowed her to feel close to many people in the group.

In the afternoon, a man worked on his isolation and on the repeated pattern of loneliness throughout his childhood. He didn't trust people, generally, because of his 'untrustworthy parents'. He felt his parents hadn't wanted him from the time of his conception. They physically beat him throughout his childhood. He was the second member of the group who felt rejected by his parents. Anne identified with this, as she also felt she wasn't wanted. Being rejected from birth caused her low self-esteem that was compounded by continual sexual abuse from the three primary men in her life. She began to talk about her experiences in the last or 'sharing' part of the psychodrama session. She said to the group: ' I was eight when it all began to happen.' In the last part of the session, 'sharing', group members relate their own experiences to that of the protagonist. From doing this, Anne gained from letting out a little bit at a time and getting used to the delicate balance of self-disclosure and support.

The next afternoon we were all set to work with someone else. It was a warm day so we went outside for a break before the session. Anne began to cry. Her anger at her children began to surface. She kicked and cried. Other members of the group were sitting beside her. Her emotion was real and immediate. The time seemed ready to work with her, and we all felt it. The person planning to work suggested that he wait and we all agreed. I took Anne to the stage.

As we began, I remembered that Anne had told me that she didn't want to talk about her children in front of the group. She was too 'embarrassed'. I wondered how she would handle this now that she felt so angry towards her children. I waited. She said she wanted to begin by talking to her children. I suggested she put her children in two empty chairs in front of her. Her anger was uncontainable. She addressed them 'If it weren't for you, I wouldn't be in this mess. I wish you were dead.'

I suggested she set up the scene at home when she first heard of the sexual assault her son had allegedly made on her daughter. She showed us her living room by putting chairs to represent the furniture. We use very few props in psychodrama, a few chairs and an empty space. As is true of listening to radio, the imagination fills in the details. I asked her to reverse roles, first with her daughter and then with her son. 'I am' statements give a much clearer perception of the role than 'She is' statements. For example, 'I am shy, I am nervous', etc. The spontaneous body language the person produces is also revealing and helpful. She began to see, in the role of her son and daughter, how each was 'set up' to sexually explore each other. They had been told never explore in any way that was sexual. 'Do not explore,' was a hypnotic induction. It produced the opposite unconscious command, 'Do explore.'

When we began the scene with the teacher coming home with her daughter, I stopped everything. 'Anne,' I spoke truthfully, 'you said you never wanted to reveal this scene to the rest of the group. Should we stop now?' I wanted to give her complete control over her self-disclosure. Her main problem in the past was that she had had no control over what happened to her. I did not, as her therapist, want to collude with that error. 'No,' she said, 'I want to continue, it must be dealt with. It's what began all this and it's what I'm thinking about now.' We continued. I asked her in her daughter's role, if it did 'begin all this'. 'Nonsense,' she said, in the role of her daughter, 'she had her own problems with abuse before all this started. We didn't do that to her.' Anne saw the sense of that.

Moreno said, 'People are more spontaneous in the role of someone else than in their own role.' (Moreno 1965) She was exploring the truth through dramatic method and it was easier to see the truth through her daughter's eyes. She played out the scene of humiliation and distrust. As her daughter, Anne begged to be believed. History was repeating itself. Her mother didn't believe her and she saw the importance of being listened to.

We then moved to a scene with Anne trying to tell her own mother that she was being sexually abused by her grandfather. The scene began when she was coming back from her grandfather's house after several weeks. Her mother refused to listen to the story. By paying absolutely no attention to her, her mother intimated that Anne was ridiculous. She dismissed it all without Anne even getting a word out. Even her distress, without the details, was not taken seriously. The little 8-year-old girl was trapped in her own silence without an ally or an advocate to speak for her. She was alone.

At that point, I asked Anne to use her tele to choose a group member to play the role of little Anne. 'Tele' is the Greek word meaning 'at a distance'. Moreno adopted it to mean 'feeling into' another person. It is a two-way system. Telepathy is usually one way. Because tele is a two-way system, the person chosen for the role often knows in advance that he or she will be chosen. She chose a shy, sad female member of the group. Anne watched the same scene enacted by others in the group. In the scene, a 'fag' hung out of her mother's mouth, as she, resentfully, did the family's washing and studiously didn't listen to anything her daughter had to say.

As Anne watched, she felt hurt. She could see the little girl's right, and need to be able to tell someone what had happened. I asked Anne if there was anyone in her life that could have helped her at that moment. She said, as is commonly spoken by the abused: 'There was no-one.' I asked: 'What would it have been like if you, as you are now, could have spoken for the little girl and comforted her?' Anne cuddled the child and said, 'This should have never happened to you. You didn't deserve it and you should have been able to tell the truth and have someone hear you.'

I asked Anne to look at the group and choose someone to enact the role of the mother she would have liked to have had when she was little. She choose an open-faced participant who was friendly and loving. The woman gladly came up on the stage. I asked Anne to express, without words, what she couldn't express to her mother at the time. Anne collapsed into the woman's arms and sobbed. She began to tell her mother how frightened she had been, how lonely she had felt and how desperately she had wanted to be protected. 'Why weren't you there?' she said, 'Why weren't you there?' Her anger started to rise. 'That bastard,' she said, 'I'll kill him.'

At that moment we began to get some of her murderous anger rightly placed. The anger came initially from Anne in the mother's role. 'Where is your father, your uncle, your grandfather? All three of them, I'll kill them,' she shouted. Finally, she was beginning to stand up for herself. Her self-esteem had found its voice at last. She had rights. I gave her a long plastic tube that she throttled, twisted and finally slapped onto the wooden stool in front of her. She chose three men from the group to enact the three perpetrators in her life. They sat in chairs in front of her. She began to hit down on the tube harder. 'How dare you,' she screamed. 'How dare you do what you did to me.' She was now herself. 'You bastards, you worms, you deserve to die.' The wish for them to be dead shadowed what she had felt for her children at the beginning of the session. The strength of these feelings belonged to these three men and not to her children. These men had changed her life history forever. She turned to me. 'I'd like to kill them. Can I?' 'How would you do it?' I asked. 'This is a psychodrama, remember, not real life.' 'I'd put them through a mincer, or I'd stab them, or I'd cut their heads off. No. I'd twist their necks.'

She completed the scene of fantasised revenge. Rage is a mild word to express what she felt in this scene. I was careful not to role-reverse her into any of the men's roles. To understand the reasons behind their action was not the task of this session. Too many victims get lost in an attempt to understand and forgive. They can trap themselves in a sea of rationalisations from which they may never return.

I gave her a cushion to simulate the action. After that her anger abated. 'I can never forgive what you did to me. Because of your own emotional poverty, you couldn't stop yourselves from doing it. You poor sods.' Turning to me she said, 'I want to say goodbye to my father. I want to accept my parents. They are the only parents I have, but I don't ever have to accept what they did. Never.' She quietly took her father in her arms and motioned to the woman who had played her mother to come back on stage. 'This is what I want,' she said. She stood holding and being held by her parents.

In this part of the session, she had the opportunity to internalise the goodness of her parents and to accept that she, too, contained the potential for goodness. She then stood facing the two auxiliary egos (those people who played the significant roles of members in her life). 'Thank you for staying with me.' She said to her children and husband, 'I want to stay with you. You are my real family now. Thank you, thank you everyone.'

After she'd finally said and done what she really felt, she looked vibrant, satisfied and spent. The rest of the group spontaneously came around her in a circle and we breathed our first collective breath of relief. The 3-hour journey was now over. It felt complete. The group members said how privileged they were to be there, and how much courage she had shown. Each person, one by one, shared with Anne their personal identification with her story. Each told which part of the session had moved them the most and what it had meant to them. If it reminded them of significant moments in their own life, they spoke about those moments. The people in the group who had been abused in their own childhood cried, individually, in her arms. One said, 'Your story is my story.' Another said, 'The details were different but my feelings were exactly the same. I felt just like you did when you wanted to kill your father.'

Someone else said: 'Thank you Anne, thank you. I realised for the first time how much support my daughter needs and how important it is that I listen to her. She hasn't been abused but she has been hurt and I didn't listen either. I have to set that right when I get home.'

The sharing went on for a long time. Anne listened, hugged, felt strong and kept mumbling gleefully, 'I did it!'

Anne slept like a baby that night. The rest of the week she participated in other people's dramas and even played roles in two of them. She shared with others more easily and had a renewed sense of confidence.

She had a difficult moment on the fourth day of the week, when a male in the group began to be angry at his neighbours, who were badly harassing him. As she watched, Anne was beginning to feel angry with him when all of a sudden she began to cry. Facing her own anger was too much. 'I can't watch this. I want to go home. I want to cuddle Jon.' She held on to me tightly. I stopped the action on the stage. The group was silent. 'Stay with it Anne, you're not going mad, you're just feeling strong emotion. Hang on. It will be over soon and you'll be alright.'

It took her several minutes to calm down. She had wanted to leave, to shut her mind off and to run away. It was easier than to ride through these new emotions, even in the safety of this group. We continued the work on stage. After several minutes, Anne said softly, 'He's not my father. Go get him!' she said, speaking to the protagonist. 'Go after him. Go on, tell him!' She was shouting out and encouraging the anger she had just previously feared. At the end of the session she continued to hold on to her new realisation. 'Other men are not my father. I don't have to be afraid of them.'

That morning, her own real father had been taken to our local hospital with another heart attack. 'What shall I do?' she asked the group. 'I want to try and go and see him tomorrow.' Our last day, I thought to myself. She'd be better off to go and see him tonight and then she'd have the support of the group in the morning. That's what she decided to do.

At 6.30 a.m. the next morning. I unlocked the back door as usual. She hugged me. 'Oh, Marcia, I did it. If only he could have been like that my whole life.' I held her quietly, and spoke calmly, 'He's dying, Anne, or he thinks he is.' 'Tell me what happened,' I said. Her visit to hospital was a real-life test of our work. It couldn't have been more timely. 'I stayed for an hour. I never thought I could do that. When I got there, he had begun to ask me why I hadn't been to see him in the last few months.' Being the oldest of seven children, she was expected to visit him. 'You knew I was ill,' he said. She and he spoke in broad Devonshire accents. 'That's why I didn't come, Dad. You know you and I argue. I didn't think it was good to argue with you if you were ill.' 'Yes, you and I argue, we do,' said her dad. She said, 'Let's not talk about that now, dad.' She held his hand. While there she also spoke to the doctor about his condition. 'He'll kill himself if he goes on like this,' the doctor told her. 'He's so anxious, he's making it worse for himself.' Anne said to me,

'He was like a little baby, Marcia, so afraid. He kept looking at me as if to say he was sorry. He has to have more tests. Now I hope he doesn't die. I can't believe it. I honestly hope he doesn't die. He's more like the father I always wanted. Maybe I'm just fooling myself, but I thoroughly enjoyed that hour. It was okay to be near him.'

As people arrived that morning for breakfast she told them her news. She almost couldn't believe it herself.

The week came to an end. Anne said: 'If it wasn't for coming here I would have left my husband and children, the people I love the most in the world. Funny isn't it? You've done a bloody good job.'

At the conclusion of this writing, Anne continues to go from strength to strength. She sees me for follow-up sessions. She reports,

'I'm a different person. The way I feel now I've never felt in my whole life. I can't explain it but I sleep and eat better. I'm not so irritable. I actually suggested that my daughter go out and enjoy herself. My husband says I'm not so uptight. And I went to see my social worker, You know, she wasn't as bad as I thought she was.'

There have been many dramatic psychodrama sessions at Holwell over the years. The expression of blocked emotions and the gained attitude changes are an important point of beginning on the road back to health. I am aware, with Anne, that it is early days in her reawakening process. Part of her current behaviour is a euphoric relief. Several weeks after this writing, she is still feeling 'better than ever'. It is interesting to note that after reading this chapter, Anne said:

'Fantastic. Seeing it on paper is just fantastic. It is the first time I really feel I've been believed. During that week at Holwell, I'd wished I'd been two people, one who'd experienced it and one who was watching it. Reading it was like watching it. I cried and laughed all the way through it. I hope many therapists can read this story.'

It is hoped by her husband, by Anne, by myself and all those that know her that her new sense of wellbeing will be sustaining and irrevocable. There will no doubt be setbacks, and support in the follow-up period will be crucial. Unlike her prior thinking that she has much to fight against, she now realises that she has much to struggle *for*.

She is planning a new career. She is full of confidence and zest for life. At her last appointment, Anne, the social worker and myself had a truthful review of what has happened over the last several months. Anne and the social worker were able to tell each other how special each has been to the other. At the end of the session, in a rather moving moment, they embraced. Again, it was something Anne thought she could never do. As she left, Anne asked for the piccalilli recipe. An unusual and unconventional combination, psychodrama and piccalilli – but one that worked.

Acknowledgements

I would like to thank Midge MacKenzie for seeing the importance of this experience and encouraging me to write it down.

To my *compañero*, Ken Sprague, *gracias* for your imaginative vision and your infectious hope for humanity, which helped me through this journey.

I give a big kiss to my daughter Maureen Heawood, who typed this with her new word processor on her days off. In the end, she had to use her nose because her fingers stopped working!

This chapter wouldn't have happened without their friendship.

And most of all I want to thank Anne, whose struggle is unforgettable.

Piccalilli

In Britain, piccalilli is served as a condiment. A tablespoonful is delicious with cheese and bread. It is also a good accompaniment to meat or vegetables. Most people who don't like piccalilli like this one for its mild flavour.

Ingredients

4 lbs cubed marrow (marrow is like a large zuccini or courgette)
1 lb cauliflower florets
1 lb onions (shallots, pickling onions or sliced onions)
1 large peeled and diced cucumber (3 American-sized)

3 oz salt
12 oz sugar (demerara or light brown)
2 pints white vinegar
4 oz dried mustard
2 level tablespoons flour or cornflour (cornstarch)
1 level tablespoon turmeric
1 bag pickling spices (tea-bag size)

Method

Layer all the vegetables in the salt (you can use 2 oz more salt), in a large bowl, sprinkle with 2 oz of the sugar and leave to stand for 24 hours. Drain and rinse the vegetables. Put the vegetables (except for the cauliflower) into a large pan with the remaining 10 oz sugar, $1^1/_2$ pints of the vinegar (set aside $^1/_2$ pint of the total 2 pints) and add the spice bag. Bring to the boil. Simmer for 15 minutes. Add the cauliflower after 5 minutes (it needs to remain crunchy). Remove the spice bag. Blend the mustard, cornflour and turmeric with the remaining $^1/_2$ pint of vinegar. Stir the mixture into the vegetables, cook for 3 minutes. Pour into jars, cover and seal.

References

Conway, A. and Clarkson, P. (1987) 'Everyday hypnotic induction', *Transactional Analysis Journal* 17 (2)

Feldmar, A. (1989) 'Did you used to be R. D. Laing?' London: Channel 4, October 3.

Miller, A. (1987) *For Your Own Good*, London: Virago.

Miller, A. (1986) *Thou Shall Not Be Aware*, London: Pluto Press.

Moreno, J. L. (1953) *Who Shall Survive?*, Beacon, NY: Beacon House.

Moreno, J. L. (1965) Conversation with Marcia Karp.

Chapter eight

Who goes there?

Group-analytic drama for disturbed adolescents

Sarah T. Willis

That old cow
She hates me
And I am worthless
　　　　　　(Young person in a session talking about his mother)

Preliminary remarks

As the warm-up begins, the group appears fragmented. Mark is dismantling
the window frame while Tony picks a fight with Ruby. Lynn is asleep and
Donna says she hates drama and she's going to be sick. The other group
members are lying almost prone in their chairs. Insolence and bellicosity
exude from every pore. The two conductors maintain a calm facade while
their brains work frantically. It seems incredible that we can ever come
together. How are we to keep ourselves from getting caught up in this
mesmerising kaleidoscope of primitive behaviour? What's it all about?
How to harness at least part of this rich mass of material into something to
be worked with?

These are just a few of the questions which confront those who offer therapy
to disturbed adolescents. The broad and bewildering range of possible
approaches gives rise to fundamental dilemmas. Should we use a one-to-one
treatment mode or work in a group? If so, what kind of group? Should we adopt
a more analytic stance, centred on in-depth exploration and interpretation, or a
more open style with emphasis on support and modelling? What are the advantages of action methods over non-action?

We, at York Road, set out to discover experientially with the young people
themselves what kind of approach would be most accessible and potentially
creative. The particular difficulties of our adolescents and my own skills and
background would inevitably influence our initial choices. The first decision was
to work in groups. Previously, several attempts by other therapists to engage our
youngsters in individual psychotherapy had broken down due to the fact that
intense, ready-made negative transference had awaited them from the start. All

adolescents are 'primarily concerned with what they appear to be in the eyes of others as compared with what they feel they are' (Erikson 1987: 235). To perform this essential new task of achieving a stable ego identity, they instinctively turn to groups and gangs. A group, therefore, seemed to be the most natural and safe context for their therapy. Before working as a teacher and a therapist, I had been a professional actress myself and so had inside knowledge of drama as a means of helping people to get in touch with their emotions and communicate them spontaneously. Thus we began, with the drama and the group. The discovery that we were implicitly applying group-analytic principles came somewhat later.

The new method that evolved is essentially a synthesis of action techniques with non-action therapy. I have called it group-analytic drama (GAD), since it brings together aspects of the theory and practice of group analysis, psychodrama, sociodrama and theatre itself. This chapter examines first, the sources from which the new method derives. Then our client group will be introduced to the reader. The rationale of why we use certain techniques will be explained. Finally, I describe how we put these and other techniques into effect, and compare the method with the classic psychodramatic approach of Moreno.

Influences: group analysis, psychodrama, sociodrama, and theatre

In this section I shall outline briefly the four main sources that have influenced the development of group-analytic dramas. Since most readers will already be familiar with the basic principles of psychodrama, sociodrama and theatre, I shall give a slightly more detailed account of the theory and practice of group analysis, focusing on those aspects that have had most impact on our method.

Group analysis, founded by S.H. Foulkes, 1898–1976, is a form of psychotherapy in small groups. Foulkes' grounding in psychoanalysis led him to recognise the existence of the unconscious mind and the complex range of psychic mechanisms associated with it, e.g. repression, intrapsychic conflict, transference, etc. In his theoretical explorations, Foulkes went beyond the Freudian emphasis on an individual's inner processes to develop ideas about the group as a totality. From gestalt and field theory ((Lewin 1951), he adopted the view that the whole is more elementary than its parts, 'the function of the group as a whole has . . . a more primary significance for the understanding of all part processes concerning its members, and not the other way round' (Foulkes and Anthony 1984: 19). Underlying this working principle was Foulkes' clear conviction that the essential nature of man is social. 'What stands in need of explanation is not the existence of groups but the existence of individuals' (Foulkes and Anthony 1984: 234–5). The social aspect is 'an irreducible basic fact' (Foulkes 1964: 109).

Foulkes has come to be well known for his use of the term 'matrix' as a conceptual construct to describe the idea of communication occurring across the group and not merely between individuals in the group. The individual might well be seen as a nodal point in a field of interaction in which 'unconscious reactions meet' (Foulkes and Anthony 1984: 29). His view of the significance of the matrix upholds the notion that all intrapsychic processes as well as all interpersonal events can have meaning only within a total network of communication.

The overall aim of group-analytic psychotherapy is to achieve far-reaching changes in the individual. In practice, however, the first objective is to make conscious the 'group unconscious', so that true feelings may be experienced fully. New outcomes to old conflicts are sought. For this objective to be reached, certain key conditions must be fulfilled. I describe here only those that also have relevance for group-analytic drama. One: the group must be carefully set up and maintained. Preserving boundaries of space, time and suitable conduct means that the group is protected from pernicious forces, both within and without. Two: 'free-floating' verbal communication (Foulkes and Anthony 1984: 59) needs to develop. The free associations of psychoanalysis have become group associations to a shared context. Since the members are seen to be unconsciously as well as consciously in contact with one another, all responses are accepted as having the value of spontaneous interpretations. Most of the work is done by the group. Three: the group works in a state of suspended action. Although non-verbal and verbal communication happen simultaneously, the emphasis is on verbal interaction. Abstinence from all other activities has the effect of supporting more extreme levels of anxiety. Thus the shared unconscious of the group is activated, and hitherto suppressed feelings are experienced and expressed (Molnos 1987: 47–61, 1988).

Therapy hinges on active participation in the group, i.e. experience of the dynamic processes in the here-and-now together with their analysis. Enduring therapeutic change will result only if emotional experience and increased insight occur in unison.

All of these strands have been incorporated to a greater or lesser degree into group-analytic drama. However, two principal features of GAD that are derived from group analysis stand out. These features are the theoretical idea of the group as a whole as a frame of reference and, in practice, the use of a non-action technique as part of the session. For more information about group analysis please see the publications by Foulkes listed at the end of this chapter under the heading, Further reading.

Psychodrama is a therapeutic dramatic process employed to help the individual. A group member becomes the protagonist in his/her own drama. Auxiliary egos are chosen from amongst the group members to play the parts of significant others. This way the protagonist can re-examine roles he or she plays in a personal network. Where someone is rigidly bound to a life script that is obsolete and suffocating, a new spontaneity may be found. Other participants, deeply involved, benefit therapeutically by virtue of the mechanisms of resonance and identification.

Sociodrama, also developed by Moreno, is a method of acting through which the members can address specified group themes, e.g. racism, domestic conflict, gender stereotyping, etc. and the roles individuals play in relation to them. The people who enact the parts represent those roles and functions rather than themselves in role. The aim is to explore feelings about particular social and family constellations. Emphasis is on interpersonal relationships and treatment is directed towards the group.

The fourth influence on GAD is theatre itself. While group analysis, psychodrama and sociodrama provide the theoretical framework for the method, my own experience in the theatre has inevitably contributed to the essence of its development. Like actors believe that great drama happens when the structure of a play is transcended by the actors' intuitive and spontaneous use of improvisation. Peter Brook's concept of the empty space, where anything might happen, where the actor 'enters the unpredictable' (Brook 1988: 8), seems not so far removed from Winnicott's 'potential space' or 'intermediate area of experience' (Winnicott 1986: 126, 15, 44), which alleviates the tension created between internal and external reality, and where imaginative playful creativity becomes possible. Winnicott said that the object of psychotherapy is to bring a person into a state of being able to play. Adolescents who have lived most of their lives in crisis have not been secure enough to play. With our youngsters in mind, we set out to create an empty, but safe space where they might learn to play.

Group-analytic drama, then, is a combination of these four important sources. Like psychodrama it aims to help the individual. It seeks to do this by means of the group, whereby the group becomes the focus of treatment. As in group analysis, the group itself is the principal therapeutic agency. There are two main links with sociodrama. No scene is directly taken from the actual experience of any group member, and all members are encouraged to become protagonists, assuming roles and freely associating to the dramatic content. We call this 'the invented drama'. The key features of this approach are the use of non-action, verbalised responses in the drama, and the low-profile, receptive attitude of the conductor during the non-directive phases of the session. All three approaches – psychodrama, sociodrama and group-analytic drama – follow the same basic sequence: a warm-up, a drama and a sharing of feelings.

Group-analytic drama

The adolescents

Intermediate treatment was set up as an alternative to care or custody for young adolescents who are experiencing school and family breakdown and who might be in serious trouble with the law. Our main objective is to help them gain more control over their lives, whilst remaining within their own community. At York Road they attend a four-day-a-week, day-care programme, which consists of formal education, including vocational skills training, activity and therapy groups and counselling. The group-analytic drama method was developed by myself, with the help of my colleagues and five groups of adolescents between the ages of 14 and 17.

All the young people come from chaotic, abusing families and have experienced in varying degrees, cruelty, sexual and physical abuse and neglect. They have lived their lives in a protracted trauma. Now aspects of this trauma are violently re-created in their social milieu. Frequently, those who come to our notice have been referred by other agencies who have become concerned about their behaviour and its effects on others. The adolescents themselves often recognise no personal difficulties. Everything that is wrong is 'out there'. They express little desire to change. In spite of this they present themselves as bewildered and lost. They do not seem to know who they are or what is happening to them. They may be depressed and withdrawn or overtly acting out. Behavioural problems include drug abuse, promiscuity, prostitution, self-cutting, suicide attempts and delinquent activities such as burglary, assault, extortion, arson and rape. Seen at close quarters they are not attractive. They are liars and rogues who can produce a staggering range of invective and abuse. They have poor impulse control and little sense of boundaries or of self. They continually externalise and project their experiences and have minimal capacity for coherent, logical thought. What's more, every good experience has to be rubbished or destroyed.

The crisis of puberty, which re-evokes all the quintessential 'modes of excitation, tension, gratification and defence' (Blos 1962: 11) that were operating in early childhood lies behind the regressive character of adolescent behaviour. It is this behaviour, characteristic of the so-called normally developing adolescent, which is magnified in the case of severely disturbed adolescents and so often becomes an obstacle to therapy. Since disturbed adolescents, more than others, lack the ability to start putting order into their fragmentation and lack the structures in which thought and action can become distinct, we need a method that helps them and us give shape to much of what is going on.

Two colleagues of mine ran an analytic discussion group with disaffected boys in a secondary school. They write:

> We didn't realise how savagely our way of thinking would come under attack, how far our feelings of containment would be shredded to the point that the room, and we in it, seemed to be a hazy soup of noise and movement where nothing was allowed to make sense for even a minute.
>
> (Ellwood and Oke 1987: 37)

Those who work with disturbed adolescents will recognise the scene. How impossible it seems, under such conditions, to find the 'common sense' in the group. Language is not yet used for self-reflection. In such groups it's a kind of ammunition. Words are blasted back and forth like bullets. Scattered, denied and painful feelings ricochet around the space. There is an absence of any real or group focus. The adolescent group is, as Winnicott says, an aggregate of isolates, each person desperately alone and not quite part of the group (Winnicott 1987: 190). They need to be helped to come together.

So the question that I asked myself was: what can we offer that the recalcitrant, alienated and highly defended young person can accept?

Eight techniques

I have listed eight features of disturbed adolescence that so often obstruct the achievement of a more reflective mode of working. These I recount here together with some therapeutic techniques and the rationale for their use (see Table 8.1).

1. *Adolescents appear or may claim to be easily bored and display a constant need for stimulation.* So, we ensure that throughout the $2^1/_2$ hour session there is a variety of tasks and pace, from participating in the warm-up, through negotiating a theme for the drama, to taking part in the analysis.

2. *Disturbed adolescents experience difficulties with anxiety and over-excitability.* Anxiety of great intensity may build up and disrupt play. Overexcitement leads to fragmentation in which playfulness cannot be sustained. Spontaneous playfulness is at the centre of our work and to develop the capacity for it is our goal. Firm models of exchange, which help reduce anxiety, can only become established if we have clearly defined and maintained boundaries. Basic rules are: no violence to persons or property, no drugs, no weapons. Acting out, in the sense that action or indeed words may be substituted for real feeling, is discouraged. The group has six to eight members. One conductor acts as custodian of the boundaries, chasing up anyone who leaves the room during the session.

3. *Adolescents may regress to an early infantile state and/or exhibit exaggerated compensatory maturity.* Both of these apparent opposites can be catered for by nurturing in the warm-up. Sometimes we take them on a guided fantasy and they curl up like 3 year olds listening to a fairy tale. We play games: some are intended to help participants start talking more openly and some are designed to help them develop and improve their vocabulary for emotions; popular children's games are also played, with the emphasis on encouraging an atmosphere of co-operation and sharing. We do exercises that foster trust, relaxation and concentration. Here is an example of a trust exercise which is also fun. Members, with partners, have to close their eyes and, without peeping, place their finger on their partner's nose. They have to accomplish this without poking out their partner's eye or ramming their finger up his nostril.

4. *Adolescents have problems with channelling energy.* To help syphon off excess energy we may use vigorous exercise in the warm-up, this in the

form of boisterous games that involve physical movement and touching. Hop-and-bump is a favourite. The aim is to hop around within a delineated area and gently knock everybody else out of it. Deep-breathing exercises, designed to ground some of the more chaotic elements once excess energy has been dealt with, are used as a matter of course in all warm-ups. The youngsters are asked to stretch up on tip-toe and tense every muscle. Slowly they may relax, bit by bit. First they wiggle their fingers, then let their hands hang limp, unlock their elbows, revolve their shoulders, drop their heads and so on through the whole body – back, waist, hips, knees, until they fall slowly onto their sides. They then lie on their backs with one hand on their diaphragms, to test the efficiency of their deep breathing, and breathe in to a count of ten, hold to a count of ten and out again to the same. Everything should be smooth and controlled. There should be no great gulps or explosive exhalations. Many youngsters need help to achieve this, although apparently physically relaxed. This exercise is usually followed by a guided fantasy.

5. *Adolescents fear too much self-disclosure happening too fast.* This is taken care of by the 'invented drama'. Scenes from real life are not explored (until late in the life of the group) as intense anxiety would be experienced and under such conditions resistance hardens almost to an impasse: 'My Dad wouldn't say that', and so on.

6. *In the group we encounter a contradiction in the adolescent; self-conscious fear of being singled out together with the dread of being excluded (which, if we were doing psychodrama with one main protagonist at a time could put us in an insoluble dilemma).* This contradiction is dealt with in two ways, so that the underlying need for the limelight and the hidden fear of closeness are reconciled with the need for inclusion. First, everyone is a protagonist in the drama simultaneously, including the conductor(s). Thus fear is reduced, and while no-one has to endure the heat of the spotlight alone, everyone gets attention. Second, the final sharing is structured so that each member takes it in turn to receive the focus of attention. We might ask the individual member, 'Who did you like in our drama? Whom didn't you like? Towards whom did you have your strongest feelings?' Each individually begun analysis quickly becomes a lively interchange between all members of the group. What happens is a series of analyses involving the whole group rather than analysis of the individual within it. The agreed norm of taking turns reassures the insecure adolescent that no one will be left out.

7. *Wrangles around authority issues frequently render therapy (or group work with adolescents in general) unviable.* Once the 'them and us' mode has been established, not much headway can be made. Paranoia intensifies. Battles ensue. All-out war or equally defensive deadlock

become the only solutions. To be overdirective or too remote as a conductor would seem to invite these responses. Bion's style of conducting, for example, which emphasises therapy of the group by a relatively remote, non-participating conductor encourages repressed basic states and a diminished sense of individual identity (Bion 1961). Foulkes' idea of the conductor as an involved observer 'keeping in the background' (Foulkes 1986: 111) seems to stand in contrast to this. The intermittently non-directive, participatory activity of the conductors in our method helps to diffuse and circumvent the danger of the aforementioned warring process holding up therapy.

8. *Last and all-pervasive there is the adolescent propensity for extreme acting-out behaviour.* Some of it is useful discharge of affect, much of it is projection of strong libidinal and aggressive drives, most of it is defensive. In adolescents, acting out is usually associated with physical action. Group-analytic drama is essentially a non-action therapy. In the drama the members simply sit in a circle and the interaction is entirely verbal. This inhibits youngsters' defensive use of action and heightens intensity of feeling.

Table 8.1 Adolescent difficulties and therapeutic techniques

Characteristics of disturbed adolescents which stand between them and therapy	Therapeutic techniques and approach
1. Easily bored; need for stimulation	1. Varied task and pace
2. Overexcitability and difficulties with anxiety	2. Clear boundaries
3. The demanding baby	3. Playfulness and nurturing in the warm-up
4. Difficulties with channelling energy	4. Vigorous action in the warm-up when needed
5. Fear of too much self-disclosure	5. No scenes from real life
6. The adolescent contradiction: self-conscious fear of being singled out together with dread of being excluded	6. Everyone a protagonist; serial analytic procedures
7. Authority issues	7. Low-profile conductor: therapy of, by and through the group
8. Extreme acting-out behaviour	8. Moving towards a non-action therapy as trust develops

Source: Willis (1988: 156)

A clinical illustration

This illustration comes from an early session in the life of a group that ran for 18 months and had eight members, six of whom joined at the beginning. Attendance was 90 per cent and we had no dropouts. There were two conductors. Here is a thumbnail sketch of the group members, all aged 14 or 15:

Donna was a pretty girl who lived with foster parents. Delinquent and chock-full of mistrust, she isolated herself and became brittle in intimate situations. Her natural family had been bursting with hostility. She saw herself as a loner and definitely not in need of our kind of help.

Tony was an effeminate Anglo-West-Indian boy. He felt out of control and frightened but camouflaged this with a sneering contempt. He had lived all his life in a series of care placements, which had broken down one after another because of his behavioural problems. He was locked in a cycle of rejections, about which he was at once triumphant and despairing.

Scott was a shy, red-headed boy, physically mature but given to tantrums. He was in serious trouble with the courts and had a view of himself as irretrievably cast in the role of villain. There was a great air of hopelessness about him.

Ruby was a tomboyish, attractive West Indian girl. When she first came to us she formed no relationships but alternated between bouts of hyperactivity, screaming and racing around the building one minute, and the next, crouching on the floor in a foetal position, sucking her thumb noisily. She stole and lied compulsively. There were instances of her smearing faeces in another child's desk.

Mark arrived from a secure unit where he had earned the reputation of being 'unreachable'. He had cold, angry eyes. He was small and frequently bullied, inviting this with subtle, constant provocation. He held rigid, dogmatic views and flaunted them in the face of anyone who tried to get in too close. Staff working with him often felt an intense rage.

Lynn was beautiful and intelligent. Her mother was a schizophrenic. Lynn experienced terrifying episodes when she lost her hold on reality and became violent and unpredictable. She was a battered child and had recently been raped on several occasions. She regularly self-mutilated and had a borderline personality.

The session began with the warm-up.

A conversation started about parents and parental figures and what they had to offer. Ruby's granny had arrived from America this morning and all she had brought were some 'horrible humbugs'. Other members talked about the death of loved ones. Beautiful Lynn, smiling ominously, sarcasm glinting on her tongue, spoke: 'When my Mum dies, all she'll leave me is a can of Guinness'. Donna and Scott arrived, whispering conspiratorially. Mark, looking like a wizened whippet, was pink-cheeked and jumpy. Ruby had earlier 'borrowed' his bike without his permission. He wanted us to know how cheated he felt. There were more desultory exchanges around the theme of death and not getting what you want. The group decided to play a game, the object of which was to memorise a list of goods bought at the market. As more items were added to the list, the prevailing mood of foggy indifference lifted somewhat. We, the conductors, suggested that the group do some physical exercise, to combat the apathy. At this point Tony collapsed into a seat, claiming to be ill, conspicuously waving a bottle of codeine.

The conductors were aware of feeling irritated! We wondered out loud if all this talk of death and disappointment had something to do with the fact that this was the last session before the Christmas break? We suggested doing some deep-breathing exercises. This idea they accepted and we then took them on a guided fantasy about being in the belly of a great ship. They curled up and Ruby sucked her thumb. The task of negotiating a theme for the drama was now addressed. Donna wanted to do something on 'being accused when you know you didn't do it'. The following associations were produced: 'guilty, deceived, red-handed, forgotten, mad'. The conductor suggested a skeleton plot: 'Someone has been accused of shoplifting and returns home. The angry shopkeeper visits the family'. Tony was to be the accused, Donna his sister. Mark, who hates grannies, wanted to be a granny. The others were to be parents and siblings, Lynn the shopkeeper.

The drama began.

There was an angry exchange between Tony and his dad. Feeling increasingly rejected, he started to talk provocatively about a gold pendant he had recently acquired by dubious means.
Ruby exclaimed: 'Never mind the pendant, what about the four Parker pens and the gold bracelet?'
Tony and Donna looked daggers at her and the conductors began to suspect that we were now dealing with information about real life criminal activities. We kept the focus on the drama, inviting the shopkeeper to speak. Lynn embarked on a tirade against Tony, using sexual innuendo and scurrility. Suddenly she came out of role, saying she wanted to go and wash her hands, which were covered in red felt-tip. She left the room.

Now the family members turned on each other. The blame was bounced around the group and eventually clung like a magnet to Ruby: 'You've always been the bad girl.' Donna, clearly the co-culprit with Tony, said to him, 'Why don't you confess? You know you did it.' Lynn, who had outwitted my co-conductor's attempts at restraining her movements, re-entered the room and the drama, bearing a trayful of cups of tea. Tony spuriously owned up. Lynn magnanimously forgave Tony but forbade him to use her shop ever again. Donna smirked.

As the drama finished, anxiety was high. They scrambled for the tray and tea got slopped. Mark leapt up, knocked Ruby's arm and Tony's tea went over Scott. A cup was smashed. Everyone became quiet. Both conductors clearly re-stated the limits, saying that no more acting out would be tolerated. Tony, chastened, went to fetch a rag. Mark appeared frightened, near to tears, and then burst into hysterical laughter. Lynn, supreme, continued to be thoroughly unpleasant, putting her feet up against the door, humming and scornful.

An analysis followed.

The colourful acting out and blurring of boundaries subsided now as each person took it in turn to talk about their feelings. The group told Ruby that they had attacked her because she was too much like a baby. Ruby protested, 'Anyway, I'm a good girl', maintaining a penetrating look of hostility. Someone retorted, 'All babies are bad.' Lynn declared that she had been ripped off and deceived in her life and that she had strong feelings about this which she was not prepared to share. The conductor pointed out that the avoidance of strong feelings in all of us had led to the explosion of tea and cups. Lynn exclaimed, 'How come you can read my mind?' I said, 'Maybe it feels like that because some of those feelings are very hard to push away right now.' 'Yeah', snarled Tony at Lynn, 'That's why you had to go and wash the blood off your hands' and he turned viciously on me, saying, 'and *you* probably don't even wash'.

Mark said that he envied Donna for doing the theft and not getting caught. He commented on how she had, during the drama, urged Tony to confess his guilt. 'That's his business' she remarked. 'He's nothing to do with me.' The group members laughed and reminded her that she had been very much his accomplice in the theft. The conductor suggested that Tony in his role did in fact represent a part of Donna, and that this part of Donna had something to do with everyone in the group. Mark said he felt his offending behaviour had nothing to do with himself and therefore he could hope to have no control over it. The others expressed similar feelings. The conductor linked this expression of helplessness with the buried feelings of rage and guilt about the separation in the coming break. Lynn agreed. 'It's like the lies your mother tells you when you're little. You think you're going into care for a week. Then you find you're in it for the rest of your life.' 'Anyway', said Tony, 'the whole experience is head-stuff and has nothing to do with feelings.' 'Why are you getting so wound up then?' asked one of the others. Tony said that in the end there had been nobody, but nobody on his side in the drama, not even Donna. Everyone had deserted him. He remembered one of his many expulsions from foster-homes and institutions and became very sad. Then it was the end of the session.

In evaluating the work we did with this group, it is difficult to distinguish the progress they made through the group-analytic drama from other mutative influences in their lives. It is possible, however, to observe that all members of the five groups made excellent advances and this compares favourably with the progress of youngsters attending only day care. After some months in the group, Tony experienced the latest in a long series of rejections: his sister threw him out of their home. Earlier he would have dealt with such rejection by delinquent acts and suicidal behaviour. This time he found words instead and he began to grieve:

> If a bucket could catch my tears
> They would fill this living-room.

Discussion

The sequence of the session

Throughout the session there is movement on a continuum away from action to a more reflective mode of communication. To achieve this, the conductors move between directive handling of the group and phases of maintaining a low profile.

The disruptive, rebellious, sabotaging forms of behaviour that can characterise the early life of the group as well as the warm-up part of the session are best viewed in terms of the underlying theme and emerging group processes. Once there was a lot of excited talk about stealing. The members recounted to each other how some of them had taken a joy-ride in an old car after the session last week and had crashed it several times. John struggled hard to be included in the enticing but frightening fantasy of collision: 'I've done worse things than that and bigger.' The previous week there had been a lot of sexual anxiety and we, the conductors, felt now that this talk of crashing cars was another way of expressing the continuing anxiety around sex. Perhaps they were also telling us that group-analytic drama feels like a very dangerous game.

Adolescents tend to think of acting as performing. So, when we first introduce them to the idea of a different kind of drama we say, 'There'll be no pulling faces or putting on funny voices. We are just ourselves, we even use our own names. It's a sit-down drama.' Towards the end of the warm-up we have to find a theme for the drama. One way is to name a current preoccupation in the group and then play a word-association game in which the members express what it makes them feel. Then the group agrees on a skeleton story. We draw up a list of characters and the group members cast themselves, mostly preferring to use their own names. They often choose roles in which they can do useful work.

Sometimes, however, the casting process is used as a resistance: for example, Ruby always opting to be the victim or Tony a dominating monopoliser. In this event we might encourage them to play dreaded roles, e.g. Ruby, an assertive mother, Mark, a friend and not an enemy. On occasions, with casting completed, someone will become alarmed and want to change roles. The conductor might be very firm and say, 'No, stick with your first decision. You don't need to be so bound up in your usual role. See what it feels like not to be.' In the choice of a story for the drama, the adolescents are drawn to themes with which they are all too familiar: abortion, getting the sack, a family member leaves or dies, parents split up, children go into care, a mixed-race marriage, etc.

It always amazes me to see how quickly the drama gets underway. Another remarkable feature is the sustained intensity of the feelings experienced. The warm-up has taken care of excessive fears, the leaping about or the saturnine mood, and now thanks to the 'invented drama' censorship, guilt, and inhibition are partially suspended. The involvement of the whole group adds to the momentum.

Perhaps there is another reason why I shouldn't be so surprised. In a sense adolescents are acting all the time. They switch constantly between thinking, performing, and acting or reacting. Intense transferences occur in real-life relationships. Conductors may be hated, reviled, respected, idealised. One is often in danger of becoming, for example, the punishing parent or the seductive friend. When it happens in the drama, this projective identification, having been lifted from its everyday context, becomes a feature of the dramatic convention and therefore more available for interpretation. Furthermore, in the dramatic context, there is no danger of the conductor really becoming one of these figures – so there is safety all round and the possibilities for therapy remain open.

The conductor has very much the role of an 'agent provocateur' in the drama, a catalyst to the psychological action who, when necessary, drives events forward. By assuming a role, the conductor neither appears as a blank screen, nor risks too much personal transparency, but presents a concrete image that has to be reckoned with alongside those of all the other protagonists. Most of this acting-in-role work has to be a fine mixture of intuition, judgement and strategy. Unlike in psychodrama, where the director follows and works with the resistances, such a strategy is adopted only to a limited degree in GAD. As in other active forms of dynamic psychotherapy (Malan 1986), the basic rule is ultimately not to collude with or follow the patient's defensive moves, but to challenge them. Relentless pressure brings the resistance more and more into the open and has the effect of 'intensifying the patient's anxiety until the true feeling is reached' (Molnos 1986: 167). This principle applied to group-analytic drama often means that the conductor, when in doubt, will refuse to play along with members' preconceived expectations. Also, defensive blurring of the boundaries between the drama and real life has to be opposed, and not interpreted.

Sometimes, during the drama, people want to come out of role, or in the analysis they slip back into role. Once, Ruby was being extremely provocative in a scene with Tony. He found himself increasingly irritated and turned to me, the conductor, who was playing a neighbour and pleaded, 'Do something about her, will you, Sally?' Tony was clearly seeking my complicity as an out-of-role conductor in his attempt to get away from the feelings evoked by the drama. As the conductor's main task here is to maintain the focus on the relationships within the drama, I stayed in role and kept to the issue that was causing him so much anxiety. As the neighbour I said, 'You do something, if you really want to.' This way I did not comply with Tony's defensive move but challenged it. Tony's resistance hardened and yet was available for further confrontation. It may be seen that through such holding and challenge of the defences, containment and therapeutic manoeuveres can go hand in hand.

After a while group members themselves learn to 'act' therapeutically. One time Stella interrupted the drama, which was about a lost baby, complaining that it was too sad and she was sure the drama would go much better if we started all over again. Other participants, remaining in role, urged her to stay with the task; one of them said, 'You can't be born again, if that's what you think.' Stella was shocked into a reappraisal of her motives for wanting a new beginning.

In the analysis we explore the feelings that have been aroused during the drama: Group-analytic principles are brought to bear throughout the whole session and receive particular emphasis now. Using Foulkes' concept of the 'group as a whole', everything that happens in the group is considered in terms of communication across a network of relationships (Foulkes and Anthony 1984: 26). We explore meaning on all levels of communication from the symbolic and dream level to the conscious and the manifest. The aim is to translate identified symptoms, which in the case of disturbed adolescents might be delinquent attitudes and behaviour, into problems that can be articulated and worked with. By looking at the relationships in the drama we can explore current ones in the group as well as transference phenomena; we can help people take back their projections and disavowed aspects of themselves. Often heated discussions develop in the analysis that are just as powerful and compelling as the drama that preceded them.

At all times during the session many non-verbal signals regulate the system of communication. They include convoluted bodily postures, changes in syntax, pitch, pace, intonation, eye contact and gesture. The more subtle cues often appear with split-second timing and are picked up subliminally. It is worth trying to pay attention to them because they are a crucial part of the whole communication.

In each session there is a progression from an action based warm-up through the drama to a non-action analysis. The conductor(s) must ensure that these three stages of the session occur. This progression from action towards non-action therapy is reflected in the long-term life of the group. As the group matures, there evolves a gradual shift of emphasis away from the games and the establishing of a safe environment in the early stages to a more mature level of functioning where open, free-floating discussion can develop in an atmosphere of mutual understanding and acceptance.

Links with psychodrama

In this section I shall start by describing briefly the two main features that distinguish GAD from Moreno's psychodrama. They concern views about what is curative in therapy. First, in GAD we maintain a distinction and a balance between action and non-action. Second, in GAD we see the group and not the individual as the primary therapeutic agent. The chief influence of psychodrama on our method will then be outlined and specific similarities in ways of working will be explored.

Moreno saw action as the essential tool of therapy. He believed that it was superior to transference in removing symptoms. He used the term 'acting out', giving it a positive connotation, to refer to a universal function of human behaviour. He believed that the psychoanalytic dislike of action was based on fear of countertransferential expression of libidinal and aggressive impulses. In fact Foulkes, and other psychoanalysts, have given the term 'acting out' a generally negative connotation because most action is seen to be used as a substitute for feeling and remembering. Modern theorists accept acting out as potentially having two opposite meanings: it may be a resistance but it may also be adaptive and an attempt at communication. Allowing for both possibilities and bearing in mind the extreme tendency towards antitherapeutic acting out in adolescents, we use a non-action drama to provide the focus for a therapy that also applies action techniques.

A group-analytic approach, which emphasises the importance of the unconscious group dynamic together with treatment of the individual as its ultimate aim, is chosen. Adolescents instinctively turn to the peer group to help them deal with pressing maturational tasks such as the achievement of separation from parents, identity formation and autonomy. In the group context a youngster can retain a safe sense of belonging while aspiring to the formation of a stable ego identity. While the group interaction effectively reproduces and expresses the pathology with which we need to work, it also presents obstacles to therapy. Paying attention to and interpreting the unconscious group processes help to contain the extreme anxiety that otherwise leads to psychic fragmentation and disruption of the session. In our work with severely disturbed adolescents, we have found that we ignore the powerful group-as-a-whole dynamics at our peril.

GAD has drawn principally from psychodrama the key concepts of creativity and spontaneity in therapy. Closely connected with these is the idea that therapy can be both fun and inspiring, and should always be playful. Moreno saw spontaneity as a new response to an old situation and an adequate response to a new one. According to Moreno it is a form of energy that cannot be conserved. It must be spent the moment it emerges. It is the arch-catalyser of creativity (Moreno 1953). He adopted a very different conceptual framework from that of Foulkes, whose terms of reference go back to the psychoanalytic language of Freud. When Moreno spoke about regression, resistances, projection and sublimation, he saw them all as functions of either creativity or spontaneity. In spite of attaching different meanings to similar processes, both Foulkes and Moreno believed that play and the pursuit of spontaneity should be key objectives in therapy. GAD has been particularly influenced by Moreno's insistence on the importance of play and his belief in the apparently limitless possibilities for exploration through drama.

Here are some core operations of group-analytic drama in relation to some of Moreno's principal techniques of psychodrama, namely: the mirror, the use of the auxiliary ego as double and significant other, and role reversal.

The mirror technique used in psychodrama is where one person acts on behalf of another, standing in for the protagonist – thus enabling the person to observe his/her performance in a significant situation with enough distance to gain insight. In group-analytic drama, sharing in the group's resistant attitude effectively parallels and adds to the mirror technique of psychodrama. For example, in a situation where an unrelentingly defiant attitude to the police is taking the drama around in circles, the conductor, or indeed the group member, might join in with an exaggerated insolence that holds up a magnifying mirror to the group's intransigence. Thus distance and insight are achieved through the reflecting and group-specific amplifying effect of what is happening. Here an individual's or a group's delusions, distorted self-images and negative behaviour can be given back immediately through dramatic heightening, ridicule – safe, because it's in the drama – irony and analogy. Adolescents are often finely tuned to and enjoy exaggeration of this kind. In spite of their disturbance, many have a facility for humour and self-mockery that offers an avenue to new experiences and insights.

In Moreno's psychodrama the auxiliary ego, whether expressed as significant other or as double, challenges the simplistic position taken up by the protagonist. The aim is to help the protagonist more fully experience and articulate previously repressed felings, thereby increasing role repertoire. There are many ways of employing this technique. I confine myself here to describing the use of the double in psychodrama and the function of the significant other in GAD.

The double in Moreno's psychodrama helps the protagonist to explore his or her innermost feelings by assuming the same role and physical position and verbalising unexpressed emotions on behalf of this person. The intention is 'not to imitate, but to feel what the protagonist is feeling' (Moreno 1965). For example, if I were the protagonist and were on the phone to my husband, saying, 'I'm sick of you and I want you to get lost', my double would assume the same physical position near to me and might say, 'I'm longing for you, but I dread letting you know and getting close.' The double is usually performed by someone who identifies very much with the protagonist. Although there is no double in GAD, the auxiliary ego as significant other may find its impetus from identifying closely with another group member. For instance, in one drama, Sharon was claiming to have rich parents who had sent her away to public shcool while they went away on holiday. After she had boasted to her friends for some time, the conductor, picking up Sharon's underlying feelings of abandonment, in the role of a jealous schoolmate, said, 'Let's face it, Sharon, you've been dumped.' Sharon's facade crumbled and in the following analysis, she and others were able to get more in touch with their feelings of hurt and rage at not being held. Joining the fantasy of the group is, of course, what we do the moment we step into role. To do this and then to oppose part of the fantasy in group-analytic drama fulfils a function similar to that of the auxiliary ego as significant other in psychodrama, confronting the patient or group with its repressed part.

In Moreno's role-reversal technique, A becomes B and B becomes A. It has several aims, principally to help the protagonist understand the other person's position, to see with another's eyes, to be in another's shoes and to shift the protagonist out of habitual defences. This procedure is replicated to some extent in our drama when child plays adult, white plays black, male plays female, habitual victim plays oppressor, etc. We have noticed that gender role reversal can dramatically release repressed feelings. In an all-girls black group recently, one member played a jilted boyfriend. In this role she surprised us with a powerful invective, filled with obscenity and self-loathing. It was the first time the group came to be in touch with its repressed, very strong feelings that had to do with oppression.

In both methods, then, we have parallel techniques to dismantle resistances and facilitate spontaneity. The reason I prefer to use the word 'operations' as opposed to 'techniques' when referring to active participation in the drama is because these operations are an inherent part of the whole group interaction and are not techniques that require conscious and deliberate application. Our method views the group itself as the main therapeutic agent. That which is so often used defensively, namely whole-group interaction, becomes the very tool of therapy.

Group-analytic drama and the adolescent

Disturbed adolescents are self-absorbed and have fantasies of onmipotence. They treat others as extensions of themselves and not as people in their own right. It is very important for such an adolescent to have access to a therapy where putting yourself in someone else's shoes (while paradoxically remaining in your own) is an integral part of the whole process. It helps develop the empathic response.

In their narcissistic isolation, adolescents have to deal with the following core-issues: dependence versus independence, the importance of peer-group relationships, solitude and loneliness, and the changing boundaries of the self, both physical and psychic. The most frequently recurring themes in our sessions are fear of attack and abandonment and sexual anxiety, and these are often linked. Early in the life of a group, and often at the beginning of a session, Klein's (1946) paranoid–schizoid position seems much in evidence. Youngsters dread being 'seen through'. They attack and feel attacked. 'What are you staring at me for?' They wear scarves in front of their faces, cover their eyes with their arms, and hold cushions in front of themselves. Many of our youngsters experience very conflicted feelings about their bodies and show an inability to relate to them in a caring way (Laufer and Laufer 1984: 73). They might attack their bodies by self-mutilating or release their anger onto another object. Anxiety around this sensitive area cannot always be contained easily. Someone once observed that the boys were showing off in front of the girls. The anxiety in the room became so unbearable that fights broke out. Thomas clutched his ears saying, 'It can't be undone – you've said it now', as if the words themselves had lodged like his pain inside him forever. Unable to tolerate his feelings of shame and invasion, he left the building and smashed all the windows in a car outside.

The adolescents feel that they are failing, but do not express their complaint by saying: 'There is something wrong with me.' Instead, they project the fault onto others – 'There's something wrong with them, they're ugly, they've got diseases, they're perverted' – and then they complain themselves about loneliness and isolation. Ideally the group and the drama should fulfil the holding function of a good-enough and strong-enough parent, enabling the adolescents to experience and express their destructive hatred of the internalised, forbidding parents in the 'dramatic' transference instead of needing to direct it at their own bodies, or at cars belonging to members of staff!

This phenomenon I have called the adolescent sexual matrix. I believe that it underpins all other changes at this stage of development.

Dramatic action is traditionally seen as physical action. In developing this method of group-analytic drama in which the accent is on a movement away from physical action towards psychic action I let go of the notion that dramatic action, or play, has to be physical. As an actress I found that not all play is action. It seemed that I did my best work in interpreting roles when I was still, i.e. motionless. This helped free me from any preoccupation with the external trappings of the part. To understand this better, one has only to think of the Greek theatre's use of mask whereby attention is focused so powerfully on the feeling and the word.

There are several reasons for an emphasis on psychic drama in our method. Acting out in adolescence tends to take the form of physical action and, while some of it may be an attempt at communication and can even be helpful in that it stimulates limit-setting, most of it is an unhelpful substitute for feeling and remembering. The adolescent's tendency to use action defensively is, however, not the only reason for the invention of a centrally non-action therapy. In adolescence there seems to be a thin line between what is real and what is playful. Children might say, 'We were only playing' when an adult interrupts a fight when, as every parent knows, the wise response is to warn, 'This will end in tears.' Since only the contrast between the consequences of the two types of behaviour shows us which kind is playful and which is not, a non-action therapy with clear boundaries helps us to work more safely with adolescents for whom playing and reality are too often one and the same.

The power of action methods should not be underestimated. With severely disturbed patients the danger is that in action therapy the body might remember what the ego cannot integrate or even recognise. On the stage delusions and hallucinations may acquire flesh – a terrifying prospect. Group-analytic drama is as much a method of restraint as it is of expression, so that the overly and diffusively, explosively expressive adolescents are not necessarily encouraged to 'let it all hang out'. In stillness, like the actor bearing the Greek mask, they too, can learn to listen to themselves, to communicate inwardly as well as outwardly. They can learn to retain their experiences and start building a coherent sense of self.

Summing up

The specific, pathological features of disturbed adolescence that frequently render other forms of therapy unviable are addressed in our method of group-analytic drama. Its accessibility to this client group is its essential characteristic. This eclectic method that progresses from an action to an analytic, non-action approach is the result of a combination of practices deriving from the fields of group analysis, psychodrama, sociodrama and theatre.

Disturbed adolescents face the possible foreclosure of their developmental process. Pathological patterns of behaviour become increasingly fixed. In the battle against the conservation of habitual roles, drama can be a powerful catalyst for change, for healing and creativity, indeed for structuring the self anew. 'Drama has the divine possibility, beyond all other arts, of inventing new animals, that is to say new instruments – Creation – is thus literally shifted into drama' (Canetti 1986: 8).

Acknowledgement

My thanks go to Dr Angela Molnos for her inspiration and help.

References

Bion, W.R. (1961) *Experiences in Groups*, London: Tavistock.
Blos, P. (1962) *On Adolescence*, New York: The Free Press.
Brook, P. (1988) *The Shifting Point*, London: Methuen.
Canetti, E. (1986) *The Human Province*, London: Pan.
Ellwood, J. and Oke, M. (1987) 'Analytic groupwork in a boys' comprehensive school'. *Free Association* 8.
Erikson, E. (1987) *Childhood and Society*, London: Paladin.
Foulkes, S.H. (1986) *Group Analytic Psychotherapy. Method and Principles*, London: H. Karnac Books Ltd.
Foulkes, S.H. and Anthony, E.J. (1984) *Group Psychotherapy: The Psychoanalytical Approach*, London: Maresfield Reprints.
Klein, M. (1946) 'Notes on some schizoid mechanisms', *International Journal of Psycho-Analysis*, XXVII, part 3; 99–109.
Laufer, M. and Laufer, M. E. (1984) *Adolescence and Developmental Breakdown. A Psychoanalytic View*, New Haven and London: Yale University Press.
Lewin, K. (1951) *Field Theory in Social Science*, New York: Harper Bros.
Malan, D. (1986) 'Beyond interpretation: initial evaluation and technique in short-term

dynamic psychotherapy. Part 1', *International Journal of Short-Term Psychotherapy* 1.

Molnos, A. (1986) 'From video recordings towards integrated thinking in brief psychotherapy. Reflections after the first European symposium on short-term dynamic psychotherapy. Copenhagen 7–11 July 1986', *British Journal of Psychotherapy* 3 (2).

Molnos, A. (1987) El nosotros en el grupo analítico. (We in the analytic group) In *Psico-sociolojía de la Salud Mental*, Ozámiz, J.A. (ed) San Sebastián (Spain): Ttartalo 47–61.

Molnos, A. (1988) *Psychoanalytic Theory in Group Analysis.* Talk given at the first meeting of the Think Tank, Institute of Group Analysis, 5 December 1988. (Unpublished manuscript.)

Moreno, J.L. (1953) *Who Shall Survive?*, Beacon, NY: Beacon House.

Moreno, Z.T. (1965) 'Psychodramatic rules, techniques and adjunctive methods', *Group Psychotherapy*, XVIII; 73–86.

Willis, S.T. (1988) 'Group-analytic drama: A therapy for disturbed adolescents', *Group Analysis. The Journal of Group Analytic Psychotherapy* 21 (2)

Winnicott, D.W. (1986) *Playing and Reality*, Harmondsworth: Penguin.

Winnicott, D.W. (1987) *The Maturational Processes and The Facilitating Environment*, London: Hogarth Press.

Further reading

Foulkes, S.H. (1964) *Therapeutic Group Analysis*, London: Allen and Unwin.

Foulkes, S.H. (1984) *Introduction to Group Analytic Psychotherapy: studies in the social integration of individuals and groups*, London: Maresfield Reprints.

Chapter nine

Issues of milieu therapy

Psychodrama as a contribution to the treatment of a case of anorexia nervosa

Joke Meillo

Introduction

Irene's psychodramatic treatment is part of the treatment in a psychotherapeutic community for adolescents. The frame of reference with which this 'in-patient clinic' works, the position occupied by psychodrama and the style of treatment will be explained first. After an impression has been gained of the clinical setting, Irene's case will be examined more closely.

For these purposes, it is necessary first to present certain general information about problems in the treatment of anorexia. We will then be introduced to Irene via:

1. Details of the case history
2. Aspects of the treatment plan
3. Family background

Only when we are familiar with the clinical setting and are equipped with information about Irene's treatment in a more general sense, will it be possible to analyse and study the psychodramatic treatment and the individual therapy (on analytic lines) added to it in the later stages of the treatment.

A psychotherapeutic community for disturbed adolescents

Adolescents from about 16–21 years of age are admitted. Many clients have a DSM III R (diagnostic and statistical manual of mental disorder – the American classification system for psychiatric disorders, that is also used in the Netherlands), like schizophrenic disorder, paranoid disorder or major affective disorder. In addition, many clients suffer from severe personality disorders, e.g. borderline personality disorders, schizoid personality disorders or schizotypal personality disorders.

An important subcategory of clients like this is a patient suffering from a pure eating disorder, which is not connected with one of the former disorders (anorexia nervosa DSM 307.10).

The psychotherapeutic community is part of a large psychiatric hospital (with approximately 1,100 patients). Twenty-five adolescents are randomly divided into two smaller communities, each having its own living room and its own team of sociotherapists, who supervise and influence the daily living climate. They see the young men and women 24 hours a day, are in close touch with what is happening in the community and outside it and support the adolescents in short individual chats. In addition, by means of various daily and weekly group meetings, they discuss mutual interactions. Using a group-dynamic method of working, they attempt to improve the quality of the living climate and thereby also create the conditions for the psychotherapeutic group treatments. The professional sociotherapy constitutes the foundation for the psychotherapeutic group treatments. In other words, it is responsible for the primary level of treatment. The secondary level of treatment is the psychotherapeutic treatment.

By contrast to the randomly constituted sociogroups, psychotherapeutic treatment takes place in groups of patients with comparable ego strengths. The psychotherapy programme consists of group psychotherapy, psychodrama and individual therapy. There is close collaboration between the group psychotherapist and the psychodramatist. Themes circulate between group psychotherapy and psychodrama group, as has been described elsewhere (Meillo 1986).

Problems that have already been discussed in sociotherapy at the level of day-to-day reality are also brought into the psychotherapy sessions, where interpsychic and intrapsychic aspects are considered. For example, the continuous rivalry of two female group members is discussed in sociotherapy. An examination takes place of the consequences this rivalry has for the other members of the group who manage to keep out of the firing line of the intense quarrels. The rival ladies' behaviour helps others avoid their conflicts being discussed. The sociotherapy works, as is shown in this example, using group-dynamic principles.

Psychotherapy (group psychotherapy and psychodrama) works group-dynamically and group-analytically. For example, there can be discussions about which fears do not need to be felt because of the behaviour of the two rival ladies and the other evasive group members. The inner struggle of the group members can be clarified and felt by putting it into words and, in addition, by concretising it in psychodrama. (When an inner struggle is made concrete, a double can, for example, be brought in or the struggle can be symbolised by two auxiliary egos who each represent one side of the conflict). By working on group-analytic lines in group psychotherapy and psychodrama sessions what occurs and is evoked in the real relationship with therapist(s) and fellow group members can be translated back into the primary relationships in the original family.

This intensive co-operation between sociotherapy and psychotherapy guarantees a reasonably effective treatment since all treatment instances are in tune with one another and work for each other.

Some comments still need to be made about the style of the therapeutic milieu. Traditionally, in therapeutic communities, there is a high level of permissiveness and work is done in a rather non-directive way (Jones 1973). The literature related to group psychotherapy (Foulkes 1975) based on the group-analytic frame of reference also assumes a non-directive, explorative style of working.

A psychotherapeutic community with a population of seriously disturbed adolescents, however, demands more limit-setting and a larger degree of direct-iveness and security.

Nevertheless, the attitude of the members of staff can be described as being characterised by as much permissiveness and tolerance as possible. The adoles-cents are allowed to learn from their experiences, which are subsequently explored. Acting out is not prevented but worked through. Limits are set when the psychic or physical safety of the adolescent is involved.

Problems in the treatment of anorexia nervosa

A great deal has been written about the origin and treatment of the illness anorexia nervosa. It is impossible, within the scope of this chapter, to give an extensive description of the pathology. It is nevertheless useful to give a brief summary of the problems that make the treatment of anorexia nervosa difficult in order to be able to assess later the extent to which psychodrama treatment is capable of reducing these problems. In general, it can be stated that clients with anorexia nervosa have a great resistance to treatment, especially to treatment that is *not* directed towards the symptom. They tend to deny any other problems such as: family problems, (not) having a personality of one's own, difficulties with peers relationships, etc. The symptom functions as a means of exercising power. A number of characteristics that anorexia nervosa clients develop strongly (such as stubbornness, ambitiousness, resistance and rationalisation), constitute the arsenal of weapons with which attempts are made to prevent the background and/or causes of the symptom being treated.

In the very earliest stage, there is often a denial of the symptom as an illness. The client is 'actually very contented and happy'; it is others who are worried and have 'talked the client into' treatment. This central problem is possibly also the reason why therapeutic schools have disagreed with each other so strongly.

Behaviour therapy schools have made an extensive study of the treatment of anorexia nervosa and have developed operant conditioning methods with the direct aim of removing the symptom (Bhanji 1975; Bianco 1972).

Hilde Bruch (1974) opened the attack on the treatment of symptoms. She proposed a psychodynamic approach to treatment and argued in favour of pro-found personality alterations by means of psychoanalytic therapy yielding insight. Her principal objection to behaviour therapy is that clients are more-or-less forced to give up their symptoms, as a result of which their self-esteem, which was already low, is reduced still further.

Of course, as the years have gone by, different approaches to treatment have remained in existence but there is agreement that, even when the weight problem (symptom) is treated first, relapse and breakdown can only be prevented by forms of psychotherapy, which also involve the personality structure in the treatment.

In this case, the environment of the clinic is considered to be the main treatment modality. For the anorexic patient, this means that the family pathology, in which the anorexia has always such power, is interrupted. The patient comes into a new environment in which being a patient is not so special any more.

The anorexic is shown to have symptoms 'just like' other adolescents. Group treatment removes the exclusivity of the symptoms. Group members do not accept resistance, the denial of the patient that anything might be wrong with the family. Adolescents can be very confrontational, which makes it possible for the group therapist to avoid an attitude that is too confrontational or negotiating. It is important that group treatment makes it possible to treat 'in situ' (Moreno 1970) the severe relationship disturbances that always accompany anorexia.

The case: Irene

Details of the case history

Irene was an awkward, stubborn child. She sucked her thumb for many years. She bit her nails and was punished for this. She lay awake at nights, listening to her mother and father quarrelling. When she slept, she had nightmares. She continued to wet her bed until she was 12 and was teased about this by her younger brother. She was a child who bottled everything up. At domestic science school, things went very well for her for the first time; she had hobbies and felt good. But most of what she did was despised by her father. She trained to be a nursery nurse but failed her examinations, after which she worked as a waitress in a restaurant.

Her attitude towards independence was: 'you're only somebody when you've got somebody else who supports you'. Narcissistic balance was disturbed. This seemed to be primarily linked with the father's attitude of rejection. Nor did her mother support her. The mother was often depressed. As a result, Irene did not dare to take any boyfriends or girlfriends home. There was little affection in the family. Irene's physical development was delayed: menarche occurred only when she was 15. Irene's basic conflict consisted of the need to become more female and adult, opposed to the desire to remain a child and to receive the cherishing she had missed.

She had a strict conscience. Aggressive impulses were rejected and directed against herself.

Aspects of treatment plan

The total length of the admission was $2^1/2$ years, followed by a further 9 months running down of individual psychotherapy. Irene was 19 on admission. She weighed 37 kg. and was 1.66 m tall. Three weeks prior to admission, her fiancé had broken off with her. He thought she was too thin and too difficult. In addition, there was also complete isolation from others of the same age. At home, the situation had grown intolerable. Her father was forcing her to eat and her mother lay awake at nights crying loudly because Irene was losing so much weight. As a result, the rest of the family was not sleeping. The final straw came when the mother found bags of vomit filled with maggots hidden in Irene's room.

Through the JPS (Juvenile Psychiatric Service), voluntary admission was arranged. The stay at the admissions centre lasted almost a year. It began with bed nursing, a 2,000-calorie diet and thereafter a programme, which was regularly adjusted according to whether weight increased or fell, designed to achieve a target weight of 50 kg.

An impression can be gained of a programme such as this by referring to the fact that there was a daily contact of only five minutes with the person regularly concerned with a particular patient's treatment.

All freedoms, such as going for walks, were removed. Over-activity was forbidden. Irene was only allowed to do what had been agreed upon. Daily weighing took place. At 41 kg, mail could be sent and received, at 43 kg, going for walks in a group was allowed, at 44 kg, group psychotherapy took place. At 44.5 kg she was allowed her own room, at 46.5 kg she was allowed trips to the beat-music room under supervision, and so on.

Things went well for 4 months. then her weight fell again. Isolation policy and a 2,000-calorie diet were introduced. Drip-feeding (500 calories) was used if food was not eaten by the evening, etc. Initially, Irene was not prepared to talk about anything other than eating problems. Gradually, issues around relationships became more accessible. When, after approximately 10 months, her weight was more or less stable, transfer to the psychotherapeutic community took place. Here also, agreement about the minimum weight of 43 kg was necessary for admission. She was discharged twice for a period of one week for breaking these agreements. After approximately 5 months (on Christmas Day), there was a serious suicide attempt leading to coma.

After return to the therapeutic community, treatment was continued with the addition of individual psychotherapy. When she no longer needed to be weighed, she was, as a symbolic gesture, given back the scales that had been confiscated. The total length of stay in the psychotherapeutic community was approximately 18 months.

Family background

Irene had an older sister and younger brother. Her father was a pilot. He was ambitious and thought Irene was stupid – more stupid than her brother and just as stupid as her mother. Her mother had been an alcoholic for at least twelve years. She had undergone a great deal of treatment. Because of the alcohol problems, there were often stormy quarrels between the mother and father and even fights at night in which furniture was wrecked. When Irene was 16, her father changed jobs. He was given a management post at the airline company. Thereafter, the mother's symptoms gradually improved. During the period of admission contact with the family remained, confined to discussions of policy for the purpose of obtaining minimal support for the treatment. Family therapy was rejected.

During the discussions of policy, the father tolerated no opposition and made blunt comments about the children. He gave his wife no support at all and she, so to speak, asked the father's permission to talk to the children with any sort of affection.

Irene initially adopted a dependent and guilty attitude and expressed her reproaches of her parents in an exclusively non-verbal way.

The psychodramas and the individual psychotherapy

The psychotherapeutic treatment will be described in terms of six 'full-circle psychodramas'. Basically, a full-circle psychodrama involves the summarising and working through of the protagonist's central problem. For example, a neurotic pattern and its origin can be clarified. In addition to these protagonist-centred psychodramas, Irene participated in a number of more group-orientated psychodramas, which will not be described here.

During the course of the treatment, it turned out to be necessary to supplement group treatment (sociogroups, group psychotherapy and psychodrama) with individual psychotherapy on analytic lines.

Individual therapy is not a standard part of the regime but is allotted as the result of a decision of the treatment team. The principle is that, whenever possible, group treatment in a psychotherapeutic community should suffice. In Irene's case, the addition of individual therapy after the suicide attempt was primarily necessary in order to give her more support and security. It had become apparent that she held herself in too much in group psychotherapy and psychodrama because of the fear of disappointing others.

In addition, it was considered that it would be possible, in individual therapy, to talk more extensively about the specific eating problems, the family and about the suicide attempt. Were this to have taken place in the group, this would have made her position too exclusive and in this way allowed her to profit from her illness.

In addition to the psychodramas, the course of the individual psychotherapy will be described. This will make it possible to show that an intensive interaction developed between psychodrama and individual therapy, made possible because the psychodramatist also conducted the individual psychotherapy. The way in which individual psychotherapy also operated as 'working through' will also be explained.

Psychodrama I

Distance and proximity

Initially, the psychotherapeutic line of treatment amounts to the termination of the special attention and other benefits that Irene derived from her illness. Her first psychodrama is directed towards looking at her relationships with other group members and at the way in which they see her. A number of scenes bring out the way in which Irene keeps her feelings at a distance and feels herself, as well as being felt by others, to be cold. By keeping quiet generally during group programmes, she makes her position safe, keeps control and does not need to compete (with all the consequences that would result in terms of the experiencing of feelings). Her fellow group members find her silence inhibiting.

The psychodrama consists of re-enacted group scenes, in which psychodramatic techniques serve to explore and bring to the surface feelings and suppressed desires. The particular value of psychodramatic techniques can be summarised as follows: Irene irritates others with her attempts to discuss her eating problems in an unemotional way. She is felt to be dull, cold, boring and uninspiring. In view of the fact that her behaviour is also controlled and well-mannered, she prevents the others, in most verbal programmes, from expressing their irritation and feelings. Re-enactment has a definite shock effect, produced by releasing, exaggerating techniques such as mirroring. Consequently, more of Irene's, and the group members', feelings are awoken and expressed. As a result, possibilities of identification with Irene are increased. If Irene succeeds in interesting the others more, they will invest more energy in her and she will be able to derive greater benefit from the clinical treatment as a whole. In addition, the directive methods of psychodrama deprive her of control. This loss of control works in a productive way, because anorexic patients always invest large amounts of energy in struggles for power.

Summary

1. The particular value of psychodrama compared to verbal therapy is that it awakes more feelings, both in the protagonist and in the other group members.
2. The psychodramatist's directive leadership is important, especially in the case of a patient with control problems.

Relationships with peers were slowly established, despite the difficulties Irene had with the unstructured aspects of clinic life such as the occupation of her free time. Things seemed to be going well. After she had twice been discharged for a week for breaking agreements over her weight, she gradually got along better at the clinic, both in her particular community and in her treatment group. Outside the clinic, and particularly at home, this was not the case. Irene's apparently increasing independence was not particularly appreciated at home. Family tensions steadily increased and were kept hidden by Irene. The working relationship between the clinic and the parents was difficult. As a result of this, those treating Irene were not aware of the worsening situation.

This all came out on Christmas Day with a very serious suicide attempt. Irene swallowed Valium pills taken from her mother's medicine cabinet. The pressure of the obligatory cheerfulness of Christmas and the obligation to eat both a great deal and a great variety of food were the precipitating factors. After she had been discharged from the hospital, she was very apprehensive about returning to the clinic but her return was well accepted and she turned out not to have lost her position in the group.

The treatment team had decided to assign her to an individual therapist in addition to the group treatments in which, for reasons of consistency, all adolescents admitted to the community participate. This had been done because individual therapy would make it more difficult for Irene to keep family tensions hidden.

There were two reasons for deciding that the psychodramatist would also be the one to conduct individual therapy:

1. The psychodramatist was a woman and Irene was less anxious with the female than with the male psychotherapist.
2. It had already become apparent on several occasions that Irene used splitting manoeuvres in order to be able to retain control. She split sociotherapy and psychotherapy, group psychotherapy and psychodrama. The addition of an individual psychotherapist in addition to group psychotherapist and psychodramatist would have given her an additional possibility of splitting.

For these reasons, it was decided that the psychodramatist would also take over the individual psychotherapy to be offered on analytic lines.

Irene greatly appreciated individual therapy. She kept the appointments diligently and enjoyed the extra individual attention that, in this therapeutic community, is given only on the recommendation of the therapist. Individual psychotherapy began immediately and the feelings of gloom, inadequacy and unwantedness, which led to the suicide attempt soon came under discussion, as did the relationship between those feelings and the eating problems. Now that Irene was capable of making this connection, it made sense to examine the eating problems as a theme and the psychotherapeutic line of treatment was adjusted accordingly.

Psychodrama II

Not eating, eating and vomiting

The second psychodrama is, therefore, extensively concerned with eating. The first scene is enacted by the group and deals with eating in the community: the exasperatingly slow eating of small amounts of food that leads to the kitchen staff (group members) not being able, not daring, to get on with their work. Not eating or eating slowly gives her a special position in the group that the group members do not know how to deal with. Many members of the group continually hesitate over whether or not they should/may say anything to Irene about this. During the group scene, Irene hears how afraid they are of hurting her but also how angry the members of the group are with her. Irene's predominant feeling at this point of the psychodrama is: she is *forced* to eat; vomiting later is *fighting back*. Attention is focused on the origin of the neurotic pattern. Scenes from her childhood at home or at grandpa's give an insight into the struggle around food that has been going on for almost all of her life.

At home, (aged 6). Irene does not want to eat. Her plate of potatoes, meat and vegetables is put in the fridge and she has to eat it up cold the following morning for her breakfast. What is more, she has to do this standing at the draining-board. She is not allowed to sit down on, for example, the pedal bin.

At grandpa's (aged ten). Grandpa has an old-fashioned little shop. You can see into the back room from inside the shop and even from in front of the shop window. If Irene does not eat, the curtains separating the back room from the shop are opened. Not eating therefore signifies: public ridicule, feelings of shame, suppressed, impotent anger at lack of understanding and affection.

What psychodrama offers here is the possibility of reliving the moment of not eating, resulting in acutely-felt insight. In addition, the situations are so harrowing that support from the group offers a corrective emotional experience.

Summary

1. Psychodrama offers the possibility of an acutely felt, relived insight.
2. The harrowing nature of the scenes results in group members starting to offer a corrective emotional experience instead of turning away from Irene as they did before.

'Working through' takes place in individual therapy. Irene slept for years with clenched fists, felt very aggressive and jealous towards her older sister and especially towards her younger brother who was always given preferential treatment. No attempt was made to conceal the message, nor did she have to read between the lines. It was said directly: 'We should have had a boy after Jennie. Sorry, Irene, you shouldn't be here. Two children is enough nowadays.'

Psychodrama III

The third full-circle psychodrama concentrates on the theme of the family and explores it in greater depth. The advantages of psychodrama come to the fore here: the possibility of the working through of intrapsychic relationships with people who are absent, *without strengthening the real link with the family.* After all, there are very pathogenic interactions between clients with anorexia nervosa and their families of origin. The contacts between client and family not infrequently serve to maintain the symptomatology and family therapists often conduct tough battles (Stern *et al* 1981).

In the early stage of a lengthy treatment in a psychotherapeutic community with adolescents, it can be of great importance not to tighten ties with the family but rather, indeed, to make them somewhat looser. In Irene's case, in addition, the family refused to co-operate in any form of family treatment. Psychodrama, then, offers the possibility of exploring the family problems with the assistance of auxiliary egos who, because they are not the real family members, will not intensify the symptomatology by means of implicit messages.

In Irene's case, this is virtually the only possibility in view of the impossibility of treating her family.

'Family ties'

The full-circle psychodrama deals with the feeling of 'being thrown onto the rubbish heap' by the family. The first scene takes place at a party. Her father says out loud that Irene is at domestic science school and that she therefore has no future. The psychodramatic adaptation of the real scene (using asides and interviews with role-reversals) results in: Mother is perhaps stupid but Irene isn't. Somebody who is no good is better off doing away with themselves.

The following scene takes place when Irene arrives home at weekends. It turns out that the parents have, in addition to the treatment policy of the clinic, thought up their own treatment policy. Irene must say what she weighs at the door. If her weight is too low, then she is not allowed to come in. If she does come in and gives her father a kiss, then he wipes the kiss off straightaway. All these scenes make it clear to us that Irene is sure of one thing: rejection. But rejection is linked to a need for her father's acceptance, jealousy of her mother and fear of being near to her father.

Summary

Psychodrama can explore intrapsychic relationships with the family, without strengthening the real relationships.

This theme was further explored in individual psychotherapy. We discussed mother's alcoholism and the fights at night between mother and father. At first,

Irene and her father had been a pair, in which Irene had had the job of telling her father when and how often her mother had drunk too much. The mother was quite a fat woman and Irene, who followed her mother's example in many ways, was also quite fat at this time.

During this period, Irene's father frequently pinched her bottom and Irene tried to make herself pretty for him. The conflicts between the mother and father became so intense that divorce was considered. Father was very kind to Irene and his behaviour towards her also had a somewhat erotic undertone. Irene became somewhat fearful towards proximity and sexuality: 'It's my turn next.' She saw to it that she steadily lost weight. Her father called her a bag of bones and despite the rejection, this made Irene feel safe.

Psychodrama IV

Excesses and shame

The fourth psychodrama deals with Irene's excesses and the accompanying feelings of shame. The scenes show her hoarding food, secretly eating the group's food and searching through the rubbish bin, eating up the cottage cheese that she finds there and that has partly gone off. Another advantage of psychodrama appears here. Re-enactment isolates the behaviour of the patient from the compulsive urge. In real life, the compulsive urge is satisfied. Here it is not. As a result, a certain distance can be created that is normally not possible. Irene suddenly sees how strange it is: I'm eating like a dog out of the rubbish bin. Her behaviour becomes more realistic and loses some of its ritualistic character. It becomes clear how strong the need is if someone is prepared to do such shameful things to gratify it.

The psychodrama is not complete at this point. Irene's excesses extend to drinking too much in the pub (c.f. mother's alcohol problem), after which she has sex with strangers in a car. The following morning, she punishes herself: 'Mother and father are right. I'm no good.' She sentences herself to not eating for several days. The psychodramatic double counter-balances the destructiveness of these scenes by highlighting the despairing positive needs that lead to this behaviour. The double highlights Irene's need to belong, as well as her longing to be able to devote herself to others instead of always having to feel that punishing, compulsive control. Helped by the double, she can verbalise her strong need for warmth and affection. The group members are moved by the fact that Irene can have feelings and show them. As a result, Irene is better understood and accepted. From this point on, she is also able to maintain some personal contacts in her daily life.

Summary

1. Re-enactment isolates behaviour from libidinal impulses. In reality, there is gratification, in psychodrama, there is not. Consequently, Irene can view her own behaviour from a distance.
2. The psychodramatic double is empathic and supportive and counterbalances Irene's self-destructive feelings.

Hereafter, the theme of sexuality could be worked through in individual psychotherapy. During the relationship with the 'fiancé', there had been sexual contact but Irene had not been able to experience any enjoyment during intercourse and certainly had not been able to achieve orgasm. This was not the case with masturbation. In other words, when she was in control, the engagement ritual, complete with party for family and friends, had increased her status. However, she had not known what to do with the fiancé and continually felt guilty towards him. Also discussed were the advantages of having a relationship with someone who is a travel guide; luckily, he always goes away again. While, on the other hand, it is a consoling thought to know that you have got a fiancé so that you can feel protected. In short, the theme was that of proximity/distance and who was in control of this.

Psychodrama V

The ideal body

The fifth psychodrama is concerned with the depersonalisation of the body. Standing in front of an imaginary mirror, Irene becomes aware of the way she experiences herself. She hardly dares to touch her own body, never mind somebody else's. She does not feel pain or hunger. She verbalises her own inner voice by means of a psychodramatic split. She chooses someone to play Irene and tells this Irene (herself) that a thin, quick, combative girl possesses a sort of guarantee in life of social acceptance. If your figure is perfect (in your eyes), then you can no longer be rejected because of it. The group is then brought in. It contests the myth in a confrontational way. Girls and boys show, in very short, snappy psychodramatic scenes, moments in which they feel attracted to someone. They try to put their reasons into words. The perfect figure is much less important for most group members than Irene had thought it would be. In this way, the idea of attractiveness is made concrete by means of psychodrama. Irene's myth is dispelled. The final scene takes place between two girls in the group. Elly, a very feminine girl, and Irene sit next to each other and dare to hold each other's hand in order to see what they feel when they do this. The link between them is that, because of their past history, both of them are frightened of men and of almost every sort of physical contact. Still in a fearful mood, they console each other.

Summary

1. Psychodrama is a technique that integrates physical experiences with intellectual understanding so that feelings can be integrated more easily.
2. The reality confrontation by means of the peer group is a powerful weapon in the struggle with stubborn internalised images.

It was only towards the end of treatment in the clinic that Irene was ready, in individual therapy, to work through aspects of transference. Generally speaking, with adolescents who are very disturbed at an early age, transference is not explicitly handled since this would result in too much regression. Attempts are made as much as possible to maintain a positive transference and a good working alliance. If the transference reactions are of such a nature (both too positive and too negative) that they disturb the therapeutic process, then this transference is interpreted. Contrary to what is often thought, a psychodramatic handling of transference phenomena is also entirely possible (Meillo 1986).

At this stage of the individual therapy, the old feeling that Irene had that she had been rejected and abandoned by her parents was repeated in transference to the individual therapist. She was afraid that I, too, would reject her and abandon her.

Her desire to achieve and her obedience served to stave off this threat. She was prepared to change for anybody who accepted her and for the time being I was that person. Only later was she able to integrate this and change for herself.

Transference was of an idealising nature but she finally manages, when challenged by me, to find something in which she can compete with me and win. She says with a beaming expression: 'I'm younger than you.'

Psychodrama VI

'Home and the clinic'

In her sixth psychodrama, conflict of loyalties between home and the clinic is worked through. She literally has her back to the wall since, because she is stuck in a conflict of loyalties, she is preventing herself from making progress. In social terms she is doing well but she is only doing moderately in terms of weight. Progress in the area of weight principally means that she is doing what is required of her at home without being first accepted there as she would wish. In addition, if she reaches her correct weight, she will no longer have a weapon to punish her parents with. At the moment, she can at least occasionally say or suggest: 'Look what you have done to me.'

That she has made social progress and has become more confident and pleasant to know does not greatly interest the family. They are obsessed with her weight. The advantage of this is that she can make social progress without this being noticed. She can allow herself this sort of progress. If her weight were to be normal, this would mean that the strategy of the clinic had won over the punishment treatment used at home. She is afraid of that guilt feeling. The treatment is too far advanced for her to retreat but she dare not go forwards.

The psychodramatic double technique also helps her in this psychodrama. The double puts the problem into words and keeps her pushed up firmly against the wall. As a result of this pressure exerted on her resistance (both figuratively and literally), she can take herself in hand and drag herself (in the form of the double who embodies the other part of herself) through the room. There is no longer any option other than to change. Not for others, but for herself.

Summary

1. In psychodrama two Irenes can be created, symbolising the internal struggle. She can experience both sides and realise how the interaction takes away her energy.
2. Concretisation and symbolisation bring her to an understanding of the consequences of her lack of progress. Rationalisations as defence mechanisms do not function in emotional dramas.

This psychodrama brought a breakthrough in treatment that, at that stage, had become bogged down. Things proceed quickly thereafter. Weight increases to a proper level and remains stable. The discharge stage begins.

From now on, individual therapy concentrates upon the ambivalence centred around independence and desires for dependency. It is difficult to give up the exclusivity and tensions involved in the obsession with eating and she wonders what she will get in return. She is afraid of being boring, of being a normal girl! She does not allow all this to be taken away from her and she talks at length about her cooking lessons. She does not give up her desire to have a perfect figure. She goes to a gym and does body-building.

We discuss all this and Irene understands very well that her cooking and body-building are linked to her obsession with food and body. However, for the time being she does not think that she can manage entirely without that obsession. In all other respects, she is getting along fine. She is living on her own and the situation at home has settled down. Now that Irene is 'better', she also receives a certain amount of appreciation from her father.

All in all, we bring the treatment to an end with feelings of satisfaction. My last encounter with Irene took place by chance – a few years after treatment had finished – in a trendy haridresser's. The encounter had a feeling of equality about it. We were both of the opinion that you did not have your hair cut by an assistant, but by the boss himself!

She said that she occasionally had relapses. She then found the temptation to go on a strict diet and to take diuretic tablets difficult or impossible to resist. In general, things were well with her. She had a job in a crèche, was still living on her own, looked nice and had adequate social contacts. But she has not managed to work herself loose from the repetition of the *oral nature* of her mother's problem. The desire to punish her mother by indulging in the same sort of behaviour is also, albeit to a lesser degree, still present.

Conclusions

A summary of the advantages that psychodrama can have, over and above a purely verbal psychotherapy, was given here after each description of a particular psychodrama. If we attempt to identify the common denominator of these advantages, then it is noticeable that they all involve the exertion of more pressure on the protagonist's resistance.

Responsible and expert psychodrama, however, is not intended to break down the client's resistance. On occasion, one hears stories about instances in which the psychodramatic therapist has unfortunately gone too far and charged down the defences of the client. Clinical practice such as this has contributed to the sometimes negative image of psychodrama (Schatzberg, Lobis and Westfall 1974).

It is of enormous importance to work carefully, particularly in the cases of clients with serious disturbances that date back to the early years of life. The therapist working with groups of clients with weak ego structures must not be non-directive, since a lack of clear boundaries can cause a great deal of anxiety in these clients.

On the other hand, the therapist must not be too directive since this can also cause a great deal of anxiety. The client feels that weak ego boundaries are being assailed and often seeks refuge behind a wall of withdrawn behaviour. The psychodramatist must offer an adequate degree of security. Overintense expressions of emotion should be cushioned and sometimes clarified or corrected. A good holding environment needs to be created. In cases where emotions are sealed up, the psychodramatist can provoke and stimulate, as well as showing by example how attractive it can be to express yourself in a more personal way.

Psychodramatic techniques are tools for exerting a little more pressure in cases where resistance is often stubborn without, however, breaking down that resistance.

Psychodramatists, who have also trained to be group psychotherapists, are often better able to avoid the dangers mentioned. They see the group as a whole of which a protagonist forms a part.

Foulkes (1965) says of the therapist:

It would be quite impossible for him to follow each individual at the same time. He focuses on the total interactional field, in the matrix in which these unconscious reactions meet. His background is always and should consciously be the group as a whole.

The accent is therefore laid less upon individual therapy in a group context. (In this case there is an increased risk that the individual's resistance will be broken down.) If the group is considered as a whole, this risk is diminished.

If psychodrama is used in a group-analytic frame of reference, then resistances are explored in the course of the initial psychodramatic session(s). When this exploration has been satisfactorily completed, central conflicts can be gradually brought up in subsequent psychodramas.

Considering the group-analytic frame of reference, the concept of 'working through' is also an important element.

In psychodrama sessions, elements from earlier sessions are systematically brought up again by the therapist and the members of the group and linked up with the current situation. This comes about through the choice of scenes and the way in which a theme is followed up in a subsequent psychodrama. But it also comes about during sharing, in which elements from earlier sessions are actively linked up by the therapist with the present session and with what group members impart during the sharing. With a certain regularity, the therapist chooses *not* to accede to group pressure to stage a new psychodrama with a protagonist or a group theme. In cases like this, the session is devoted to 'working through'. Enquiries are made into what is being done with worked-through material in order to avoid group members, as a form of resistance, constantly wanting to present 'exciting or traumatic' material, for example, with a view to acquiring a better position in the group. This procedure is also present in Irene's series of six psychodramas.

The first session was entirely devoted to the working through of the resistance to the course of treatment as a whole. The fact that Irene becomes aware of this resistance, combined with the effect, which should not be underestimated, of being the focus of attention for the group for $1^1/2$ hours, means that this psychodrama is productive and can make itself felt in all aspects of the living environment of the clinic. This phenomenon is also present in subsequent psychodramas. It is apparent that psychodrama has a considerable power of attraction, a certain aura about it, that other programmes can clearly benefit from.

A closer look at the second psychodrama shows that although the neurotic pattern is indeed worked through to a greater extent, this takes place on the basis of the symbol of resistance: reluctance to do certain things, etc. It is only in the third and following psychodramas that aspects of Irene's central conflict can be explored on a regular basis. Only then has an adequate level of security been built up for Irene in the treatment group and only then is the working alliance with the therapist of a quality adequate for making such psychodramas possible. In this respect, the role played by admission to the therapeutic community must constantly be kept in mind.

If one views the treatment as a whole, it must be concluded that the effect of psychodrama is increased by the addition of individual psychotherapy on analytic lines. Lange and Hartgers (1986) state that, in cases like this, there is a question of 'cross-fertilisation' between individual and group psychotherapy: the group functions as a practice ground for what is discovered and worked through in individual therapy and, conversely, the group yields content material for the individual therapy.

Rutan and Alonso (1982) state that a combination of group therapy and individual therapy unites the advantages of both. In individual therapy, it is more possible to learn to grow attached to one person via positive transference and to develop a feeling of security. In the group, one grows used to the proximity of several peers while, because attention needs to be divided, not having to be constantly in the limelight and thereby acquiring security again.

Finally, it must be emphasised that a stay in the psychotherapeutic community, with an extensive package of sociotherapy and psychotherapy, creates a holding environment that makes the working through of Irene's problems possible. Because all aspects of the clinical environment are well in tune with each other and because the treatment is relatively long and intensive, the treatment can achieve a certain degree of personality reconstruction. Consequently, recovery is of a more than superficial nature and the chance of a relapse, even with such serious disturbances, is relatively low.

References

Bhanji, S. (1975) 'Operant conditioning in anorexia nervosa', in J.H. Masserman (ed.) *Current Psychiatric Therapies*, vol. 15, New York: Grune & Stratton, pp. 59–64.

Bianco, F.J. (1972) 'Rapid treatment of two cases of anorexia nervosa', *Journal of Behavior Therapy and Experimental Psychiatry* 3: 223–4.

Bruch, H. (1974) 'Perils of behaviour modification in treatment of anorexia nervosa', *Journal of the American Medical Association* 230: 1419–22.

Foulkes, S.H. (1965) *Group Psychotherapy. The Psychoanalytic Approach*, 2nd edn, Harmondsworth: Penguin Books.

Foulkes, S.H. (1975) *Group-analytic Psychotherapy, Method and Principles*, London: Gordon & Breach.

Jones, M. (1973) (ed.) *Beyond the Therapeutic Community*, New Haven, Connecticut: Yale University Press.

Lange, S.G. and Hartgers, M.J.W. (1986) 'Individuele psychotherapie in een psychotherapeutische gemeenschap voor adolescenten: een contradictie?' *Kinder- en jeugdpsychotherapie* 1 (the Netherlands).

Meillo, H.J. (1986) 'Psychodrama and the groupdynamic/groupanalytic frame of reference', *Journal of Psychotherapy* 3: 157–67 (the Netherlands).

Moreno, J.L. (1970) *Psychodrama Vol I*, Beacon, NY: Beacon House.

Rutan, J.S. and Alonso, A. (1982) 'Group therapy, individual therapy or both?' *International Journal of Group Psychotherapy* 32: 267–82.

Schatzberg, A.F., Lobis, R.A. and Westfall, M.P. (1974) 'The use of psychodrama in the hospital setting', *American Journal of Psychotherapy* 28.

Stern, S., Whitaker, C. A., Hagemann, N.J., Anderson, R. B. and Bargman, G.J. (1981) 'Anorexia nervosa: the hospital's role in family treatment', *Family process* 20: 395–408.

Further reading

Bruch, H. (1975) 'Behaviour therapy on anorexia nervosa' (letter to the editor), *Journal of the American Medical Association* 233: 318.

Chapter ten

Hide and seek

The psychodramatist and the alcoholic

Gillie Ruscombe-King

First the man takes a drink,
Then the drink takes a drink,
Then the drink takes the man,
Then the man has a fall.

(Japanese proverb)

Introduction

'I feel as confused as when I was on the beer' (a distressed man, who has used and abused alcohol for many years, in his first psychodrama group).

Alcohol contains a drug that acts as a depressant on the central nervous system. It arouses excitement, garrulousness and gaiety as it depresses the inhibitory centres normally 'raised' in social and interpersonal dialogue. In moderation, alcohol changes the state of consciousness. In excess, it promotes loss of emotional and physical control. With habitual use and abuse, it becomes physically addictive, psychologically eroding and socially destructive. The occurrence of any or all of these three would indicate to the author the diagnosis of alcoholism. The World Health Organization defines alcoholism as follows:

> Alcoholics are those excessive drinkers whose dependence on alcohol has attained such a degree that they show a noticeable mental disturbance or an interference with their mental and bodily health, their interpersonal relations and their smooth social and economic functioning; or they show the prodromal signs of such developments. They therefore require treatment.
>
> (WHO 1952)

For the physically addicted, tremor, nausea and in some cases, hallucinosis may, if not treated, be only abated by alcohol. Personal confidence and self-esteem can be shattered by creeping dependence on an alternative source of strength, potentially leading to a breakdown of interpersonal and familiar relationships. Isolation can result, which, in turn, can exacerbate the craving for escape. And so, the 'roundabout', a term often used to describe the alcoholic syndrome, continues to revolve.

155

Causation of alcoholism is a complex entity, created by the interaction between personality, social factors, psychodynamic roots and possible genetic predisposition. The task of the psychodramatist is to explore these entities and help the alcoholic off the roundabout. However, the specific characteristics of guilt, passivity, low self-esteem and paranoia that present in the alcoholic's personality perpetuate the need for reliance on people of influence and those who will provide help. And yet, that need arouses intense anger and hostility. The recipient of such an encounter is immediately bestowed with feelings and anxieties, not openly expressed even before a relationship has developed. Such is the dilemma that faces the psychodrama director in the therapeutic encounter with the alcoholic. In the author's view, it is this that creates rich, challenging and indeed rewarding psychodramatic work. The 'tensions', as expressed in the opening statement, between director, client and other group members, become an outstanding and dominating feature of the psychodramatic journey in a way that is seen less clearly with other client groups, because of the deep, underlying craving for dependency and comfort for which the alcoholic is searching.

Imagine the scene – a large, burly man, roughly spoken, deeply rooted in a 'labourer's' lifestyle:

'How can I possibly do this? I am not a child and I have not come here to be treated like one.' Or, a young, homeless man, with poor social connections: 'You are the only person that has ever. . . Do I have to leave tomorrow?' Where do these statements come from and how does the psychodramatist respond?

When working with alcoholics, there is a need for a clear understanding of the origins of the syndrome, and the nature of the complexities that will arise for both the alcoholic and the psychodramatist.

The author's experience has been gained from working in an NHS regional alcohol unit, which provided detoxification and a psychological treatment approach, implementing group-analytic and psychodramatic group methods.

The origins and development of alcoholism

The structure of personality is created and influenced by interconnections between an individual and his environment... If that environment is inconsistent, overindulgent, hostile or brutal, the individual's instinctive and infantile needs will be rebuffed. For survival, the individual adapts, through despair, rage and helplessness and his needs become buried, suppressed or even extinguished. Such suppression creates anxiety, emotional conflict and guilt.

For the alcoholic, studies have shown that maternal care is lacking, often inconsistent and rejecting (McCord 1960). Paternal figures have shown to be harsh, punitive, rejecting and, at time, ineffectual (Kessel and Walton 1965), but McCord stresses that it is the inconsistency of care that is a major contributory factor. Karl Menninger, in his book *Man Against Himself* suggests that:

the alcoholic pattern should be viewed as a progression; frustration in the oral stage leads to rage against the parents; this rage is suppressed because of guilt and is replaced with feelings of worthlessness and inferiority. . . . These feelings lead, in turn, to addiction.

(Menninger 1938)

As the infant develops, he will find different ways of shielding himself from the internal and external conflicts that surround him. Some children become shy and socially uneasy, isolated and picked on at school. Others become outwardly tough, strong and 'Jack the lad'. Some remain protected with few demands. Others are expected to assume a parental role from an early age. What can emerge is a complete denial of the reality of the situation in which they find themselves as a suppression of dependency needs takes place. Denial is a common defence mechanism associated with the alcoholic's personality: 'There is nothing wrong with my Dad, he just . . . .' Instead, relationships become fantasised, and unreal: 'My Mum was just wonderful.' They learn to detach themselves from real emotional needs and experiences and 'talk' about issues in a reasonable way: 'Things are OK at home.'

Fear of emotional expression becomes great, sometimes associated with punitive authority from the past: 'I told my Dad that I was hit at school so he sent me packing with a thrashing to toughen me up.' Internal fears cause tension fiercely controlled in the face of inconsistency, leading to rigidity of mind and emotionality in an attempt to establish order out of emotional chaos: 'I can't come and play as . . . '. Conversely, overprotective parenting creates apathy, passivity and lack of emotional engagement, preventing exploration of expression and maturation: 'My Mum will do it. She does everything.'

Rebuffed from reassurance and affection, the individual may keep searching from adult to adult to satisfy inner rejected needs. Self-esteem can only remain low as the experience of rejection continues. Trust of the individual's own personal sense of expression and trust of interpersonal contact is hard to develop, contributing to a defensiveness and 'independence' that is masking highly dependent desires and needs. Through defensiveness and denial, feelings are avoided. Decisions and disclosures are resisted and soon become inaccessible: 'There is nothing wrong with me, I don't know what you are making such a fuss about.'

The desire for relationships is often heightened in order to find someone to take care of unresolved needs. The level of maturity can be inappropriate for a mature adult relationship and the 'normal' adult role is not assumed. Craving for past and obsolete relationships with parental figures prevents exploration and appropriate mature affairs with peers. Reinstatement of relationships similar to those experienced with those of influence from the past may be sought. Fear and anxiety surrounding latent sexuality or unterminated parental dominance may promote avoidance of engagement in relationships and lead to denial of intimate and sexual needs. Few of these relationships can be satisfactory and many can

157

become unproductive, destructive and unfulfilling. Yet they become repeatedly re-enacted and will reappear clearly in the treatment setting.

Dependency

On the discovery of alcohol later in life, the 'infant' within the adult experiences the solace and comfort for which he or she has been searching for many years. Alcohol becomes a stable, constant support that promotes self-confidence, reduces personal inferiorities and unleashes unresolved anxieties. It facilitates expression of those aspects of an individual's personality, conscious or unconscious, that cannot be expressed without the influence of the drug.

Such is the onset of psychological dependency. But with the dependency comes the exacerbation of the original conflict that the individual was striving to beset. And hence anxiety is increased, social confidence is eroded and emotional rigidity becomes more entrenched. Irrational, unreasonable behaviour will persist, creating great strain for those around them. Violence, debt and possible unemployment lead to greater interpersonal friction. Families break up; homelessness can result. Self-injuries and suicides are common.

Conversely, relationships may emerge that may protect the individual from the responsibility of their inappropriate behaviour, perpetuating the 'unconditional love' that the alcoholic seeks (Blane 1968), and sustaining the highly developed defence mechanisms described earlier.

Changing attitudes

It is at the point of realisation that alcohol has failed to fulfil the inspired fantasies for which it was primarily sought, that an altered attitude towards continued drinking may emerge. Chronic physical addiction and poor health may enforce hospitalisation. Sudden trauma, the loss of a relative or the sense that 'I just can't go on' may expose a secretive drinking pattern that already embraces psychological and physical dependence. If physically addicted, the alcoholic may be tremulous, agitated, nauseous, sweaty and restless. Concentration is poor, with feelings of irritability and confusion, some paranoia and suspiciousness, directed at those around them. As the physical symptoms abate, aspects of the 'dependent' personality emerge, with craving, self-preoccupation and the realisation of the pending loss of alcohol. This phenomenon has been enlikened by many to a grief reaction, with accompanied anger, sadness, romanticisation and longing for the lost object. Yet it can be reversed, by choice, by the reinstatement of drinking.

Alongside the withdrawal phenomena, poor psychological functioning is exposed, with excessive inhibition in the absence of alcohol. Poor self-esteem is disguised, sometimes by hostility and irritability. Slowly, the extent and the consequences of drinking behaviour emerges, with the sense of guilt, anguish and self-recrimination faced, perhaps for the first time, without the escape of alcohol. Such is the picture first seen by the psychodramatist.

In response to the emotional turmoil of withdrawal, defences will be heightened accordingly. Denial of the full extent of the difficulties may be exposed: 'I have cracked it this time.' Intellectualisation may prevent expression of the true sense of pain and loss: 'I'll buy my own house and start again.' Secretiveness and avoidance of contact may block any exploration of what is going on. An individual may promote the 'plight' of another, in deference to himself, through identification with that plight but as a deflection from his own needs: 'But look, *he* is homeless, what are you going to do for *him*?' Projection, 'a common defence against mental pain' (Main 1975), by unconsciously lodging uncomfortable and painful aspects of one's own personality on to another's and only seeing them in that person, is frequently used by the alcoholic. His entire relationship with alcohol, in spite of its inanimation, could be seen as a projection: 'Alcohol is wonderful. Alcohol will be the death of me.' With relationships, the alcoholic can pick out others and project his discomfort on to them: 'Don't trust him, he is a loser.' 'She looked so revolting when she came in drunk.' Such projections, if left unchallenged, encourage pairs to form, to reinforce the projection, and distance the pain even further: 'You saw her the other day, didn't you, Bert?' This, in turn, can lead to splitting, where some people tightly hold one belief and another holds others equally firmly. The fantasies become confirmed and the realities are never tested. Ostracisation and withdrawal can result.

The way forward

In my opinion, therefore, the task of the psychodramatist is to help the individual explore those defence mechanisms to allow him or her to find out what lies behind their formation. This must be done in the *absence* of alcohol or other mood-altering drugs, as the drinking itself is a defensive manoeuvre against self-discovery. Clear guidelines need to be laid down at the beginning of the therapeutic encounter, stipulating total abstinence during the course of treatment, consistent and punctual attendance of all groups, with a clear outline of the times of the groups. Without these clear guidelines the psychodramatist is unable to tackle inconsistency and avoidance; indeed, an exact enactment of the defence mechanisms the individual needs to explore. The psychodramatist has to be equally consistent and exemplary to enable sufficient stability and trust to develop to allow the defence mechanisms to be explored within the individual, within the group and between the individual and the psychodramatist. It is only by providing a setting of consistency and clarity that the alcoholic can begin to explore what has always been denied and has never been available to him or her.

To clarify my point I refer to current psychoanalytic thinking and theory. All aspects of an individual's personality will influence and contribute to his or her relationship that he or she encounters in a therapy setting. 'Few are free in their attitudes towards such issues as parental authority, dependency, God, autonomy and rebellion – all of which often come to be personified in the person of the therapist' (Yalom 1975). Such a phenomenon is described as transference. There is considerable debate about specific definitions of transference, well described by Sandler, Dare and Holder (1973), but no-one disputes its genesis in Freudian theory (Freud 1955). For the purpose of this chapter, the description by Greenson (1965) is of help: 'Transference is the experience of feelings, drives, attitudes and fantasies towards a person in the present which are inappropriate to that person and are a repetition, a displacement of reactions originating in regard to significant persons of early childhood.' Greenson emphasises that: 'In order for it to be considered transference, it must have two characteristics: it must be a repetition of the past and it must be inappropriate to the present'.

Moreno, writing at the same time as Freud, and of course the father of psychodrama, lays much more emphasis on tele, which he describes as 'an objective system of interpersonal relationships' (Moreno 1977: 231). Tele is the ability of the therapist to empathise, to take the role of another in any situation and the ability to assume their feelings. Moreno also goes on to say: 'Underlying every transference process projected by a patient are also complex tele relationships. Many factors which are uncritically assigned to transference are true tele relationships' (op. cit.). The two viewpoints seem to come closer in what Moreno describes as 'distorted identification' where feelings are evoked in the present (not necessarily towards the therapist) that are not congruent to the situation, but are restimulative of past experiences (ibid: 383).

Whatever the professional and clinical orientation of the psychodramatist to these issues, perhaps the most important statement for this chapter is the acknowledgement of the presence of tele and/or transference, the sensitivity to make therapeutic use of such processes and as Yalom points out, to work towards a resolution of any incongruities. 'If the therapist maintains his flexibility, he may make good therapeutic use of these irrational attitudes towards him without at the same time neglecting his many other functions in the group' (Yalom: 94). Failure to acknowledge these group phenomena will restrict the therapeutic potential of the group process. To quote Yalom again, transference is 'either an effective therapeutic tool or a set of shackles which encumbers his (the therapist's) every movement' (ibid: 191).

Meanwhile, the specific characteristics of psychodrama as a form of group psychotherapy focus on action. It is an enactment, through active participation, for the individual of the perceived present and historical truths to promote self-discovery. Psychodrama is also, in the author's experience, a group enactment of the interconnection of individuals' collective defence mechanisms that perpetuate the protection of pain and emotional difficulty. Without exploration, they remain unconscious. Commonly, in groups of alcoholics there is much discussion about alcohol as a replacement for the bottle through which they have formerly communicated. Long stories can give the group a 'sip-by-sip' account of misdemeanors, excitements and scares in the course of drinking. It can begin to feel as if the bottle is present and is being passed around! Such discussion creates barriers against more personal and intimate engagement with other group members.

Collective resistance against the psychodramatist strives to retain the limited potency and strength over the fantasised power of the authority figure. Simultaneously, anxiety is generated through fear of lack of containment and punishment and may lead to apparent compliance and apathy. Collusion with other group members of delinquent or evasive behaviour may render the psychodramatist less effective. Emergence of the individual as leader, dominant and talkative, may prevent group exploration. So, too, with pairings and splittings as 'secrets' are divulged to a privileged few. Projective mechanisms are common where an aspect of an individual's personality is seen in another but the ownership is not consciously acknowledged. Hatred, envy and rejection of the other for this characteristic can result. Collusion with denial prevents challenging; the search for comfort and intimacy creates pairings that resist exploration and can promote isolation, jealousy and sibling rivalry in relation to the group and the affections of the therapist. There may be group flight away from these and other difficult issues with discussion (commonly about alcohol) not appropriate or sensitive to the treatment situation. Mechanisms of denial and intellectualisation, well known to the alcoholic, can make the phenomenon hard to address. However, exploration of the existence and enactment of group mechanisms is a vital source of material for individual growth, and without exploration, self-discovery can once again be denied and frustrated.

For the alcoholic, self-exploration through action is scary. The psychodramatist's journey has to begin by harnessing and acknowledging the anxieties and resistances to the 'perceived' situation – attitude to therapy, attitude to the psychodramatist and to the perceived understanding of the psychodramatic process. As the journey continues, through each stage and technical aspect of the psychodrama – warm-up, role reversal, scene setting, auxiliary work, catharsis – the process needs to embrace individual pain, individual defences against pain and the group phenomenon that may be preventing that individual from truthful expression of that pain.

The psychodrama

Here follows some technical description of aspects of the psychodrama process with description of four individuals' journeys through that psychodramatic process. All four case profiles described participated, at different times, in a three-week residential treatment programme at an NHS regional alcohol unit. The main focus of the programme was the psychodrama group. The groups were closed, with a stipulated beginning and end, included men and women and had six–eight participants. The author was, in each case, the director. She had the help of a co-director and both were consistent to their role for the three-week period.

The warm-up

A good warm-up has been described as the creation of 'an atmosphere of openness in expression without the fear of being ridiculed or ostracized and is thus a required process for generating spontaneity' (Treadwell, Stein and Kumar 1988). The alcoholic is highly tense, suspicious and lacking in confidence at the start of a group. Because of this, caution is needed when using 'classical' warm-ups. To suggest an active, 'playful' warm-up is to dive into their deepest area of difficulty, previously only expressed when drinking and therefore commonly reminiscent of being ridiculed and losing control. The acute discomfort of this experience can be uncontainable and is dealt with in two ways. It either gets 'thrown' at the director – 'I am not an infant at school', 'This is stupid. How dare you treat me like this' – or the participant becomes more withdrawn and suspicious. Clearly, this material is vital for the alcoholic to explore. However, the feelings surface quickly and intensely before the alcoholic has sufficient strength, trust and capacity for self-expression to make use of the experience. He can therefore become defended to the stress aroused by the experience, repeating patterns of the past, rather than being facilitated by its potential. It is only through slow, sensitive, interpersonal work, with plenty of time for sharing anxieties and hostilities, that real trust towards the psychodramatic process and the director can be gained. Going too fast creates defensiveness and suppresses spontaneity.

Warm-ups create group cohesiveness. The alcoholic feels persecuted and anxious. Interpersonal work with the whole group is vital to reduce high levels of tension. It is important for the director to be mindful of the group mechanisms that may be disrupting cohesion – group denial, talking of drink, exclusion of the therapist. All these factors need to be considered when thinking about choice and direction of warm-up. In the author's view, every session can be started with a period of reflection, perhaps silence, discussion or debate depending on what is spontaneously presented by the group members. It is an approach more commonly used with well-established groups familiar with the process of psychodrama. However, the director is then able to tune in to individual and group anxieties, to outside information pertinent to group members, and to individual and group defences that may be preventing exploration.

From this information, the director can choose a more active, engaging warm-up that is compatible with the already spontaneous expression of material – a quiet, passive group may need an active warm-up to create energy; a highly talkative and anxious group may need a more focused, interpersonal warm-up to release anxiety and provide more intimate expression. Throughout, the director needs to bear in mind what each individual might express when drinking, or when disinhibited, and therefore what is so hard to reveal when sober. However, all expression involved in the warm-up process is of great importance to the alcoholic as it is perhaps a 'here-and-now' enactment of feelings and thoughts that have hitherto always been avoided, denied or drowned by alcohol. The acknowledgement and connection with those feelings needs to be shared and integrated before any in-depth psychodrama can take place. Affirmation through each stage of the psychodrama process is important before continuing self-discovery.

The following is a case profile of Tom, describing his response to warm-ups and the consequent work he went on to do.

Tom

> He was a young, single man, quite outspoken and 'chirpy', a 'Jack the lad', fresh, slightly baby-faced with a bewildered expression. Put into care at an early age, he described great inferiority at not having a 'home' and considerable envy towards those who did. He had been drinking since his early days and had amassed a considerable criminal record for petty crime when drinking. He had not faced sobriety before and had been abstinent for a few weeks.

> It was the first group that Tom had attended. The group was anxious but talkative, making determined statements about future change. Tom contributed quite freely, boasting a little about his drinking pursuits and expressing some anger about lack of care from the police. To focus the group to more personal interchange, and help with introductions, the director requested the group to throw a cushion to each member, stating their first name and then something they noticed about that person. The response was energetic, with lighthearted banter. After a few exchanges, the cushion was again thrown to Tom, whereupon he slumped into a corner, holding the cushion, quivering and speechless. He pushed away all approaches to offer help, and when the director went forward, he shouted: 'Go away, I hate this stupid exercise. Is this meant to help me? You're just like my stepmother, she used to hit me with a stick!'

> The overwhelming feelings of such painful material shocked the group into silence. Tom was in pain, feeling persecuted, and highly suspicious of the director and her motives. Because of his fear and prior associations, he was unable to reach the support available. Other group members were instantly reminded of the pain experienced at the hand of 'others' and the loss of trust of those in charge. The responses were mixed. Some became withdrawn and preoccupied, others became agitated and tried to talk to Tom. One man turned to the director and said: 'What the hell are you doing this to Tom for?'

> The group felt unsafe and frightened with little trust in the director. Tom, meanwhile, felt scared, uncontained and vulnerable, with insufficient strength and trust to work with the material aroused. The director suggested

that the group made a circle around Tom and sitting with the group said:

'I think I remind you of those in the past that have been cruel or unpredictable. Perhaps we can share those experiences together, which may help Tom to tell us more about the pain that he is feeling now.'

There followed a tentative sharing about bad and mad parents. Tom became more relaxed and was able to offload some of the very painful memories he had been carrying for years. He hinted that he only remained in the room because he was jammed in the corner. Nevertheless, he began to feel safer in himself. The intensity of feeling had subsided without resorting to the pub and the session ended there.

Clearly, Tom's response to the warm-up was uncommonly explicit but the author would argue that every individual has the potential to respond in such a way. The response can be denied or defended against. The task of the director is to be true to those defences, working within the safety of the group.

Role reversal and auxiliary work

At the beginning of the next session Tom was present. There was considerable anxiety about what we were going 'to do', and whether it was going to be so intense. It seemed that the group felt very out of control, handing over their fears, and at the same time their needs, to the director (a role commonly taken by alcohol). Mindful of this and the need to continue the process of warm-up from intrapersonal conflict to interpersonal work, but aware of the lack of group safety and ego strength, the director asked the group to think of someone in their lives, past or present, who might have helped them with their fears and needs.
Another group member spontaneously said: 'The only friend I have ever had is the bottle.'

For the alcoholic, the importance of alcohol and its representation has to be worked with, even mourned, before any significant shift of emotional independence can start. The group had not yet used the stage area where they were 'put on the spot' or 'put in the hot seat' as they saw it. Those comments are easy to ignore, but clearly express low self-confidence. Nor had the group used role reversal or auxiliary work – strange and bewildering ideas for those who feel emotionally out of control. Each step has to be taken sensitively to see where anxiety and resistance lie.

The director put forward two empty chairs on the stage, one to represent alcohol and the other for the group member. She asked each person, in their own time, to come forward and make one statement from each chair. Response was mixed, some confused, some anxious at having alcohol present.

Tom was wary to come forward and said (as Tom to 'Alcohol'): 'I hate you. You make me feel lousy.'

Tom as Alcohol:

'I don't force you to drink me.'

After each person had had a turn acclimatising to the stage area and role reversal, the director asked if anyone would explore the dialogue further. Tom stepped forward.

Tom to Alcohol: 'I hate you.

Tom as Alcohol: 'Why? I have done nothing wrong.'

Tom to Alcohol: 'Cos you get me into such trouble and then I get copped.'

Tom as Alcohol: 'A lot of people have fun with me. I don't force you to drink so much!'

Director: 'I want to keep you in role as Alcohol and ask anyone who feels like Tom to come and be Tom.'

Kevin comes forward to be Tom.

Moreno said: 'The growth of the reversal strategy of the child is an indicator of the freedom from the auxiliary ego, the mother and the mother substitute' (Moreno 1977: 63) This is vital growth for the alcoholic, often paralysed by a deep-seated sense of isolation and entrenched perception. Through the direction, the director hoped to further Tom's exploration of his abuse and dependence on alcohol in the absence of past appropriate parenting. The dialogue continues:

Kevin as 'Tom': 'I never have fun anyway. You make me feel so wretched.'

Tom as Alcohol: 'So why do you go over the top?'

Director: 'Reverse roles.'

Tom as Tom: 'I suppose I am searching for something. But you are just like the rest; no bloody good either!'

Kevin as Alcohol: 'I don't know why you say these things. You hate yourself for drinking me. Now that is a different matter. But don't keep dumping things on me!'

Tom as Tom: 'Oh shut up. I don't want to hear any of that stuff.'

Director to Tom: 'Do you think there was some sense in that?'

Tom: 'I don't know, I will have to think about it.'

The sharing involved discussion about how alcohol could be 'blamed' for problems and conflicts. Tom was beginning to explore his projective systems of hate and bitterness, formerly tied up with past relationships. He was not 'prepared' psychologically to reintegrate the projection and further psychodramatic work was not yet appropriate.

Scene setting and catharsis

In the opening discussion of a further session, Tom spontaneously began to talk about his early experiences in care and specifically about his hateful relationship with his stepmother. His material seemed 'ripe' for work, yet he remained emotionally defended from the extent of his pain. He seemed to feel stronger to tackle his unresolved difficulties, and when asked if he would like the stage area, he said:

Tom: 'Well, I can't go on hating all my life.'

Director: 'Are you still wary of me?'

Tom: 'I don't know what the hell is going to happen, but I need some help.'

Director: 'If you feel unhappy about the way things are going, you tell me. As a child, you never had the power or the opportunity to say stop. So where shall we start?'

Tom: 'Let's start with that cushion game. The others know that.'

At this suggestion, the director was mindful of two main issues – the extent of Tom's self-punishment, integrated for so long, and the need to support the group who felt unsafe and wary. The director, too, needs to remain in tune with his or her own response to emotive, painful material. A director can only be effective when working within his or her capabilities. This issue is addressed in greater depth at the end of the chapter.

With these thoughts in mind, the director suggested that he should choose someone to be Tom (so that he was not alone) and for Tom to be the cushion thrower, stating the punishing words that were still with him. Tom chose Frank, another young person with some childhood experiences in common, and with whom he had 'palled up'. With Frank as 'Tom', Tom threw the cushion to him and said:

'You're just no good.'

'I can't do anything with you.'

'You're such a bad little boy.'

'How dare you raid the larder?'

The statements continued.

Director: 'Become Tom, and Frank stay as your double. Who could be the cushion thrower?'

It is important to notice who is picked for different roles for a clear sociogram of group interaction. Both projective mechanisms and 'tele' – 'a mutual exchange of empathy and appreciation' (Greenberg 1975) can be at work.

Tom chose Albert, a large forbidding man, an ex-teacher with a tight, curt manner. Albert agreed to the role and in action, Tom quite quickly became frightened and agitated.

Tom: 'Don't do that,' he said in his defence, 'I am only little. It's not my fault. I hate you.'

Director: 'How old are you and where are you.'

Tom: 'I am in the garden and *she* (pointing at Albert) has a stick in her hand. I'm only three or four, very little.'

Tom began to sob.

Director: 'Shall we find someone to be your stepmother, or shall we ask Albert to stay?'

Tom: 'I can see her standing there; he can stay if he wants.'

Checking with Albert that this is acceptable, the director reminded Tom that this was psychodrama, and with the help of his double he could tell this person what he thought and felt.

Tom struggled with this, switching from considerable rage to feeble helplessness. The group was alert and tense.

Director: 'Who, Tom, could have helped you in this situation?'

Tom (looking up with wide eyes): 'Auntie Joan. I was her favourite. I used to crawl into her bed at night.'

(Positive as well as negative aspects of one's personality can be bestowed onto others, leaving the individual void of those strengths and comforts. Role reversal can facilitate some reclamation.)

Director: 'Be Auntie Joan, and Frank stay as Tom. As Auntie Joan, what do you say to Tom?'

Suddenly, the scene was not so bleak. With reassurances and comfort, Tom, in role reversal, could rediscover loveable, well-appreciated aspects of himself. He had found the 'good' mother within him. With the choice of Jane as auxiliary, he could begin some integration of those aspects, and with her help he was able to put at rest some of the hostility towards his 'punitive, rejecting mother'.

Tom: 'Auntie Joan, you liked Sarah.'

The drama ended with a playful, happy scene, with Tom sitting on a wall with his girlfriend – an appropriate, adult relationship which called on some of his wit, humour and talents: 'What is that bull doing in that field next door?'

The group ended in laughter.

In the sharing, it was important to clarify with Albert and Jane how they had felt in role, to replace misconstrued perceptions from group members and indeed to acknowledge identifications and similarities with the roles for both the enacted 'good' and 'bad' parent.

Rehearsal for living

In the following session, Tom was generally more buoyant. His stay in the group was nearing completion – a testing time as pending separation from the intimacy and support from the group restimulates feelings of past separation and loss (Arroyave n.d.). His return, potentially to a lonely, isolated existence with some rekindled resources, but once again faced with the threat of alcohol, was appropriately daunting.

To build on personal strengths and to bring the 'outer world' in, some rehearsal work can be helpful. Commonly, meeting old drinking pals causes some awkwardness, when there is encouragement, even mockery and disdain, to return to old haunts. Scenes of either past experiences (possibly failed) or potential future encounters are usefully enacted. Strategies for the preservation of sobriety (and for the alcoholic, the preservation of 'self' in an alcohol-orientated society) can be practised, experienced and strengthened.

Tom's enactment was of interest. He chose a scene in a pub where he was 'a regular', in which, by some present, he was protected, lent money, etc; by others, he was the source of ridicule and mockery – 'Here comes piss-head'. In rehearsal he was able to remain independent of both 'camps', not needing to gain esteem by siding or pairing, or to be abusive or intolerant of the other. He had, with support at least, reclaimed some of the projections, both negative and positive, which had left him emotionally void. With integration, he can tackle a life-long attitude to alcohol, the very problem that can potentially erode personal strength. Such are the requirements of a sober life.

Jo

The next case history illustrates the use of role reversal and auxiliary work as a way through the clouded perceptions of the alcoholic's approach to 'authority'.

> Jo, a man in his fifties, with four children is facing divorce because of his heavy drinking, had always been a good worker; tries hard: 'I am here to save my marriage.' He drinks in secret as well as with work chums. He has stopped drinking for three weeks, appears compliant and eager to please.

When Jo was first in the group, he seemed quick to volunteer for action, would enliven group members as a 'co-therapist' and would ignore their resistances. In preparation for full psychodrama, the director might ask each individual to describe, in role reversal, a significant object or article of clothing, as a warm-up to individual issues and to gauge individual and group anxieties about expression and disclosure. Jo was always the first to come forward, speaking in a flat, slightly strained but 'prepared' voice. Something was pushing him forward, but he was unclear of his needs. His actions were beginning to block and therefore deny the more conscious anxieties of other members. The director's sense was not to perpetuate the situation, as he was not warmed up, and his contributions were defensive in nature, yet she remained aware of his desire to please.

During another group member's vignette, Jo was asked to play the role of a heavy drinking partner. In this role, he became more assertive and determined.

> 'How dare you push me about. I do have a head on my shoulders. I may drink heavily, but I am not such an idiot as you think I am.'
> In the sharing he was able to acknowledge that he frequently argued with his wife when intoxicated, before he got too drunk.

Once the group is familiar with scene setting, role reversal and auxiliary work, the director might introduce a protagonist-centred warm-up, based on past or present relationships, moving slowly with the group resistances.

Jo was slowly becoming aware of the nature of his difficulty with his wife and women, and in turn, he became more preoccupied, and less needy of acceptance from the director. Much less boldly, he volunteered a scene with his wife. He was putting up some shelves, at her request, knowing all the time she would be critical of the result. The first enactment showed him taking the criticism, feeling hopeless and dejected and sneaking off for a drink before attempting to rectify the situation. At the suggestion of the director to express what was not being said, the second enactment was different. Empowered by his former auxiliary work, he was able to vent some of the rage and hurt he had felt in the relationship, and express his timidity at leaving the marriage because of his need for constant approval. Quite quickly he was able to make connections with his relationship with his mother. With even greater trepidation he described a scene in a small sitting room. He was the eldest of a large family and was constantly blamed by his mother for the behaviour of the other children, and never praised, even rejected, for what he did achieve.

Mother: 'Go and tell your brother to turn the radio down.'

Jo: 'I just have.'

Mother: 'Well it's still too loud. How many times do I have to tell you these things?'

In order to gain the love that he craved, he never answered back. Too scared of the withdrawal of the minimal affection he did receive, be became bidding and compliant. In psychodrama, he could express some sadness and rage not acknowledged for so long, and for which alcohol had been such a solace.

In group terms, there was some relief through the expression of rage as a greater understanding of Jo's position emerged, freeing the group of unconscious currents. In the sharing, there was some identification with his experiences. However, even after such a frank and open psychodrama, the group sharing can be uneasy and often sticky. Others can be thrown back by the powerful nature of the enactment, and are not sufficiently emotionally buoyant to clarify the identification straight away. They may remain fearful of expression, embarrassed and unable to overcome the hurdles of self-disclosure. In the director's experience, the sharing can be the most difficult stage of a psychodrama, and can demand sensitive modelling and individual facilitation, in order to support the protagonist and the whole group. It is for this reason the director commences the following session with a period of reflection and sharing, to pick up the threads of any undisclosed sharing from the previous psychodrama. Jo seemed more relaxed in the sharing, and his relationship towards the director became clearer and therefore more free and easy and more appropriate.

Catharsis

John

He was a large, strong man in his early thirties, on his second marriage, dismissive and denying of his alcoholism. He was jocular, only getting help because of 'the wife'; patronising in manner towards the male participants and flirtatious with the female group members, and a combination of both of these towards the therapist, yet always polite. He remained rather aloof and maintained dominance by talking intellectually. He was clearly scared to engage and was frightened, not only of the psychodrama but of his own inner process. He was wary to participate in others' psychodramas, feeling tight, rigid and fearful, defending himself through denial. His position caused irritation amongst other group members – an unconscious response to their own resistances and fears. The director felt untrusted, slightly patronised and kept at arm's length.

His first involvement with the psychodrama process came when he was picked by a female member to enact the role of her abusive, drunken husband. He played the role well but defended himself from the sharing by splitting away from the role. However, the next day he talked about his own drunken behaviour. He seemed prepared to explore his thoughts further, was jocular but co-operative. He described a scene in a pub, with a girl-friend, where, to his total consternation, he vomited into her drink. His response:

'Oh my God, what have I done? Whatever would my mother say? She would be disgusted.'

When asked if he could talk to his mother, he replied:

'She would not believe it. I have always been so perfect in her eyes.'

Indeed in enactment:

John's mother: 'You have always been such a good boy.'

John: 'But mother, look what I have done. There are bits of me that are not so pretty.'

John's mother: 'Oh that was just a little mistake.'

Here is revealed a contribution to the origins of John's denial of himself, his problems of revealing himself to the group and his dilemmas of self-disclosure in front of a female therapist. He felt belittled by his admission, and because of the nature of the enactment, some discomfort towards the director. It is important for the director, when working with strong defences, to be sensitive to a 'catharsis anxiety'. He or she may need to handle the rebound from a disclosure of guilt, regret, anger, anxiety and commonly, a sense of betrayal: 'I never meant to say so much about my wife.' Similarly, the responses in the group may be dishar-monious or angry, when a very different side of someone's personality, as in John's case, is revealed.

John felt sheepish, the group felt awkward. Perhaps what is vital is to acknowledge the existence of the 'catharsis response'.

Director to John: 'Perhaps you are feeling a little concerned about what you have told us, and perhaps others can share in that discomfort.'

Through the acknowledgement and possible integration of the catharsis anxiety, greater work towards future catharsis is possible, if the anxiety is diminished. The task of the director is to facilitate independence and autonomy, free of dependency on others. Moreno describes this as 'the infant growing away from the matrix identity' (Moreno 1977: 63).

Individuals' response to group dynamics

Continuing with John, he became consistently irritable with another female member of the group. At her instigation, the relationship was explored. In a sculpt, she placed him towering over here like a large bear. In role:

John: 'I must be big and tough; I cannot allow you to smother me.'

In role reversal: 'I can't cope if you loom that large. I can't get near you.'

John: 'I can't let you get too close as you will trample on me.'

In role reversal: 'You remind me of a big bear, fierce and tough on the outside and soft as butter inside.'

John: 'I can't cope with being soft. It is being weak and pathetic.'

The dialogue reminded John of his experience with his first wife. She left him as he compensated for his perceived weakness by heavy drinking. He could not bear that rejection and chose to dismiss her himself. Hence the irritation with the group member. This mechanism is known to be so strong that it can force participants to leave a group setting if it remains unexplored. While rejecting, John simultaneously craved praise and support – an exact enactment of his presentation in the group.

Exploration of individual and group processes in the psychodrama group

Caroline

She is a married woman, with several previous marriages and children now in their teens. She has been known to the alcohol services for many years, has some periods of sobriety, but when drinking has severe and frightening withdrawal symptoms. She has recently been detoxified and is desperate for 'a last chance'. She feels guilt ridden and angry about her failures. When sober, she is always beautifully turned out.

When first in the group, Caroline was highly anxious, fiddling with her finger nails and looking at the floor. Her tension was mirrored by other group members who were ill at ease and preoccupied. Any form of 'playful' warm-up would have been forced and the silence was heavy and

171

suspicious. An introductory name game lightened the atmosphere, although there were references to feeling self conscious and stupid. Personal esteem and self-confidence were low and there seemed to be an unspoken craving for alcohol to relieve the anguish. The director asked the group to think what would be most helpful for each participant, and opened a 'magic shop' to enable exchange for some tensions.

Caroline came forward and said she did not deserve anything from the shop as she had been such a failure. The director asked her to swap roles with the shopkeeper.

Caroline as Shopkeeper: 'How can I help you?'

Caroline: 'I don't know! I am not worth bothering about.'

Caroline as Shopkeeper: 'Doesn't it help to tell us that you feel so bad?'

Caroline: 'Yes.'

Director: 'Choose someone to be the shopkeeper.' (Caroline chooses another female member.)

Shopkeeper: 'What do you want from me?'

Caroline: 'I want to run away and hide.'

Shopkeeper: 'But where would you go?'

Caroline: 'Down the gutter, I suppose.'

Director: 'Reverse roles.'

Caroline as Shopkeeper: 'Well, why not try and come in here first and just see what we have in here?'

Director: 'Reverse roles.'

Caroline (goes in): 'I feel better in here, but I am still unsure what to ask for.'

The director asks the other group members to come into the shop and share similar feelings. Thus, the process of engagement with the group began and the extent of isolation reduced. As the group progressed, Caroline was often picked for auxiliary roles, not as she saw herself – weak and guilty – but as they saw her – sharp, quick and assertive. While not discounting this image, she said:

'That sounds just like my husband. He is arrogant, pigheaded and I hate him. He puts me down all the time.'

When asked by the director to choose a scene to explore their relationship, she replied: 'I can't think of a specific scene as he is always like this.'

Director: 'Introduce him to us.'

Caroline: 'He is big, strong and tall.'

(Caroline stands on the tallest piece of furniture she can find, stands firm and upright, hands on hips.)

Caroline as Husband: 'Well, there is nothing wrong with me. I have my business, I have my cars. You are the problem as you keep drinking all the time.'

(Caroline, in role, looks assertive and strong.)

Director: 'Reverse roles and choose someone to be your husband.'

Caroline: 'I can't do that, he is too hateful. Anyway, I can see him standing there.'
Director: 'Let's ask someone to play the role.'
James volunteers, a large bullish man, who although unclear to him, had a strong identification with the role. The dialogue continues with James high and strong.
Caroline: 'Why do you always put me down?'
Husband: 'You always make stupid mistakes.'
Caroline: 'But I clear up all your muddles.'
Husband: 'And then go and hit the bottle – a fine way to carry on.'
Caroline: 'But why don't you give me any praise?'
Director: 'Reverse roles.'
Caroline as Husband: 'Don't be pathetic. What's the matter with you, you're not a child. I'm so busy.'
Caroline as Husband to Director: 'Gosh I feel good up here. She looks so pathetic from up here. There really *is* nothing wrong with me.'

During the scene, the director was alerted to the misconstrued perceptions of each partner, and the 'untruths' were not being challenged. In psychoanalytic terms, the projective identification from Caroline to Husband of power, strength and autonomy empowered her husband with these attributes to the exclusion of everything else. So he became that person for her. For Caroline, those aspects of her personality were lost into the projection and she was left diminished, disempowered and vulnerable, particularly to drinking. She continued to get looked after, and her husband had someone to contain his failures and weaknesses. The director's task was to make conscious and work with the mutually entrenched projective system.

Caroline as Husband: 'You'll never be any different.'
Director: 'Reverse roles.'
Caroline: 'Well, I have come here for treatment, haven't I?'
Director: 'How can this be different?'
Caroline: 'He'll never change. I just want some strength to keep fighting.'
Director: 'Like you felt when you were him?'
Caroline: 'Yes I suppose so, but he would never give it to me.'
Director: 'Who do you feel empowered by?'
Caroline: 'Members of the AA. I get a lot from going to their meetings.'

With the help of another group member – a female, interestingly – she was asked, in role, what she did need from her husband and to clarify what she could find elsewhere. Her journey through the group encouraged her to individuate and to discover herself as a person, away from alcohol, and only from such a position could she begin to tackle the origins of such a destructive relationship. Her relationship with the director was always pleasant and co-operative. Things may have been different if the director had been a man.

In group terms, Caroline's enactment had a profound effect. James, who had played the role as husband, became agitated and indignant in the sharing.

James: 'How could anyone be like that? He is like an animal. I never want to be like that.'

His sentiments were echoed by the other men in the group. At the next session, in spite of the repeated rejection of the image of this man, there was continuous and intense discussion about him.

A: 'I feel haunted by him.'

B: 'What did you say that he said?'

James: 'I never want to meet a man like that.'

It seemed to the director that Caroline's husband had 'joined the group' and what he represented was very present, if denied and projected back to its original source.

Director: 'I am wondering what this man represents for each member of the group as he is being talked about continuously. I will put an empty chair here and ask you to come forward in your own time and tell him what he does remind you of.'

James leaps up and says angrily: 'I think you are a horrible man. I never want to see you. Goodbye.' (He sits down urgently, looking flustered and defiant.)

Andrew: 'I think you are too big for your boots.'

Bert: 'My wife says I am like you when I have been drinking. I find it hard to believe, but I am scared she might be right.'

(This was an interesting connection for Caroline, as she was always seen as 'the drinking partner'.) Bert agreed to set up a scene with his wife describing these accusations. At resolution, he acknowledges:

'I know I am a pig when I drink, that I smell, I urinate, I say hurtful things, but inside I feel bad, I feel weak and I do need you.'

From this enactment, Caroline could continue to disentangle some of the distorted perceptions of her husband.

James sat transfixed, became preoccupied and withdrawn and only several sessions later was he able to acknowledge his weakness and his need to empower himself with alcohol, leading to a dismissive, rejecting attitude to his wife. Thus several enactments contributed to the dismantling of the mutually held defence systems of the group members. Individuals could begin to reclaim through conscious acknowledgement, aspects of their personalities hitherto denied and defended against. It is only by encouraging a shift from an absolute entrenched state of perception that the alcoholic can begin to move forward emotionally and psychologically and by this reduce the vulnerability to drink.

Attitude of director towards clients

Considerable emphasis has been placed on the attitudes and feelings of the patient or client towards the director or therapist. What of the feelings and thoughts the director may have towards the client? The introduction suggested the task of the director was to facilitate the individual to 'step off the roundabout'. In the author's opinion, unless great caution is taken, it is all too easy to get swept onto the roundabout (fast moving) and subsequently fall off together or separately, neither being of therapeutic value. Indeed this may add to an already long list of 'failures', personal and therapeutic. How can this happen? The pathology (and survival) of alcoholics have promoted them to defend, deny and deceive themselves and those around them, in constant search for the intimacy and approval for which they crave and yet for which they feel constantly rejected. For the director, there may be, and most likely are, aspects of the clients' personalities with which he or she can consciously or unconsciously identify, can have empathy for, be endeared and even infatuated by. Conversely, feelings of repulsion, rejection, hostility, suspicion and fear can commonly be experienced amongst a widely varied client group. Storr says: 'Most of the traits we most deplore in others have their place within the recesses of our own psyches' (Storr 1979). Moreno echoes this by saying 'Mental processes in his (director's) own mind have a definite affect upon his conduct during the psychodramatic work' (Moreno 1977: 228).

The alcoholic often seeks 'rescue'. For personal and professional esteem, it may become easy to slip into the position of rescuer, for the helper to help the helpless for the helper's sake, a feeling of potency possibly more comfortable than the identification with the feeling of helplessness. 'The actively, projectively helpful will unconsciously require others to be helpless while the helpless will require others to be helpful' (Main 1975). Such patterns will perpetuate helplessness, arouse frustrations and increase potential for rejection. No response is 'bad' as long as attitudes are acknowledged and explored openly, through discussion. If submerged, disowned or discarded, then antitherapeutic interaction can take place. The director is equally at risk, slipping into defence mechanisms against his own frustrations, anger and commonly, despair. Projection back onto the client is all too easy: 'He is so passive. He is a waster. I am sure he doesn't want to stop drinking.' All assessment, thoughts and ideas need constant airing, discussing and clarifying through processing or supervision to establish the source and boundaries of personal material. Both Storr and Moreno would strongly encourage self-analysis for greater understanding of these processes, in order to maintain clear facilitation of patients in treatment.

Attitudes towards personal and group boundaries need constant analysis, with clear understanding for the decision for action: 'I am sorry I can't come to the group today, I have to go to the dentist.' By challenging a statement like this, the director may arouse considerable rage and resentment, yet may penetrate important avoidance anxiety that will ultimately facilitate group engagement. To leave the statement unchallenged, the avoidance belongs to the director, allowing the alcoholic to spiral once more into his chaotic unstructured world. It is important to remain mindful of the opening proverb altered for the illustration of this chapter:

First the man takes a drink,
Then the drink takes a drink,
Then the drink (the therapist can) take the man,
Then the man (and the therapist can) have a fall.

Conclusion

It is difficult to predict whether the use of psychodrama with alcoholics as illustrated can influence future drinking behaviour. I believe that the experience of psychodrama provides an opportunity for the rediscovery of personal potential common to every individual. In the alcoholic, that potential has been drowned by alcohol. The use of rediscovered potential demands decisions and every individual retains the choice of returning to drink or of continuing to build on rediscoveries.

Acknowledgements

It has been the sharing of such rediscoveries that has given me inspiration to do this work. I will always be grateful to those clients who have allowed me to accompany them on their journey. I am indebted, too, to Marcia Karp who remains a constant source of inspiration, and to the late Dr Fernando Arroyave, without whose support and encouragement I could not have made my own journey.

References

Arroyave, F. (n.d.) 'Group analytic treatment of drinking problems', in T. E. Lear (ed.) *Spheres of Group Analysis*, Naas, Co. Kildare: Leinster Leader Ltd.
Blane, H.T. (1968) *The Personality of the Alcoholic. Guises of Dependency*, New York: Harper & Row.
Freud, S. (1955) *Five Lectures on Psychoanalysis*, standard edn, vol. 2, London: Hogarth Press.
Greenberg, I. (1975) *Psychodrama*, New York: Souvenir Press.
Greenson, R.R. (1965) 'The working alliance and transference neurosis', *Psychoanalytic Quarterly* 34: 155–81.
Kessel, N. and Walton, T. (1965) *Alcoholism*, Harmondsworth: Penguin.
Main, T. (1975) 'Some psychodynamics of large groups', in L. Kreeger (ed.) *The Large Group*, London: Constable.
McCord, W. and McCord, J. (1960) *Origins of Alcoholism*, London: Tavistock Publications Ltd.

Menninger, K. (1938) *Man Against Himself*, New York, Harcourt Brace & Co.

Moreno, J.L. (1977) *Psychodrama 1*, New York: Beacon House.

Sandler, J., Dare, C. and Holder, A. (1973) *The Patient and the Analyst*, London: George Allen & Unwin, ch. 4.

Storr, A. (1979) *The Art of Psychotherapy*, London: Secker & Warburg.

Treadwell, T., Stein, S. and Kumar, V. (1988) 'A review of psychodramatic warm-up techniques for children, adolescents and adults', *Journal of the British Psychodrama Association* 13 (1): 5–18.

Weiner, H. (1965) 'Treating the alcoholic with psychodrama', *Group Psychotherapy and Psychodrama* 18: 21–49.

World Health Organization (1952) *Expert Committee on Mental Health*, '*Alcohol Subcommittee, second report*' W.H.O. Technical Report Series, no. 48.

Yalom, I.D. (1975) *The Theory and Practice of Group Psychotherapy*, 2nd edn, New York: Basic Books Inc.

Further reading

Blume, S. (1968) 'Psychodrama techniques in the treatment of alcoholics', *Group Psychotherapy and Psychodrama* 21: 241–6.

Blume, S. (1974) 'Psychodrama and alcoholism', *Annals New York Academy of Science* 233: 123–7, April.

Edwards, G. and Gross, M.M. (1976) 'Alcohol dependence: provisional description of a clinical syndrome', *British Medical Journal* I: 1058–61, May.

Feasy, D. (1984) 'Psychodrama is group psychotherapy', *Journal of Drama Therapy* 13 (1) Autumn.

Marrone, M. (1979) 'An approach to analytic psychodrama', *Journal of Drama Therapy* 13 (1) Autumn.

Monroe, C. (1986) 'An effective treatment for the alcoholic', *Journal of British Psychodrama Association* 1 (2): 30–6, Winter.

Powell, A. (1986) 'Object relations in the psychodrama group', *Group Analysis* 19: 125–38.

Ruscombe-King, G. (1983) 'Psychodrama – a treatment approach to alcoholism', *British Journal of Occupational Therapy* 46 (7), July.

Speroff, B.J. (1966) 'Psychodrama with alcoholics – two brief paradigms', *Group Psychotherapy* 19 (3–4): 214–19.

Van Meulenbrouck, M. (1972) 'Serial psychodrama with alcoholics', *Group Psychotherapy and Psychodrama* 125: 151–4.

Chapter eleven

Doorway to the past

Use of action techniques with adult children of alcoholics and co-dependants

Kit Wilson and Elaine Eller Goldman

There has been an increasing focus worldwide on children and adult children of alcoholics as a population-at-risk of alcoholism and a wide variety of other emotional and physical dysfunctions. Children of alcoholics are likened to survivors of the holocaust, or to Vietnam veterans – they have survived the daily traumas of parental alcoholism – but they carry the scars deep in their psyches.

All over the world today national and local media coverage has led to a demand for treatment. Attendance at conferences and workshops for adult children of alcoholics has exceeded all expectations. The excitement engendered has the characteristics of a social movement. Therapists and counsellors are rallying to provide services to meet the expressed needs of this population.

Psychodrama and other action techniques are particularly suited to addressing the specific recovery process of ACOAs (adult children of alcoholics) and co-dependants.

Traditional verbal psychotherapy often does not break through the wall of denial and access the emotions stored deep in the self. Real healing seldom occurs until these feelings are re-experienced and released. When this experiential catharsis is coupled with the cognitive learning inherent in the psychodramatic process, there is the possibility of a powerful boost to recovery.

In this chapter we will discuss some of the typical stages of recovery experienced by an adult child. We will then give examples of psychodramatic techniques that would be helpful at that stage. Prior to beginning, however, it is important to state briefly some of the basic premises that provide the foundation for today's family disease concept of alcoholism and other addictions.

Chemical dependency is a progressive disease process. The label 'chemical dependency' includes alcoholism and all other dependencies on chemicals, including cocaine, prescription drugs, narcotics and a wide variety of street drugs singly or in a mix. The lifestyle differs with different drugs – a street junkie's lifestyle is very different from the lifestyle of a female closet alcoholic. A fast-lane Yuppie coker will lead a different life from a frightened young dealer. However, the disease process, the problems, the effects on self-concept and on personhood, the steady progression of the illness are predictably similar no matter what the drug. And the effect and progression in the family system are the same whether the drug is alcohol, cocaine, marijuana, heroin or valium.

'Everyone whose life touches the alcoholic is in one way or another affected by his disease, but its direct consequences fall on the members of his immediate family' (Wegscheider 1981). To survive the inconsistency, chaos and confusion created by the chemical dependency, children develop patterns of coping that may be dysfunctional or emotionally unhealthy. These may be carried into their adult life. For example, children often do not learn how to identify boundaries – where *they* begin and others end. With unclear boundaries the family becomes an undifferentiated emotional mass. A family member caught in this trap is called a co-dependant. Co-dependency is an obsession or dependency on people or things outside the self to the point of neglecting the self and having little self-identity (Lerner 1987).

Alcoholic family systems are typically closed with rigid rules and rigid roles. Adults who have grown up in these systems need as much help as the alcoholic. This is true whether the chemically dependent person is still using, recovering, no longer present or dead. Treatment for adult children is not aimed at helping the family help the alcoholic. That is a different issue addressed in a process called intervention. Adult children must focus on their own areas of dysfunction in order to begin to heal themselves.

Preparation for change

The cardinal rules in alcoholic families are: 'Don't Trust, Don't Talk About the Real Issues, and Don't Feel' (Black 1981). Action techniques are excellent interventions for addressing these rules. Action techniques derive from psychodrama, which is based upon the theory, philosophy and methodology of Jacob L. Moreno. The use of 'action' facilitates constructive change through the development of new perceptions.

Trusting

Trust is a therapeutic prerequisite. Adult children must learn to trust both therapist and group before beginning the work of recovery. They must also learn that they can set limits in the therapy process as well as in life. In any group, trust is imperative if interpersonal feelings are to be explored.

It is important to remember that choosing and using an exercise or technique depends upon the type of group, the size of group and the time allotted to the entire session. Finally, the director's overall assessment of what the group is ready to do is most important. We use a number of simple exercises to warm the group up to each other and to the facilitators. This subsequently creates the beginning of trust in the group. When structuring any exercise, we feel it is important to be clear, to give one instruction at a time and to be aware of the comfort level of the group members. At every stage, our questions and structure reflect our purpose. In a small group we might pose a question to each member in turn. It can be helpful to start by asking the group to close their eyes or look at the floor in order to try to focus on themselves. You may need to 'settle' the group by having them take one or more deep breaths. Ask them to focus on your question, give them a moment to do so. Have them open their eyes when they are ready. Be aware of your *purpose* when choosing a topic and delving further with an individual. Here are some examples:

What is your strongest feeling today or in the last few days?
Describe yourself (the kind of person you are) in a picture or an image.
What one person or event in your life makes you angry?
What one thing in your life makes you sad?
Who has been a significant influence in your life (positive or negative)?
What about *yourself* are you most proud of?
What one behaviour or action would you change if you could?
If you could be anyone or anything in the world, who or what would you be?
Describe a significant object you have or had in your life.
What is something that you like to do (and are able to do) that you haven't done in a long time?

Expand on these or develop your own, but keep in mind your purpose. Don't forget to share your own response to the question. You may choose to do this last, or first as an ice breaker. In a large group the members may be divided into subgroups of four to eight, or a group may be divided into dyads and given a simple task that will help them to know each other and begin to feel more comfortable in the larger group. Upon completion of the task in the small group, the group is assembled again into the larger group and invited to share the experience.

There are also more sophisticated trust and risk exercises such as 'the blind walk'. For this exercise divide the group into pairs. Designate one partner of each pair as the leader. Designate the other partner of each pair as the blind person. Instruct the blind people to close their eyes. Instruct the leaders to *non-verbally* lead the blind person and give them as many sense experiences as they can find in the environment. This can be inside, outdoors or a combination. Consider your group, setting or other factors that might limit or enhance the experience. Give them whatever time is needed to do so as you observe the level of interaction. Then reverse the process. You may want the group to keep the same partners. You may want them to divide into the opposite roles and have the new leaders choose the one they will lead (or vice versa).

When all group members have had experience in each role, close with sharing. Remember, however, it is more difficult to reach a trust level with ACOAs because of their life experience. Therefore, before using an exercise like 'the blind walk', be sure that your group is ready for it.

Talking about the real issues.

Denial remains the primary symptom for adult children of alcoholics. Since they grew up in silence about the alcoholism, as adults they are still caught up in protecting themselves and other family members from the painful facts. One of the first steps in recovery is accepting the role that alcohol played in their family of origin.

The chemically dependent family is organized around alcohol or drugs and around the chemically dependent person. Family members are usually so caught up in protecting the system, saving face and surviving, that they are often unaware of what is happening. One of the first steps in recovery is increased understanding of the role alcohol or drugs have played in their family relationships. We need to break the rule that says: 'Don't talk about the real issues'. For this reason this first stage of recovery has been called *emergent awareness*.

'It is the stage in the recovery process when adult children of alcoholics begin to become aware of the psychological, physiological and genetic vulnerabilities that they acquired as a result of being raised in a family where there was an alcoholic' (Gravitz and Bowden 1985).

One of the ways to help ACOAs to 'see the alcoholism' and 'talk about it' is to use the action sociogram. This is a symbolic representation of the dynamics of the relationships within a specific group. Used with the ACOA, it serves to clarify relationships, recognise 'old messages' and gain clearer insight into the influence of alcohol on the family system generationally.

For our purposes we do two action sociograms with ACOAs. The first with the present family of the ACOA and then with the family of origin. First the individual chooses a member of the group to portray each of the significant others in their sociogram (i.e. wife, husband, children). Then the ACOA describes each in turn. On occasion, when appropriate, we may include someone to represent 'alcohol' and its place in the family dynamics. After experiencing the 'symbolic picture' of the present family structure as well as the family of origin, the ACOA can see the similarities and differences in the two families. This increases insight into the role that alcohol plays across the generations.

Here is a recent example of the visual power of the action sociogram. A male ACOA placed himself standing, on a chair, in the place of 'power', in his present oriented sociogram, with his son unable to communicate with him. He then showed us his family-of-origin sociogram. He placed his mother (the alcoholic) on a chair, with himself unable to reach her or communicate with her. As he became aware of the similarities and of how his son must be feeling, he immediately came down off the chair and dealt with his son in a different manner.

Feeling

Acknowledging the chemical dependency in the family and beginning to identify oneself as an ACOA often brings relief and even excitement. The 'Don't talk' role has been broken and the conspiracy of silence is finally ended. There is a new freedom to be open and honest.

However, the initial good feelings are often followed by a flood of less pleasant emotions – anger, shame, extreme sadness – all a part of the natural process of grief. Typically, a chemically dependent family is a container of unresolved grief. The losses involved in being a part of an impaired family are enormous – loss of childhood, loss of parents, loss of hope. Hand in hand with the need to grieve is the need to complete unfinished business that cannot, for whatever reason, be completed in life.

An ideal technique to help the ACOA deal with 'unfinished business' is 'The empty chair'. This is a role-playing technique in which an individual can speak to the significant other as they have never been able to do. The empty chair is a powerful exercise and must be used judiciously and by someone well trained in dealing with strong emotions, grief and anger. We structure the empty chair and find a volunteer who has some unfinished business with a significant person in their life. This is often someone who is no longer alive. When we allow the ACOA to say what he or she has been unable to say in life, we can often enable a catharsis of old angers and/or a piece of grief work that has been long overdue and may be causing some present difficulties.

The examples of work using the empty chair are numerous and range from a catharsis of years of unresolved anger at the alcoholic and abusive parent to deep grief work over the losses that are inherent in the life of a ACOA.

The ACOA will need help in working through the feelings. Just feeling may be a frightening experience because another family rule, 'Don't feel', is being broken.

An example of work accomplished with the empty chair might be an ACOA who is first able to cathart anger at the alcoholic parent and/or the parent who did not protect them from the alcoholic. Then he or she is finally able to cathart the tears and pain about the 'lost love' from the abusive parent.

Another technique is to have the ACOA write 'the letter' they have never written. Writing a letter that has never been written to someone significant – dead or alive – encourages the ACOA to deal with unfinished business in a safe, controlled and supportive atmosphere. The empty chair and the letter often develop into much needed grief work.

The structure of The Letter is as follows:

1. Often there are people to whom you wanted to say something and did not. Writing a letter is a way to do this.
2. What kind of stationary are you going to use?
3. Will you use a pen or pencil?
4. What date is on the letter?
5. Who is the person to whom you are writing?
6. Describe their personality in a word or two.
7. Write the letter.

8. How are you going to sign the letter?
(Use surplus reality)
9. Role-reverse the protagonist into the person receiving the letter.
10. While in role-reverse, have the protagonist describe (him/herself).
11. While in role-reverse, have the protagonist write a letter to (him/herself).
12. Role-reverse the protagonist back.
or,
13. Stop after point 8, use no role-reverse, only the passage of time.
14. What kind of response might you get?
15. Or, how does it feel now that you've written the letter?

Share

Often, after doing this exercise, participants really *do* write the letter.

Changing

The second stage of recovery for adult children of alcoholics involves dealing with core issues: ways of behaving learned in childhood and carried on today; feelings and attitudes about alcohol and drugs, issues of trust, dependency, and control, problems with intimacy and sexuality, boundary issues (Gravitz and Bowden 1985). At this time, after the initial wave of feeling has abated, it will be helpful for the adult child to be protagonist in a full-core psychodrama session.

A 'core' or 'classic' psychodrama is a session of approximately $1^1/_2$ hours during which the ACOA can explore whatever basic problems he or she wishes. The psychodrama encourages and provides a direct vehicle through which the individual re-experiences the central issues of his or her life. Instead of talking about the problem, the ACOA is plunged again into the midst of his or her own reality, as if for the first time. It is here that the true power of psychodrama lies. The emotional catharsis, the realisations that can take place in this experience can be so immediate, so vivid and so intense as to make a lasting impact.

Rehearsing

It is not always necessary or therapeutic for an adult child to deal directly with other family members who are still in denial, still enmeshed or still using. However, at some point in the recovery it may become important to visit home, check perceptions with a sibling or go to a wedding, funeral or other family occasion. These encounters can be very scary, particularly in early recovery. Often preparation and rehearsal is a helpful way of providing advance support. Role training is rehearsal for life situations. It is designed to help the client change specific behaviours and/or to enable one to practise new behaviours. The ACOA uses real events to demonstrate their reactions in a specific situation. Then, within this framework, we can show mirrors or use other psychodramatic techniques for insight or clarification as the ACOA is prepared to change the unwanted behaviour.

For example, in a role-training scene we might see the ACOA preparing to face a parent by becoming fearful, belligerent or nervous and being unaware of how he or she warms up to the coming event. We could use a mirror to show the ACOA what he or she is doing and then help them practise other behaviours.

Playing

In a family governed by rigid rules and the need to protect and save face, there is often a lack of spontaneity that retards creativity and the ability to have fun. Roles are reversed and children grow up to be 'little adults'. The need to stay in charge and control all situations leads to a family unable to relax, let loose and experience enjoyment. Family members have never learned to play. Spontaneity exercises are helpful in releasing that 'spontaneous child', within us all. Towards that end we use a number of 'spontaneity exercises' and some 'story playing'.

These exercises are designed to enhance and increase spontaneity, creativity and group co-operative effort. Primarily, they generate fun and laughter and help the ACOAs to feel like children. They range from pantomiming historic events, places, seasons, to playing out a story, fable or fairy tale.

'Story playing' is a group exercise where each member of the group takes a role or part in playing out a story or fairy tale. When doing these exercises, have fun! They will increase group cohesiveness and foster spontaneity and creativity. Allow members to experience roles not usually taken.

Some clients may be just as resistive to *play* as they are to showing other feelings. Encourage involvement on *some* level. Maintain the physical safety of the group.

Have several group members suggest different stories, fables, fairy tales, etc. Choose one story (this may be a 'sociometric' choice, a majority choice by a show of hands, or some other method. It is usually best for the group to choose). Sometimes it may be necessary to outline the story *very* briefly. Decide what characters will need to be portrayed. Remember, you may add characters or have people portray objects, etc. (Include a narrator if needed.) Have the group members volunteer or choose each other to play each character. Have the characters set the scene. Play out the story. Allow the group to portray the story in their own way. Close with sharing about the overall experience and the specific feelings while playing the characters. Was it different or similar to roles they take in life?

Choosing

Finally, adult children of alcoholics begin a process of choice making. They begin to accept responsibilities for their decisions, commitments and growth.

They need a structure and a vision to proceed with their recovery. This is the spiritual stage of recovery.

The final exercise addresses many of the problems of the ACOA and, for us, has become a powerful closure for our sessions. In the 'magic shop' only abstract qualities (i.e. courage, trust, hope, patience, the ability to show feelings, etc.) are traded for specific personal qualities of the individual (i.e. fear, anger, hopelessness, distrust, etc.). In the shop one is required to make choices and decisions and to be responsible for oneself.

For this exercise we create a special 'shop', a shopkeeper and an assistant. The shop operates only on the barter and exchange system and within this framework the ACOA comes to grips with the choices made in the past and the ones desired in the future. For example, an ACOA might want to 'buy' the ability to show feelings, but the shopkeeper will only be willing to trade if the ACOA gives up the wall of distrust he or she keeps around him/herself. Although the magic shop begins in fantasy, as the bartering proceeds the exercise moves from fantasy to symbolism and finally, to reality.

Believing

If self-esteem is the bedrock of the psychic structure, it is easy to see how adult children of alcoholics, developing in an atmosphere of tension, crisis, chaos and unpredictability, are constantly fighting for psychic survival.

Moreno said: 'Human beings have two important questions to answer, Who am I? and Where do I fit?' He said that how well we answer these questions is a measure of how fully we experience our lives (personal communication).

This is the core of the adult-child struggle: A search for identity, a solid self, comfortable boundaries – a search to discover who I really am. And a search for a niche, for relationship, for a sense of belonging – a search for an environment where I fit and will be nurtured.

Therefore, if we can aid the ACOAs in their search for trust, honesty and feeling, *vis-à-vis* the past, perhaps they can then come to trust and believe in themselves.

Psychodrama and action techniques involve the adult child of an alcoholic in experiencing their search at all levels: emotional, intellectual, physical and spiritual.

References

Black, C. (1981) *It Will Never Happen To Me*, Denver, Colorado: M.A.C. Publishers, Chapter 3 pp. 31–52.

Gravitz, H. and Bowden, J. (1985) *Guide to Recovery: A Book for Adult Children of Alcoholics*, Homes Beach, Florida: Learning Publications Inc., p. 29.

Lerner, R. (1987) Speech, Seattle, Washington, 31 July.

Wegscheider, S. (1981) *Another Chance: Hope and Health for the Alcoholic Family*, Palo Alto, California: Science and Behavior Books, Inc., p. 76.

RULE 43

Chapter twelve

What we are doing here is defusing bombs

Psychodrama with hard-core offenders

Jinnie Jefferies

In a room in Grendon Prison, a woman assistant lies on a mattress on the floor, covered by a blanket. Kneeling beside her, John is at his mother's deathbed telling her how it felt to be beaten and degraded by her when he was a child. John's mother died quite unexpectedly during his sentence. There are tears in his eyes.

Director: What is happening as you talk to your mother here?

John: I feel a lot of hate towards myself.

Director: What is the sadness about?

John: Regret, hate, love. I keep looking at myself for excuses, but I can't find them. I say my mother is to blame. I don't know whether she is.

Grendon

John is one of 260 men who have chosen to serve part of their sentence at Grendon Prison, which was built in 1962 to provide a treatment regime for prisoners with serious behaviour and personality problems. All prisoners wanting to come to Grendon must be referred by their medical officer. The average stay is about two years, but at any time either inmates or staff may decide to terminate treatment. At the end of their stay, prisoners return to their Dispersal prison for reallocation.

When they arrive at Grendon, prisoners are assessed and allocated to a wing. They have single cells that, unlike other prisons, remain unlocked during the day to allow free association. A wing population includes sex offenders, murderers and those who have committed violent crimes or drug-related offences. There is a non-violence rule, and men who commit acts of violence are transferred out of Grendon. In another prison, many of these men would serve the whole of their sentence on 'rule 43', which allows them virtual isolation. Many men choose this regime rather than risk associating with other prisoners because they are fearful of what might happen to them if the nature of their crime became known.

While on the wing, prisoners participate in intensive group therapy. They are required to attend a group regularly to talk about themselves, their relationships and their offence. They also have to attend a large community meeting that provides a forum in which small groups are fed back and deals with issues that concern the community. Prison officers take an active part in group therapy; they provide valuable role models and relationships that the prisoners would not otherwise experience. There are also work parties and education classes, but therapy has always had the highest priority at Grendon.

Psychodrama is a weekly input for the prisoners on three wings; there is a 2-hour period each week for twelve weeks. It is staffed by the psychodramatist, sometimes helped by a female assistant from another department. These assistants are not trained in psychodrama, but their presence can be valuable when an auxiliary role in the drama needs to be played by a female. At the beginning of each twelve-week series, group members themselves receive some training in auxiliary and doubling techniques, for use in later psychodramas.

Those who want to attend the psychodrama sessions have to discuss their intentions with their small group. At the 3-monthly assessments, staff may discuss with a prisoner the possibility of his attending psychodrama as part of his treatment plan. Before each twelve-week session begins, the selected prisoners are interviewed by the psychodramatist so that they can discuss the areas of work they would like to address. After this interview they make a contract to remain with the group for the whole twelve weeks, because the psychodrama group operates as a closed group.

After each weekly session, group members feed back to the community and their small group; the psychodramatist feeds back to uniformed and civilian staff in the presence of the wing therapist. In addition, the session is recorded in the Daily Occurrence Book so that staff coming on duty are aware of what has happened during the session.

The client group

Most of us abhor violence and cannot conceptualise how an individual can inflict pain and suffering on another. We have little understanding of how this can come about, and our tabloid press verbalises our hatred of these actions with such headlines as 'Animal', 'Brute' or 'Fiend'.

Many of those who come to Grendon, like John, are unhappy, alienated and distressed. What has happened to some of these men is often more destructive than their crime. There are numerous cases of men who as children were beaten, degraded and abandoned by one or both their parents; tales of violent incest, extreme cruelty, of children whose hands were placed on electric fires, who were fed with their own faeces, or were required to give sexual satisfaction to mothers and fathers. There are stories of strangers who took advantage of their vulnerable years, and of children helplessly witnessing scenes of violence between loved parents or becoming the chosen object of redirected anger. Lacking in self-esteem and confidence, and angry at having been deprived as a child of what was rightfully theirs, they make an attempt in adult life to redress the balance of these early damaging experiences. 'The tendency to treat others in the same way as we ourselves have been treated is deep in human nature' (Bowlby 1988: 91). In an attempt to assert themselves, these abused men redirect their negative feelings away from their parents and onto those members of society usually viewed as weaker than themselves.

In addition to their offences some prisoners beat their wives, and abuse or abandon their children. As soon as their relationships become threatened, or they run into difficulties at work or financially, they respond by repeating the familiar pattern of dealing with stressful issues: Dad and Mum argue; Dad hits Mum; anger is redirected to the child and Dad leaves for the pub, or for ever. They have no other model.

Attachment theory

John Bowlby's writing on 'attachment theory' and its clinical applications (Bowlby 1988) support what I have discovered through my work as a psycho-dramatist working with these issues. Moreover, it provides a theoretical framework to help understand what is happening to these men in Grendon.

Bowlby believes that the kinds of experience a person has in childhood, and the kinds of attachment created, are crucial to the development of personality. 'Early experiences affect both whether the individual expects later to find a secure personal base or not, and also the degree of competence he has to initiate mutually rewarding relationships when opportunity offers' (Bowlby 1979: 104). It is through mutually rewarding relationships and the repeated interaction with others that a healthy personality develops.

Research supporting Bowlby's ideas indicates that many individuals suffering from anxiety and insecurity, or showing signs of dependency, immaturity and low self-concept, have been exposed to pathogenic parenting, resulting in much partially unconscious resentment persisting into later life, usually expressed away from the parents towards someone weaker (Henderson 1974). Such a person, says Bowlby, is also likely to be subject to strong unconscious yearnings for love and support that may express themselves in aberrant, care-eliciting behaviour such as half-hearted suicide attempts, or conversion symptoms (Bowlby 1979).

The view that negative self-image may in some way be bound up with the propensity to offend is a long-standing one in criminology (Cohen 1955; Hewit 1970; Kaplin 1975). Confirmation that there exists a link between low self-esteem on the one hand and hostility and aggression on the other has come from a number of sources (Green and Murray 1973). Rosenbaum and de Charms (1960) view low self-esteem as being associated not only with apparently meek, withdrawn or self-effacing individuals but also with those whose social behaviour takes quite the opposite form – aggressiveness, forcefulness and assault.

In seeking to understand extreme examples of violence in families, Bowlby makes a link between anxiety and anger as a response to the risk of loss of specific relationships. These are of three types: relationships with parents, with offspring and with a sexual partner. 'Each type is shot through with strong emotion . . . . A person's whole emotional life, the underlying tone of how he feels, is determined by the state of these long-term committed relationships' (Bowlby 1988: 80). He views angry behaviour as functional, serving to maintain these vitally important long-term relationships. Maladaptive violence within families is understood by Bowlby as a distorted and exaggerated version of a behaviour that is potentially functional, especially attachment or care-eliciting behaviour.

In studying the effects on personality development in children who have been assaulted physically and psychologically, Martin Rodeheffer (quoted in Bowlby 1988) found that they were depressed, passive and inhibited, but also angry and aggressive. Bowlby's observations of young children who had been ill-treated and abused show with unmistakable clarity how early in life certain characteristic patterns of behaviour become established. He says, 'A significant proportion of rejected and abused children grow up to perpetuate the cycle of family violence by continuing to respond in social situations with the very same patterns of behaviour that they developed during early childhood' (Bowlby 1988: 92).

John

John's psychodramatic work provides evidence to support Bowlby's theories and other research in this field.

> As John moved from his mother's deathbed to the scene of his offence, he told the group that he had no understanding of his crime. 'The police knew me as a geezer who went out and had a fight and did a bit of shoplifting and burglary, but they didn't know I'd go out and rape a woman. I didn't know it myself.'
>
> On the night of his offence he had been discharged from hospital having cut his wrist and nearly lost an arm in the attempt. His arm was in plaster. In the reconstruction of his crime, John grabs his victim, played by a female auxiliary.
>
> John: 'I don't know what's going on. I don't know what's happened. I'm sorry.'
> The victim lies sobbing on the floor.
> John: 'Mentally I've hurt her. I must have degraded her. We stood crying for ten minutes. I was doing more crying. I was going mental.'
> Director: 'Show us, don't tell us.'
> John and the auxiliary just stand crying; tears fall from John's eyes as he remembers the scene, as the 'there-and-then' of his actions is experienced in the 'here-and-now' of his emotions.
> John: 'I didn't hit you, did I?'
> Rather than interrupt John's flow with a role reversal, the auxiliary shakes her head.
> John: 'Every time I start thinking about what I did to you I just want to pick

up a glass and smash it into my arm. I keep wishing I had lost my arm, that the doctor hadn't been able to save it. It sounds crazy, but I want to rip myself to bits. I hate myself for what I have done to you. The only person I wanted to hurt was my Mum. God knows what was going through my head that night, because I don't.'

After the offence he walked around for two weeks, sleeping in bushes in parks and drinking. With the few props we have in the room we construct the symbols of a bush and ask John to do his roaming and to settle under the bush when he is ready. He is asked to speak his thoughts out loud.

John: 'I keep looking for excuses, but I can't find them. I say my mother's to blame, but I don't know if she is. I don't know if it's just me wanting to hurt a woman for some reason. It's hard to forgive myself, it's just filthy what I've done. I did worse by committing a rape than my Mum ever did to me. I hope I'll get to understand it.'

John gets up, roams the room and stops, roams and stops again.

John: 'I just want to be able to trust people and love people and hold people because it must be lovely to be able to comfort somebody, to say "You're all right" and "I like you", things like that. It must be nice.'

Psychodrama at Grendon

Psychodrama at Grendon is based on the best available research. This demonstrates that negative and antisocial behaviour is often the result of low self-esteem, lack of self-confidence and is an expression of unconscious anger and resentment about what happened in earlier years and the inner world of transference objects.

The psychodramatic experience provides a forum for the prisoner to consider in detail how his modes of procuring and dealing with emotionally significant others may be influenced by the experiences he had with his parents during early childhood. For Bowlby, treatment entails reversing those experiences in the most honest way possible (Bowlby 1979). Psychodramatically this means taking the prisoner back to the primary source of his suffering: the 'there-and-then' becomes the 'here-and-now' so that he has access to those repressed emotions. He is encouraged in the psychodramatic setting to express and focus his negative feelings on their source of origin and is helped to understand how he comes to displace these feelings and transfers his inner world onto others. John raped a woman rather than deal with his feelings about his relationship with his mother, his childhood and his own feelings of inadequacy.

The director picks up on John's statement: 'The only person I wanted to hurt was Mum'. John has already made the connection himself between his present actions and past feelings. The director helps John set the scene. Mother is in the bathroom where he found her bleeding, having cut herself.

193

In real life he said nothing, shut the door and left her to go downstairs to dial 999; but now he is asked to confront her.

John: 'I wanted you dead many a time. Sometimes I think that if I had let you die I would have been a better man now. I hate you. (There is a long pause as John views the sight of his helpless mother.) Why did you beat me?'

At this juncture it is important for John to reverse roles with his mother so that he can struggle with, and hopefully come to understand, why his mother did what he accuses her of, and how she felt. By reversing roles with significant others in his life (this may include the victim), the prisoner learns to see events as others see them and comes to a clearer understanding of the interactions as they occur. In doing so he adjusts his own view.

Mum (played by John): 'You remind me of your father and I just wanted to hurt you. You are always sticking up for your father and telling people I am bad.'

John (played by another prisoner): 'But I loved Dad. Why didn't you love me?'

Mum: 'I just think I hated you. I hated you and your Dad. You are just like your father – selfish, mean and cruel.'

John: 'So are you. You drank, you didn't look after the children. You didn't.'

Mum: 'It's true, I couldn't take the pressures. I thought I would just make you run the house, look after the kids.'

The director instructs the auxiliary to take back the role of mother, knowing it is important for John to talk about something he has never talked about in real life. (Remember, John's mother died while he was in prison.)

Director: 'You never talked about these things.'

John: 'No.'

Director (sensing the feelings John is experiencing, and venturing to verbalise them for him): 'And it doesn't matter that she has been dead for six years; these feelings burn inside you?'

John: 'Yes, they do.'

The action is taken up. The auxiliary is asked to feed back the information to John which he found for himself while playing the role of his mother.

Mum: 'I can't help drinking; look at the strain I'm under with nine kids.'

John (back in his own role): 'You didn't do anything. You wouldn't go to the toilet, you used to mess in the bucket and say, "Empty it, wash it".'

Mum: 'Empty it, wash it out.'

As the auxiliary picks up the clue John gives, she brings a 'here-and-nowness' to their interaction. John begins to shout, expressing his anger.

John: 'I hate you, hate you! I should have let you die. You kept doing it in front of the kiddies. You made me clear up your own sick. You abused me.'

A prisoner from the group indicates that he wants to come up to double for John.

Double: 'In fact, you are not much of a mother.'

John (taking up the double's statement): 'No, you're not much of a mother.'

Double: 'And what hurts most of all is you don't love me.'

The double's statement stops John in his tracks. He has helped John get to the bottom of his issue with his mother. John struggles with his tears.

John: 'That's true. What hurts me is you don't love me. I think every mother should love her son.' (turning to the director and coming out of role) 'She caused me a lot of damage.'

The director instructs John to tell his mother about the damage she caused by not loving him. At this stage he begins to make connections between the past experiences and his present behaviour, and his difficulty in making personal relationships for himself.

John: 'You made me leave home when I was 16. The only thing I knew was drink. I just sat in pubs drinking; you just ruined my life by what you got me to do to you, by not loving me. I always questioned people when they said "I love you". I always needed to ask "Why?". If they tried to hold me or put their arms around me I used to push them away, I couldn't take it. I thought they were going to do the things you did, be all lovey-dovey and then kick me in the teeth.'

John is asked to tell his mother what he wanted.

John: 'All I wanted was for you to love me. All I want is a wife and two or three kids. That's all I ever wanted. I've never wanted to be rich. I just want to be able to provide for my wife and kiddies and be happy. Why didn't you love me? Why did you get drunk?'

He is then asked to reverse roles and to discover her story for himself.

Mum: 'I'd been married for fifteen years when I found out your Dad'd had an affair with another woman. Your father did a dirty one on me and that broke me up, knowing he had been sleeping with another woman. I know I had a problem with my health, like I got fat. Your father was a jockey, so I understand how he felt but I didn't think he'd do that. When I put on weight he hardly slept with me. I was only happy when I was drunk.'

Having begun to understand his mother's position and having expressed his own anger, the action moves on and John has the opportunity to have for himself what was deprived of in his early years. 'All I wanted to do when she was drunk or in a bad mood was to go up and hold her, but I was scared.'

Psychodrama in its use of 'surplus reality' offers the emotionally hungry prisoner the experience, perhaps for the first time, of finding out what it would have been like to be held, to be told he was loved, to receive tenderness rather than cruelty.

In the final scene his mother lies dying in hospital and John hears what he thinks and hopes his mother might have said, if he had been there to make his peace before she died. The auxiliary takes John's hand, but he pulls it away: it is too early to accept physical contact, for the only contact he has known is either being abused, or abusing others. After the session John talked of how he looked forward to the day when he could grab hold of 'that woman' (the auxiliary) and hug her.

Mum: 'Hello son, I didn't think you'd come. It's good to see you. I feel bad when I see you because things went wrong. Things were good at first, but they went wrong.' (She reminds him of the better times and tells him she loves him.)

John: 'Yes, they were good.'

The director notices that John is overwhelmed by feelings he cannot express, and he is 'stuck'; she instructs another member of the group to come in as the doctor and tell John that time is running out for his mother. As he does so, the tears begin to run down John's face.

Director (to John): 'Let me ask you: before your Mum dies, can you find it in yourself to forgive her?'

John: 'No.'

Realising it is still too early to repair the damage, the director asks John what he does want to say to her.

John: 'I can understand some of the things you have done. I can understand what my Dad has done. I do care for you but I don't love anyone; but I can understand some of these things.'

The doctor draws a blanket over the mother's body and John tries to leave the room in tears but is restrained from doing so.

Many of these men find it easier to hide tears behind anger, and for most of them the tears in psychodrama are the first they have shed in public for many years. Being held by another prisoner as he cries, John is asked what inscription he would want to put on his mother's gravestone. 'I love and forgive you', he says. He has made his journey, interweaving between past and present, present and past. As the group comes round to share their own experiences with John, he experiences the understanding, support and sense of caring that he did not have as a child.

As a prisoner explained on the BBC Radio Four programme 'Actuality' in 1985:

Prisoners have never had love and care. That's all they are asking for. A bit of that and you will have more success than by beating them and chaining them up. You won't do it that way because all that does is harden them. They've lived with that all their lives; they can handle it. But show them love and care, and see how they can handle it. I've seen guys crack up because they don't know how. I've done it myself. I don't know how to handle love and care, and that's what hurts. That hurts worse than any imprisonment. People come along and say we love you: we haven't had these feelings before.

Practical implications

Naturally there are difficulties in running a psychodrama group in such an environment. To start with, the group is made up of prisoners who have committed very different offences, and there is no-one so intolerant of prisoners as fellow prisoners. The psychodrama and the protagonist depend on the support of the group; this means that introducing psychodrama and building group unity cannot be hurried. If they are, one pays the price later as the work intensifies and the director looks to others for support. Comments from other prisoners like: 'I've no time for sex offenders' or 'You're an animal' or 'I feel intimidated by your violence' do not provide a setting that encourages prisoners to share their feelings about themselves or their offences.

During the early sessions it is important for the director to make sure that everyone, whatever their offence and however well they can articulate their feelings, has space to explore issues that need to be explored, however disturbing these issues are to the others. Using psychodrama warm-ups helps group members begin to share of themselves, and to realise that in order to help each other this group (in contrast to other groups they experience) needs to be supportive, facilitating and encouraging, rather than confronting. If the action is stopped by another prisoner passing judgement on what is happening in the psychodrama space, all can be lost. Many weeks of building up to the stage where a father who had killed his child dares risk looking at his actions or holding the murdered child in his arms, can be lost by a hostile comment; the protagonist is forced back into his world of isolation and self-recrimination, once again unable to speak about the unspeakable.

As well as these initial difficulties, there is the fact that prisoners (particularly those of a violent nature) often fear the emotional side of psychodrama. 'If I lose control, what then?' is a familiar question expressing real fear. Their inability to control their violence brought them into prison: also, acts of violence against each other lead to them being transferred out of Grendon. Experiencing emotions that have not been dealt with before raises anxiety as to whether the whole group – protagonist, director and the other members – can survive the emotions that need to be expressed.

A prisoner, Tony, came to a session and warned the group of the intensity of his anger towards his uncle, who had forced him to eat his faeces before sexually abusing him. The group noticeably withdrew, not knowing whether they, or the director, could contain this anger. No-one wanted to volunteer to play the role of the uncle, fearful for his own safety in the face of such negative transference. At such times the protagonist and the group are in different places. However warmed-up and ready to work the protagonist is, it is inadvisable to go ahead if the group is not warmed up to the protagonist and to the issue and to itself. It is essential to acknowledge the group's need for some form of containment, and its unreadiness to deal with certain issues. We are not dealing here with people who fantasise about aggressive acts: these men have turned fantasy into the 'Actual' (Coln 1990). The director relies heavily on the group to use restraining and containment techniques; often group members will physically restrain the protagonist so that, against this restraint, he can verbalise his emotions. For many, this is a critical way of working. They know how to put these feelings into actions, usually at the expense of others. The task here for some is to find the words that have been overwhelmed by the action. For others, it is important to find the correct resting place for actions as well as words.

It was several weeks before the group felt able to address Tony's work. Together we found creative and psychodramatic ways of making it safe for everyone, including the protagonist, without robbing him of the chance to express the anger he was frightened to show at the age of 12.

More often than not, angry outbursts are followed by tears of regret and remorse for what they have done, and for not receiving what was rightfully theirs as a child. For many of us tears are a natural expression of emotion. For these men, who have been brought up in an environment where to be a man is to adopt an unfeeling macho image and where one is beaten for crying, the psychodrama session may be the first safe and acceptable place to share these feelings. One prisoner serving 17 years for armed robbery, known for his toughness within the system and with a reputation as a mercenary with many names in his 'body book,' wept his first tears as he watched a fellow prisoner work. When he had cried as a child, his father had taken the belt to him or put him in the street to be beaten by bigger boys, to toughen him up.

In such a setting one constantly asks oneself, as director: 'What more do I need to achieve in this session?' One can ruin the impact of a session by attempting too much. It is vital to keep to the contract. To take the prisoner, without further negotiation, beyond what he has asked, or wants, to do is to put it all at risk. One needs to curb one's enthusiasm to achieve more, and to accept that there is a fine balance between encouraging, and recognising when it is enough simply for a prisoner to be present, without participating.

These men have their own vulnerability. Some have tried to take their life, having had time to realise the full extent of their offence. To journey down this path again, to go beyond the despair for what they have done to their own despair is a journey to be taken cautiously; one's professional judgement about how much and at what moment is essential. The prisoner who eventually held his murdered child in his arms could do no more for the first set of sessions than stay in the room while others explored issues and shared experiences and emotions. The next step was for the director to double the feeling he could not yet put into words. The comforting touch of others, the words of encouragement and assurance that he was doing alright, led him to the work that had to be addressed.

Conclusion

In bringing together my own experiences, research and the ideas of Bowlby and other advocates of attachment theory and its clinical application, I have found psychodrama a most effective and efficient way of working within this setting. Psychodrama includes dramatic representation of self, one's behaviour, beliefs and feelings; like other psychotherapies it is based on the knowledge that a person has the ability to be self-correcting when given accurate information about his behaviour. Research undertaken at Grendon shows that psychodrama has an effective role to play in correcting the emotional experiences of prisoners and improving their self-concept (Jefferies 1987).

As the prisoner, Tony, described the process:

> What we are doing here is defusing bombs. What do you think you're gonna get from me if you put me in a cage for eight years and pump me with a stick; what do you think you're gonna get? You're gonna get me worse than when I came in and the same goes for everybody else. It's serious business, this. It quite annoys me actually when people say psychodrama is a lot of cobblers. You should come with me for half an hour and I'll do one on you.
>
> ('Actuality' BBC Radio Four, 1985)

I wish we could defuse more bombs in more prisons. I do not believe that people are born criminals, rapists, murderers or child abusers, although I acknowledge that some of them have pathological problems that manifest themselves in antisocial behaviour. As a society we have to accept responsibility for the way we are with each other. Sadly, we look for panaceas: but however horrendous the crime, simply locking these men up for 23 hours a day without trying to achieve some change in attitudes and behaviour during their imprisonment is to return them to society more hopeless and embittered than when they were sentenced. Instead, psychodrama has shown that it can change attitudes and behaviour; it offers a far more humane and constructive approach to the treatment of those convicted of serious crimes.

References

Bowlby, J. (1979) *Making and Breaking of Affectional Bonds*, London: Tavistock.

Bowlby, J. (1988) *A Secure Base – Clinical Applications of Attachment Theory*, London: Routledge.

Cohen, A. (1955) *Delinquent Boys – the Culture of the Gang*, New York: New York Free Press.

Coln, H. (1990) *The Place of the Actual in Psychotherapy*, London: Associated Press.

Green, R. and Murray, E. (1973) 'Instigation to aggression as a function to self-disclosure and threat to self-esteem', *Journal of Counselling and Clinical Psychology* 40: 440–3.

Henderson, A. (1974) 'Care-eliciting behaviour in man', *Journal of Nervous and Mental Diseases* 159: 172–81.

Hewit, J. (1970) *Social Stratification of Deviant Behaviour*, New York: Random House.
Jefferies, J.I. (1987) 'The effect of psychodrama on the self-concept of prisoners', unpublished M.Sc. thesis, University of Surrey.
Kaplin, H. (1975) *Self Attitudes of Deviant Behaviour*, Pacific Palisades, CA: Goodyear.
Rosenbaum, M. and de Charms, R. (1960) 'Direct and vicarious reduction of hostilities', *Journal of Abstracts and Social Psychology* 66: 54–61.

Further reading

Becker, H. (1963) *Outsiders, Studies in the Sociology of Deviants*, New York: New York Press.
Bois, K. (1972) 'Role playing as behaviour change technique', *Psychotherapy: Theory Research Practices* 9: 185–92.
Charney, M. (1975) 'Psychodrama and self-identity', *Journal of Group Psychotherapy* 28: 118–27.
Cooley, C. (1922) *Human Nature and Social Order*, New York: Scribner.
Fine, L. (1978) 'Psychodrama' in R. Corsini (ed.) *Current Psychotherapies*, Illinois: Peacock.
Goffman, E. (1959) *The Presentation of Self in Everyday Life*, New York: Double Anchor.
Goldstein, J. (1971) 'Investigation of doubling as a technique for involving severely withdrawn patients in group psychotherapy', *Journal of Counselling and Clinical Psychology* 37: 155–65.
Kaplin, H. and Meyorwitz, J. (1970) 'Social and psychological correlates of drug abuse', *Social Science Medicine* 4: 203–25.
McGuire, J. and Priestley, P. (1985) *Offending Behaviour Skills and Strategy of Going Straight*, London: Batsford.
Marshall, W., Christie, M. and Lanthier, R. (1979) 'Social competence, sexual experience and attitudes seen in rapists and paedophiles', a Report to the Solicitor-General, Toronto: Ontario Research Psychiatric Center.
Mead, G. (1968) *Mind, Self and Society*, Chicago: University of Chicago Press.
Rosenthal, S. (1976) 'Effects of psychodrama on self actualisation and perceived locus of control', *Dissertation Abstracts International* 38 (1–B): 378, July 1977.
Toch, H. (1969) 'Violent men enquiry', in *Psychology of Violence*, Chicago: Aldine Press.
Wickland, R. (1978) 'Opinion change and performance facilitation as a result of objective self awareness', *Journal of Experiential Psychology* 1978 7.
Williams, S. (n.d.) 'Personality differences between rapists, paedophiles and normals', Kingston, Ontario: Penitentiary (unpublished).

Chapter thirteen

The drama of the seriously ill patient

Fifteen years' experience of psychodrama and cancer

Anne Ancelin Schützenberger

We are not troubled by events but are troubled by our perception of these events.

(Epictete)

Introduction

Fifteen years ago, after working for 20 years with psychotics, I started to perceive a connection between mental and physical problems and to wonder if psychodrama could also be applied successfully to the very sick and terminally ill. I thus began to work (sometimes in co-operation with those responsible for the medical care and sometimes just adding psychological help to classical medical care) with individuals suffering from cancer.

Aristotle, Plato, Galen, Freud, Jung, Moreno – all recognised man as a whole person. The approach is an ancient one, but for those who only believe in hard science, the link between mind and body has had to be proved. Recently, with the discoveries of the new sciences (psycho-neuro-immunology and psycho-neuro-endocrino-immunology), the medical and scientific community has begun to develop an understanding (on a more scientific basis) of the influence of the mind over the body. Many new neurotransmittors have been discovered that form the link between an individual's frame of mind and his body (in health or illness) (Ader 1981, Solomon and Moos 1964, Solomon 1985, Bahnson 1989). In cancer, as in any illness, we find, when we listen carefully to the patient, a psychosomatic and somatopsychic component to the problem. Because of this unity of mind and body, we have to take both into consideration if we want to help the patient to get well again. We try to provoke a spontaneous remission; to reduce the chance of death; to challenge the prognosis, the 'predictions' of the medical diagnosis (which are based on statistical probability).

In 1986, Bernie Siegel, a well-known American surgeon, wrote a book called *Love, Medicine and Miracle*, describing work surprisingly like my own, which I have been doing for 15 years. Siegel emphasised the theory of Carl and Stephanie Simonton (Simonton *et al.* 1978), that the health of cancer patients could be greatly improved with help, support, hope, physical exercise, relaxation, positive visualisation, mental imagery and psychotherapy; the primary objective being the shift from passive helplessness and hopelessness to active co-operation in regaining hope and health.

Siegel's personal contribution to this approach is his experience as a surgeon in a hospital and his wonderful humour and warmth. My personal contribution to this approach (to be described in this chapter) is the use of psychodrama and the genosociogram (Ancelin Schützenberger 1985).

As a result of a family event that affected me greatly (the death of a cousin from an apparently 'curable' breast cancer in 1974), I did some research that led me to the Simontons' first article on this subject (Simonton and Simonton 1975). I then started to work, on an experimental basis, with volunteer patients who were seeking any help they could find with their terminal cancer.

To everyone's surprise, as well as my own, in many patients, the general metastases disappeared, their health improved, and they lived or survived in good spirits. Some recovered and are (still) living a pleasant life, in good health, 10 to 15 years later.

These improvements could be called 'provoked *spontaneous remissions* of long duration', a situation Bernie Siegel describes as 'teaching your patient to become an *exceptional patient*, with a better quality of life and a longer life expectancy' (Siegel 1986).

The drama of the seriously ill patient

When someone is told that he has a cancer, it understandably has a devastating effect – most people feel 'hopeless and helpless' (Seligman 1975), and they let themselves become passive victims of a so-called fatal illness (cancer is not always fatal, as about 45 per cent of all treated cancer patients survive at least five years after diagnosis). Severe illness goes with depression and passivity, which is a bad clinical sign for recovery.

The first thing to do is to help the patient regain the hope that he or she may recover, and to help him or her to become active again and to fight for his or her life. The patient has to do his or her part of the job in order to help the physicians and surgeons do theirs.

For most patients and their families, some questions are frightening, for example: Why cancer? Why me? Why him/her? Why now? They feel they are the innocent victims of unknown and unfair circumstances, with no chance or ability to fight against the cancer. Many people suffering from a cancer with a 'reasonable prognosis' (i.e. those that according to the statistics may be cured in most cases) lock themselves in and 'let themselves die' – in a way 'fulfilling their own prediction' (Rosenthal and Jacobson 1966; 1968) that cancer is fatal. This is in spite of the fact that cancer is not the primary cause of death in our society (the first being cardiovascular illnesses, including heart attacks).

Table 13.1 Simonton Method: evolution of 152 patients with a diagnosis of 'terminal cancer'

		Attitude of patient					
Reaction of the patient		Non-cooperation. Instructions not followed	Non-cooperation. Instructions rarely followed	Usually followed instructions	Followed instructions and showed some initiative	Total co-operation. Followed instructions implicitly and explicitly, believes firmly in improvement	Total
Net remission of symptoms and spectacular improvement	Excellent	0	0	0	11	9	20
Improvement in symptoms and in state of health	Good	0	2	34	31	0	67
Slight improvement in symptoms	Average	0	14	29	0	0	43
No improvement in symptoms	Poor	2	17	3	0	0	22
	Total	2	33	66	42	9	152

Source: Simonton and Simonton (1975) in Ancelin Schutzenberger (1985)

The first step, then (in addition to good medical treatment and care), is to help such patients to look at life–death issues, at their expectations (Rosenthal and Jacobson 1966; 1968) and to reject the idea that cancer means death. It is important to stop them predicting and eventually provoking their own death, to help them to accept treatment more readily and to help them survive cancer. In other words, to give patients hope, care, support, love.

In this chapter we present a powerful adjunctive method (derived from the work of the Simontons) to help the patient to live with serious illness and treatment, and to 'fight for his life' (LeShan 1977) – to 'get well again' (as Carl and Stephanie Simonton put it), or to become (in Bernie Siegel's words) an 'exceptional patient'.

One of the objectives of this method is to help the patient to live, to live fully and in as good health as possible, to help him or her to face whatever may happen. In some patients it may be possible to stop the evolution of the illness and even to promote recovery, stopping fatal outcome (see Simonton's statistics with 152 terminal patients (Simonton and Simonton, in Ancelin Schützenberger 1985)) (see Table 13.1).

We have been using this method for about 15 years, extending it from cancer patients to various other very ill people, including those with AIDS. It is, of course, a method to be added to the usual medical treatment ordered by the physicians. The method can be summarised as follows:

1. Find a 'cause' for the present illness (in an interview or by giving a 'life events and stress questionnaire'); this cause is usually related to dramatic or difficult life events with overdose of stress (Holmes and Rahe 1967; Table 13.2) or to an 'anniversary syndrome' (Hilgard 1955).
2. Help the patient to overcome stress by regular relaxation exercises and positive visualisation techniques.
3. 'Tame' the medical treatment by psychodrama, group psychotherapy and positive visualisation of issues such as the surgical operation, chemotherapy, radiotherapy; to consider various possible outcomes; good results of treatment, remaining as it is or total recovery, and eventually talking about anxiety and the fear (or fact) of death or impairment.
4. Advise the patient to do some physical excercise, at least twice a week.
5. Help the patient overcome resentment.
6. Find the 'secondary benefits' of illness (and even death), and via visualisation and psychodrama, find a way to solve life problems in a way other than by death or near death.
7. Help the patient to create a support group and build an 'extended family' to help him or her to fight against illness and stress, to regain good humour and to find *joie de vivre*.
8. Make everyday life as pleasant as possible: start by making a list of at least 25 pleasant things to do (some gratis, some inexpensive, some

eventually very expensive – it is not forbidden to dream!). See that some of these things can be done now (even in hospital), some soon and some later on. The list is written down, visualised or enacted in psychodramatic vignettes (a short role play or psychodrama). This will help the patient to open up his blocked future, regain some hope and live his present situation differently, and more pleasantly.

9. Find out the patient's 'predictions' for the outcome of his or her illness, and eventually help him or her to change the bad or deadly ones, i.e. 'reprogramming' his or her life script. Make the patient draw the illness and the fight against it.

10. Very often, death, accident and illness are linked with past personal and family events, over three or more generations. Invisible 'family loyalties' and 'anniversary syndromes' join the patient to their family history. A complete family tree, with 'sociometric ties' and important life events demonstrates these links. This is the 'genosociogram'.

The patient with cancer

Why illness now?

In order to try to answer the dramatic questions: Why cancer? Why me? Why now? many of us use the 'Life events questionnaire' of Holmes and Rahe (1967) to link illness with excess stress. Of course, we know that many research studies have failed to prove the direct link between stress and cancer – even if, clinically speaking, the link is often obvious. It is not so much stress as the reaction to stress that is important. The scientific evidence for this lies in the recently discovered neurotransmittors in the nervous and immune system and on the number and quality of the white cells (the body's natural killer cells), which vary in patients depending on their frame of mind (Ader 1981; Solomon 1964 in *Advances*; Solomon 1989; Bahnson 1975 in *Advances*; Bahnson 1989; and collectively in *Advances* 1984, 1985 and 1989).

For most people, who do not believe in psychology, the link between illness and difficult life events (like the death of a spouse or a child, loss of work or expected promotion, loss of a love object) makes good common sense. People understand that this kind of loss and stress can lessen their strength and weaken their immune system, thus leading to illness.

Once the patient feels that his or her illness is linked to stress and loss, it helps him or her to overcome the destructive feelings of hopelessness and helplessness and to hope to be able to reverse the situation, cope with it and thus to get better.

Usually, we ask the patient about life events that have occurred some 6 to 18 months before the discovery of the cancer (although we know that many cancers take years to appear, nevertheless in some cases, after some dramatic life events, cancer can appear suddenly) (see Table 13.2). In any case, it makes sense to the patient.

Anne Ancelin Schützenberger

Table 13.2 Social readjustment rating scale

Life events in the past 12 months	Value	Personal value
Death of spouse	100	
Divorce	73	
Marital separation	65	
Jail term	63	
Death of close family member	63	
Personal injury or illness	53	
Marriage	50	
Fired from work	47	
Marital reconciliation	45	
Retirement	45	
Change in family member's health	44	
Pregnancy	40	
Sex difficulties	39	
Addition to family	39	
Business readjustment	39	
Change in financial status	38	
Death of close friend	37	
Change to different line of work	36	
Change in number of marital arguments	36	
Mortgage or loan over $10,000	31	
Foreclosure of mortgage or loan	30	
Aggression	30	
Long-term sickness of a family member	30	
Drug addiction or AIDS in the family	30	
Change in work responsibilities	29	
Son or daughter leaving home	29	
Trouble with in-laws	29	
Outstanding personal achievement	28	
Spouse begins or stops work	26	
Starting or finishing school	26	
Change in living conditions	25	
Revision of personal habits	24	
Trouble with boss	23	
Change in work hours, conditions	20	
Change in residence	20	
Change in schools	20	
Change in recreational habits	19	
Change in church activities	19	
Change in social activities	18	
Mortgage or loan under $10,000	17	
Change in sleeping habits	16	

Table 13.2 Social readjustment rating scale cont.

Change in number of family gatherings	15	
Change in eating habits	15	
Vacation	13	
Christmas season	12	
Minor violation of the law	11	
Personal, recent, other life events	??	
Personal total		

Source: Adapted from Holmes and Rahe (1967)
Note: This scale includes stressful events such as death of a spouse, divorce, loss of a job and other painful experiences. It also includes events such as marriage, pregnancy, or outstanding personal achievement, which are generally thought of as being happy experiences. These, too, are causes of stress. One can die of a happy as well as of an unhappy announcement. While stress may predispose to illness (for 49 per cent of those having a score of more than 300 in 12 months), the significant factor is how people evaluate it personally and how each person copes with it.

Usually, when asked what happened to him or her recently, in the last year, the patient him/herself discovers the difficult events: the death of a child, burglary, financial problems, a long-hoped-for promotion that he or she did not get, the loss of a love object. He or she can feel and remember how much such events have affected and depressed him or her and can recognise their link with the cancer or other illness.

The patient then starts to work on his or her feelings and reactions (over-reactions). These are worked through in psychotherapy or psychodrama.

According to Lawrence LeShan (1977) the situation is much worse if the loss of a love object in adulthood is a repetition of another childhood loss, especially a loss that occurred when he or she was not allowed to cry and mourn (such as the loss of a beloved granny or nanny or home-help, a divorcing father, a beloved dog or other mother–father substitutes). Psychodrama helps a lot, by bringing hidden pain out into the open, by allowing tears and the mourning of losses or by giving a 'surplus reality'.

To find meaning in one's life is very important (Franckel 1959). Then once the patient has found out why he or she has a cancer and linked 'as a matter of course' his/her illness to life events, it is possible to help him or her to decide whether these events have brought so much sadness, anger, sorrow, resentment or discouragement that he or she no longer wants to live (i.e. wants to let him/herself die) – or whether he or she chooses to reverse the course of action and now wishes to fight for his or her life and try to get well again.* The patient will then manage to get over these events, and adopt a different attitude towards life. For example,

---

* Cancer is a multifactorial illness, and thus has at the same time many 'causes'. One of them may be linked with feelings about life events; this is the only one on which the patient and psychotherapist can work.

some people prefer to die (of cancer) than to divorce, or lose an inheritance to a brother, or survive a child. Confronted with near death, however, they may prefer to give up death and live (although possibly a somewhat different life).

Very often, this recovery is linked with new choices of life style or to a faith, or to a passion (for a person, a sport, an art, a challenge). The first battle is won.

Overcoming stress: relaxation

The first objective of this approach to illness is to get the patient out of hopelessness and helplessness by identifying the stressful life event(s) that made life so difficult or even impossible for the patient. The next important objective is to give the patient all the necessary resources to fight stress; through support, relaxation, positive visualisation and physical exercise, and by being as happy and well as possible at all times.

The patient needs some very simple relaxation exercises, easy to practise by him/herself at any time, anywhere, and taking no more than 10 to 15 minutes. Therefore, we use simple relaxation techniques. It is best to practise them 3 to 5 times a day – every 3 hours, say – for a maximum of 15 to 20 minutes; for example, when waking up, in the middle of the morning, after lunch, in the middle of the afternoon and before going to bed – in fact, every day. If possible, relaxation exercises once a day with the whole family are also desirable; they also need to relax.

We use a very simple approach, derived from the Jacobson method (Jacobson 1938), tensing then relaxing muscle by muscle, and focusing on the breathing, something that nearly any patient can practise alone after half an hour of training. It is usually easy to find people able to teach such methods. Relaxation tapes, or various relaxation books may also be of use.

Visualisation of the body and the cancer

Once the patient is relaxed (it takes some 8 to 11 minutes), he or she is asked to visualise in his or her mind the work of his or her own white blood cells, immune system and treatment. First, he or she has to see him/herself and body and visualise the red blood cells going everywhere, to feed the body. Then he or she visualises the white blood cells performing a surveying task: detecting, attacking, destroying or taking away anything harmful to the body, like microbes, viruses, malignant cells, even cancer secondaries. This can be done either very realistically (with the help of medical books or plates), or with symbols, by using mental images, or even cartoon characters. Some people will visualise and draw knights fighting dragons, others will see huge vacuum cleaners or powerful waterfalls.

This could be acted out later on in psychodramatic vignettes: a short psychodrama of the victorious fight . . . the white blood cells running after the cancer cells and killing them, or taking them gently by the arm to the outside door. The patient can then be encouraged to talk to his or her own white cells to encourage them to fight harder and harder. Again, psychodramatic short vignettes are very powerful and helpful.

The patient then visualises his or her treatment, sometimes the operation, or chemotherapy, or radiotherapy or whatever, and visualises the beneficial effect of it, of how it will cure him or her and how he or she will get well again. The patient then visualises him/herself in good health again, happy and in a good frame of mind. Then, still relaxed and in alpha waves, he or she has to repeat the Coué motto (famous Dr Coué's, repetitive injunction to oneself): 'Every day, in every way, I am getting better and better'.

Illustrating the fight against illness

The patient is asked to draw the image of his or her illness. These drawings are analysed, and if the illness is seen as being more powerful than the defences, at first it is talked about and anxiety or ambivalence about death analysed, then the patient is encouraged to see the white blood cells as strong, powerful, dynamic and aggressive and to see the malignant cells as poor and weak, defeated by the white cells. One effective approach is to have the patient make a weekly drawing of the white cells and the immune system, and of the action of the body and the treatment against the illness. We analyse these drawings, 'understanding their deep meaning' and the ambivalence to recovery. We then comment on the changes and improvements. The therapist can see whether the patient is an optimist or a pessimist, and whether he or she is really fighting (or not) the illness. Often, the drawings reveal much hidden despair under a smiling surface, and even a wish to die. The patient is often struck by his work. It is discussed and worked through in psychotherapy and eventually in psychodrama.

Psychodrama and visualisation of treatment and its results

Most people are more afraid of pain, the loss of a part of the body, an operation or treatment than of death. Therefore, we use psychodrama to prepare them – a projection into the future and a taming of the unknown, using a full session rather than a vignette. We often act out the anticipated operation as realistically as possible: the patients usually ask the surgeon, the nurses and former patients for many details in order to prepare themselves for the operation.

We talk with the patient, who is often afraid of the operation, afraid of an accident like a forgotten instrument in the tummy, an unforeseen death on the operating table or pain and complications afterwards. We perform a psychodrama with three possible outcomes: an accident during the operation, a death on the table, a successful operation with a painless recovery. The patient chooses the one he or she wants to begin with. Very often, we face all three possible outcomes in a very powerful psychodrama.

Most of the time, the patient is 'sure' he or she will die on the operating table and starts with this psychodrama. When the patient is 'dead', we ask if he or she is sure he or she wants to remain dead; (such a patient very often wants to be 'dead' and to be finished with hospitals, problems and illness – sometimes as a revenge on his family or colleagues) and to see the love and sorrow expressed over his or her dead body. If the patient does not remain 'dead', the outcome is then good. Then, we act out, in psychodrama, the death, the grief of the family, and the burial. Once 'dead and buried', the patient often opts for a new psychodrama with a different outcome: recovery and good health.

Thus, having expressed the hidden fears and worst anxieties, the patient is more free to face the operation in a good and relaxed frame of mind – which of course is a real help to the surgeon and the operating team. The results of the treatment are, therefore, better. The same method can be applied to chemotherapy or radiotherapy.

Lina

One patient (let us call her Lina) was a graduate student in our University, who had a sarcoma of the right arm, with a bad (terminal) prognosis. She was 25 years old and unmarried. Her father was an officer in the French army, very strict and old-fashioned and disapproved of her way of life; he would have liked her to have been either a bright son, or a quietly married daughter staying at home, with children. At Paris's leading cancer clinic, he was told that his daughter had only two to three months left to live, and this only if her arm was amputated. He was even offered euthanasia to help her out, as terrible and unbearable pain was shortly foreseen. Fortunately, he told his daughter. Lina wanted to study and work, and was not interested in living a short time without her arm. So, she spoke with her professor and dean, who sent her to me; she came to us to fight for her life and use our approach. She survived and got better, but not without ups and downs: lung metastasis (which disappeared) and an arm nearly broken a year later because of the cancer in the bone. She found a surgeon who agreed to try and keep her arm, with only a minor operation, to consolidate her shoulder with a piece of hip bone (her arm having been damaged by a previous operation and radiotherapy). As she put it: 'I am sure to die' from the hip operation. Later, in psychodrama, she linked this fear to the fact that her grandmother had died from an accident involving a broken hip.

We first went into her family history, and she found out that her grandmother had had two accidents, she had *not* died from the hip accident. She was then able to accept the operation, although still extremely afraid of it.

We performed a psychodrama of the operation. During a role reversal, she played the surgeon, and the patient (Lina) 'died' on the operating table. Once she was 'dead', her 'family' came and cried and she was 'buried'. Again, during a role reversal, she acted the role of the parson and said:

'Poor Lina, such a nice girl, what a pity she died so young, she never had a chance to have a child of her own, a nice home of her own, she could not become a teacher and have a life as she had wanted it.'

After that, Lina asked whether she could change her mind and perform another psychodrama with a different outcome: this time a successful operation and recovery.

Then she was operated on in reality; it was a difficult operation, something the surgeon was attempting for the first time: taking a piece of her hip bone to rebuild and consolidate her fragile upper arm. At that time, some 15 years ago, there were no cases of recovery from sarcoma unless the whole arm had been amputated. The real operation was successful, with a quick recovery. Within a few months she managed to do and have what she had said in the psychodrama would be impossible.

She is now – 15 years later – well and in good health, and to everyone's surprise – as her recovery was not expected – with both her arms. She has a profession she likes, a flat overlooking the sea, a companion and a lovely, strong, healthy little boy (called Angelo). In a way, the psychodrama of her death and burial made her live as she had dreamed.

That psychodrama was so vivid, what she described she wanted from her life so clear, and what was missing in her present life (a child, a house, a job) so obvious – that she turned her prediction of death into a prediction of life and success. The projection into the future, or 'surplus reality' (Moreno 1953), became reality for her. She was the first person (at least in France and probably in the world) to have recovered from a sarcoma of the arm without the arm being totally removed.

As Robert Rosenthal said (Rosenthal and Jacobson 1968), there is often an 'automatic realisation of predictions'. A kind of 'Pygmalion effect' was working for Lina. This was increased by the visualisation being made more powerful through psychodramatic preparation for the treatment. It was really amazing to see Lina going to the operating theatre with shining eyes, sure that she would wake up after the operation (alive and well) and recover and live a happy new life of her own choice.

Meeting the future

When someone is seriously ill, there is a need to prepare for the immediate future: many arrangements have to be made because the patient might be admitted to hospital, is in need of practical help and so on. All the life situations of the patient may be acted out in psychodramas, and many small vignettes enacted to prepare the patient for the new and unexpected situations he or she is going to meet: facing the doctor, going to hospital, receiving treatment (chemotherapy, radio-therapy, operation), recovery, leaving hospital, shopping for new clothes that would be nice to wear and which would, in some case, help to hide the loss of a breast or a limb.

If the operation might deprive the patient of a part of his or her body (a breast, a leg, an arm), it is often useful to help the patient to say farewell to the part of the body that will be cut away – 'Goodbye and thank you' – to mourn it, and then to see him/herself with a repaired body, cheerful and in good form. Vignettes or psychodramas activate the process of mourning, parting and preparation for new roles and ways of handling the body.

Margaret

Margaret, who had breast cancer, was a nice woman in her early forties, an accountant, divorced, with a child. She was very much afraid she might lose her boyfriend if she was left with only one breast. She was afraid she might become ugly after the operation, and lose her womanhood.

We discussed her body in the group, and she said that her breasts were very small, like a boy's (she described them as 'like eggs, sunny side up'), but that she nevertheless needed them both. She did not believe that, after the operation, she could have her breasts reconstructed and indeed, could, if she wanted to, have any kind of breasts together with a normal feminine lifestyle. So, in a psychodrama, we created a parade of well-known, well-endowed film stars: Gina Lollobrigida, Rita Hayworth, Brigitte Bardot, Sophia Loren, Liz Taylor, and so on.

After much laughter and pleasure, Margaret chose one of the less well-endowed movie stars, and she saw herself with these sorts of breasts, now knowing and 'seeing' that her breast would be reconstructed a few months after the operation. She even decided to have her second breast operated on in order to make it a little bigger. So she went to the operating theatre with hope, looking forward to being more beautiful in the future, and being sure that everything would be fine. She woke up in the recovery room with no pain at all, to the surprise of everyone in the ward, and made a very rapid recovery. She now has the kind of nice breasts she had always dreamed of. She bought (before the operation, in psychodrama) and later on in real life, bathing suits and low-cut dresses that enhanced her body, and she has kept her boyfriend. Margaret is now (six years later) a mother, making a new life for herself, in good health, working normally and happy.

The anniversary syndrome and the genosociogram

There is often a link between stressful life events and illness; the Simontons' method is based on overcoming stress, through relaxation, positive thinking and psychotherapy. We have found, however, that, in many cases, there are no obvious major stressful life events before the onset of illness. How might this be explained? We have discovered that, very often, there is a repetition of a family situation or difficulties, a kind of 'anniversary syndrome'. Very often, people develop cancer exactly at the same time of life and at the *same age* that a very close person in their family got it or died of it.

We had a patient – Katherine – who developed cancer at the age of 36, exactly the same age as her mother was when she developed and died from cancer many years previously. Let us take the further example of Mary's family. Her grandfather died at the age of 76 on 12 May 1976, her mother (the eldest daughter) died of cancer on 12 May 1982; three years later her uncle died in a car accident (which may have been suicide) also on 12 May and a year after that her grandmother, Mary, 'let herself die' on the anniversary of her husband's death, 12 May.

Simone de Beauvoir died ('let herself die') during the night of 15–16 April 1986, exactly six years after the death of her partner, Jean-Paul Sartre, who died on 15 April 1980.

These are typical examples of the anniversary syndrome, a difficult life event (terminal cancer, a car or plane crash) happening on the *same date* or at the same age as somebody else from the immediate or extended family, as if the heart no longer has the will to live and 'lets go'. Additionally, there is often a link across generations: the patient develops terminal cancer at the same age his grandfather died, and he has a child of the same age as his father was when the grandfather died (see genosociogram in Figure 13.1). In other words, the same family structure appears.

Genosociogram

Having discovered many such anniverary syndromes in terminal patients, we have developed the genosociogram to explore these invisible repetitions. The term 'genosociogram' comes from the word 'genealogy' – the family tree – and the sociometric relationship between people. A genosociogram is more complete than the genograms used in family therapy. There is a link with sociometry. The family therapist Nathan Ackerman used to visit Moreno and then started to use genograms and 'family sculptures'.

A genosociogram is a classical family tree completed with important life events and using the concepts of Morenian sociometry (Moreno 1953; Ancelin Schützenberger 1971; 1985). It shows (over three to five generations) births (including miscarriages and stillborn children), marriages, deaths (and their causes), important illnesses, accidents, alliances and ruptures, levels of education, professions, places of residence (and moves), important life events, losses of love objects, what is known and unknown of some lost branches and people who have moved far away from the family. Sociometric relations, social atom, and psychological 'family account books' (Boszormenyi-Nagy and Spark 1975) with their 'debits and credits' and resentments are also included.

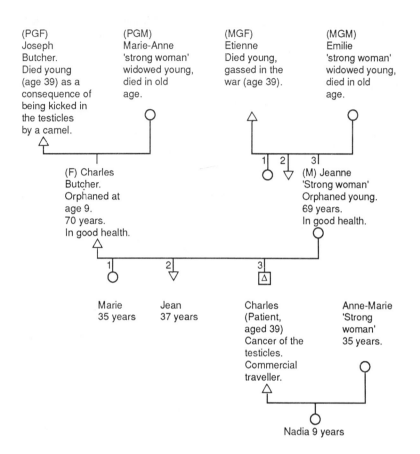

(PGF)
Joseph
Butcher.
Died young
(age 39) as a
consequence of
being kicked in
the testicles
by a camel.

(PGM)
Marie-Anne
'strong woman'
widowed young,
died in old
age.

(MGF)
Etienne
Died young,
gassed in the
war (age 39).

(MGM)
Emilie
'strong woman'
widowed young,
died in old
age.

(F) Charles
Butcher.
Orphaned at
age 9.
70 years.
In good health.

1   2   3

(M) Jeanne
'Strong woman'
Orphaned young.
69 years.
In good health.

1   2   3

Marie
35 years

Jean
37 years

Charles
(Patient,
aged 39)
Cancer of the
testicles.
Commercial
traveller.

Anne-Marie
'Strong
woman'
35 years.

Nadia 9 years

Figure 13.1 Invisible family loyalties – genosociogram of Charles

Source: (Clinical case from *Vouloir Guérir*, Ancelin Schützenberger (1985)
Note: It could be said that Charles's illness, risk of death, his transgenerational links and his family loyalty were all inherited: disease affected the testicles, just as in his paternal grandfather's case, and then affected the lungs, like his maternal grandfather, who was gassed, and at the same age (39 years). He agreed to be operated on, but refused all other treatments (chemotherapy, radiotherapy). It is as if, as the son and grandson of butchers, he only believed in the power of the knife. All the women in the family are said to be strong women; both grandmothers were widowed at an early age. In addition, his father lost his own father at the age of 9, and his daughter risks being orphaned at the age of 9, as he considers himself already lost, and his wife also risks being widowed young. There is a kind of 'script' or repetitive scenario of death at age 39 for the father, with a child aged 9.
It is also possible to comment on Joseph (PGF), struck down in his prime, and on the repetition of the wives' names (Marie-Anne and Anne). On pointing out all this to him, he can attempt to 'reframe' and change his 'script' for losing life (an early life) into a script for gaining life: it is possible to love your grandfather without dying like him, at the same age.
Key: △ Son; ○ Daughter; (F) Father; (M) Mother; (PGF) paternal grandfather; (PGM) paternal grandmother; (MGF) maternal grandfather; (MGM) maternal grandmother; △ Sick subject, eldest son, third child.

The genosociogram (Figure 13.1) helps every person understand his/her life and 'life script', his or her professional and personal choices, taking into account family heredity and heritage (conscious or unconscious) over several generations. It is a way to show clearly some of the unconscious trends and repetitions of the nuclear and extended family, and discover its various roles, dynamic myths and legends, hidden family secrets and repetitions (choice of spouse(s) or of illness and death, of profession, of family style, ways of looking at life).

We use a genosociogram in individual and group psychotherapy (with psychotics as well as with cancer patients), in family therapy, and also in training groups, and training students of psychology, medicine, nursing and post-graduate training of professionals.

This work is undertaken as follows: the patient draws his genosociogram from memory and eventually does research about facts only afterwards, if needed. What is not known, or is forgotten, might be as important as what is known (i.e. the facts of a secret or a loss of memory).

With cancer patients and other very ill patients, we usually take notes during the first interview of the 'case history' in the form of a genosociogram and look at it together; very often it becomes obvious to the patient from which event, repetition or anniversary syndrome his or her illness or his or her feeling ill at ease springs; the similarity – the repetition – of accidents, illnesses, names, ages, dates, links between birth and death, strikes the patient. Unconscious identifications become obvious. The red thread that runs in the family becomes apparent and thus, the link with illness.

When working with his or her genosociogram, on seeing the repetitions over many generations, the patient often has a glimpse of unsaid or hidden truths, of family secrets and invisible 'ghosts'. The French-Hungarian psychoanalyst, Nicolas Abraham, makes the hypothesis that in some difficult instances, it is as if a ghost (of father or grandfather) was hidden in a body 'crypt' within two or three generations, hunting and speaking for the hidden or unfair, until he is heard (Abraham with Torok 1970). The patient himself discovers 'invisible family loyalties' or links between illness or sickness and family deaths. He sees multigenerational repetitions of good or bad health and of happy or pathological ways of life. It helps the patient to see clearly what was going on in his or her family and in him/herself; it helps the patient to reverse unhealthy or dreadful death trends and frees him or her from these repetitions.

Life following death – the replacement child

Very often in a family, there is a birth just after a death. This is a different kind of anniversary syndrome, as if life were springing up again after an important death. (There are many more births after a war than in normal times.) Sometimes the child born after a death of a sibling is a 'replacement child', and his or her life can be difficult if the mother has not mourned and said goodbye to her dear one.

Vincent Van Gogh was born one year after the death of his older brother, Vincent, and was given the same first name. It was forbidden in the Van Gogh family to speak about the death of the first Vincent. As we know, the second Vincent had a difficult life, was unable to marry and was often ill and locked away in mental homes. When his brother, Theo, married and had a son, he gave the name of Vincent to his new baby. A few months later, Theo wrote a letter to his brother Vincent, who was in a mental institution in Arles, France, saying: 'I hope that this Vincent will be happy and able to live his life the way he wants to'. When he received this letter, Vincent killed himself, as if it was impossible for him that there might be two Vincent Van Goghs living and happy at the same time. Theo died soon after he was informed about the suicide of his brother.

In the same way, Salvador Dali always knew who Salvador Dali was: he (Salvador) was his elder brother in the cemetery, after whom he was named, and who died before his birth. He used to visit his brother's grave every week with his mother. He explained that he started to play the fool and become eccentric in order to create a distance and not be confused with the sweet dear boy who was under the earth.

Dali has painted the famous *Angelus* of Millet 46 times – a painting representing two peasants praying over a basket of potatoes in a field. When recently, Millet's painting was X-rayed, it was discovered that a child's coffin had been painted earlier and then cover over by the potato basket. In a private letter, Millet said that a friend of his asked him to cover up the coffin with the potato basket – a pentimento. When Dali learned this, he said that he had always felt that this painting was related to a child's death.

A child born after a family death is not always a replacement child and does not always have a tragic history; it depends on whether the mother has finished mourning the death, or whether she is still in sorrow, in depression, missing her dear, dead child and seeing the dead child when she looks at her new baby. The French psychoanalyst, André Green (1975), speaks of the 'dead mother' to describe the mother who is so deep in sorrow after a death that she is dead to the world, nearly dead herself, in deep depression or psychosis, and how much this affects the new child that she holds in her arms. Very often, the child of this 'dead mother' will have a difficult life, suicidal tendencies or suffer from schizophrenia or other kinds of problems.

Very often, when a patient discovers that his mother was a dead mother, still mourning when he or she was born, it helps to understand and overcome the feeling of being dead inside, unwanted, not having a place of his or her own to live. Often, it is through a genosociogram that this can be discovered, and then worked through in psychodrama.

The genoscoiogram helps to discover and understand the 'invisible family loyalties', and the identification of the patient with a dead or difficult member of his family. It helps the patient to undo these ties and remove him/herself from the situation.

Other factors to improve health

Overcoming resentment

To overcome resentment is not to forgive those who have hurt you, it is just to overcome the resentment, to stop keeping it in the oven, heating and reheating it. It is most unhealthy to keep resentment with you all the time and to brood upon it. It is much better to overcome it and to be able to put your energy into something positive for yourself and not go about hating people who have hurt you, remembering the bad and the unfair, feeling sorry for yourself or being eaten up inside. Good memories, good feelings and happiness uplift the body. One of the simplest ways to overcome resentment is to wish good to those who have hurt you (see Simonton method). Often it is not so simple and needs psychotherapy, psychodrama, group analysis. Death scenes, killing production, explanations with role reversal are often enacted.

Physical exercise

It is very important for the patient to do some physical exercise regularly, if possible, one hour twice a week. Any kind of physical exercise or sport will do, according to the physical capabilities of the patient. If this is not possible, mental imagery of walking, running, swimming can be used, or even moving a hand or arm in bed.

Making life as pleasant as possible – enjoying the present

Life is usually not very pleasant when one is ill, because of pain, sorrow, anxiety and difficult or unpleasant treatments. Therefore, it is very important to be able to do some pleasant things every day, even little things, and to be able to look forward to these pleasant things when waking up or going to sleep. There is a pleasure in anticipating pleasure, and happiness reduces pain and contributes to good health.

The patient is asked to make a list of 25 things he would like to do now (at home or in hospital), and later (some gratis or not very costly, some regardless of the impossibility), for example:

- drinking a cup of coffee or tea;
- buying or receiving flowers;
- listening to music;
- looking at a cloud in the sky, or at the sunshine;
- feeding a bird, etc.;
- receiving a visit from a friend;

and to list things that could be done later, for example:

- going on a trip;

- going to the theatre;
- learning to play the piano;
- learning how to make a tapestry;
- spending the weekend with friends, etc.;
- finishing building a house;
- marrying off one's son or granddaughter.

Plans can also be made for the future. Some can look extravagant, like going round the world or climbing a tall mountain; others can be more mundane. Experiences proves that, when somebody wants something very much, he or she usually manages to get it, and this determination can help improve his or her health. (Recent research on psycho-neuro-immunology shows the impact, via neurotransmitters, on white blood cells.)

Carl and Stephanie Simonton, in their book *Getting Well Again* (Simonton *et al.* 1978), give the example of a woman with terminal cancer, with only three weeks to live. When asked about her last wish – what she wanted to do with her remaining time – she said she wanted very much to take a trip around the world, but never had the money to do it. Simonton suggested in discussion that she might use her last weeks to do what she wanted to do. She realised that if she could use her savings and sold everything she had, including her furniture, possessions and car, she could buy an around-the-world ticket and fulfil her wish. Simonton encouraged her and asked her to send a postcard from every place she visited.

The postcards started to arrive, and went on arriving even after the deadline, because she did not die. When she came back from her tour, her cancer had gone, there were no metastases. Though she had no flat, no job, no home, she was in good health, very happy and able to start a new career and a new life.

Preparing children for operation

Children awaiting surgery present a very special problem in our hospitals; they are afraid of the unknown, they are alone (i.e. without their mothers), sometimes the operation has to be delayed, and they wait on the stretcher or bed, often passing down a long corridor on the way to the operating theatre, which is dark, narrow, badly lit, often underground – and depressing. The child is not allowed to take his teddy bear or favourite toy into the sterile theatre, and, of course, his parents are anxious.

In a French state hospital, with the agreement of the head surgeon, we developed a programme with the nurses who worked with us, using our version of the Simonton method, together with role play.

At the first out-patient consultation, the child is invited to bring his teddy bear or doll; the nurse (after a few hours of training in role playing) enacts a drama with the child. She listens to the chest of the teddy bear and explains that the teddy is ill and needs to be taken care of. Then the child is given the stethoscope and is asked to listen to the heartbeat of the nurse, and then of the teddy. In case of emergency, a doll could be made with a towel or paper and pen.

We have asked the hospital laundry to set aside the old and torn surgical garments; these were recut in various children's sizes, so that the children could play doctor in real operating clothes. The chief surgeon even agreed to have pictures of himself taken, with and without his mask and cap, and these were hung on the wall in the children's ward. The hospital also agreed to buy toy models of hospital rooms and theatres, and a few old stethoscopes were given for the children to play with.

When the child enters hospital before his operation, with his teddy bear, the nurse makes a diagnosis of the teddy bear's illness and asks the child to help her to treat the bear. The teddy is given an injection and is then operated on by the child and the nurse, bandaged and put to bed. The child is encouraged to play with the surgery toys and clothes and is allowed to give injections and pills to his teddy, and bandage it.

After the successful operation on the teddy, the child is, through role reversal, sucessfully 'operated on' by the nurse, then the nurse is 'operated on' by the child. Vignettes of the operation are enacted to enable the child to express his anxiety and fears. Some special situations can be 'worked through' like teaching the child to 'say goodbye' to an arm or a leg, or helping the teddy to walk with a foot missing. The hospital also bought some pairs of teddies and furry animals, one for the ward for the child to play with, to be exchanged with the other, sterile one at the entrance to the operating theatre. The City Council also paid to have paintings done on the ceiling of the underground corridor on the way to the operating theatre of successful operations on teddy bears, Snoopy dogs and Mickey Mouse characters, so that the child, when lying on the stretcher, could look at the ceiling and see interesting and comforting interactions, and successful post-operative recoveries.

This programme has now been in operation routinely for more than two years. The anaesthetists were pleasantly surprised to discover that the children who had been thus prepared needed only 40 to 60 per cent of the usual dose of anaesthesia, and that they were relaxed and happy.

Conclusion

About 2,000 years ago, Galen noticed that happy women recovered much better and more quickly from cancer than unhappy ones.

An Oxford physician recently discovered that what is much more important for the outcome is not the diagnosis or the prognosis of an illness, but the way the patient reacts to being told about the illness. It is not so much the amount of stress or the seriousness of the sickness that matters, but the manner in which the patient looks at it. Half of a bottle of wine is seen as nearly empty by the pessimist, and nearly full by the optimist.

This skill can be encouraged in patients who can be taught this method of coping with stress through using relaxation, visualisation and psychotherapy (role play and psychodrama). It can easily be learned by patients and their families, by doctors and nurses, psychologists, psychotherapists and so on. Patients can be helped to feel better, and the terminally ill to *live* longer with a much improved quality of life. Sometimes even complete recovery is possible; some patients from the early years of this work, fifteen years ago, are still well.

> Do remember to forget
> Anger, worry and regret
> Love while you've got love to give
> Live while you've got life to live
> (Pet Hien)

Hope and tender loving care change life.

References

Abraham, N. with Torok, M. (1970) *L'Ecorce et le noyau*, Paris: Aubier Flammarion.
Ader, R. (1981) (ed.) *Psycho-neuro-immunology*, New York: Academic Press.
Advances (1984 and following) (Journal of the Institute for the Advancement of Health), vols I (1984) to VII, New York NY 10022.
Ancelin Schützenberger, A. (1971) *La Sociometrie*, Paris: Editions Universitaires.
Ancelin Schüzenberger, A. (1985) 2nd edn revised, completed 1987, *Vouloir Guérir*, Toulouse: Eres, Paris: La Meridienne.
Bahnson C.B. (1989) Discussion in round table on stress, cancer, AIDS, and psychoneurimmunology, Tenth International Congress of Group Psychotherapy, Amsterdam.
Boszormenyi-Nagi, I. and Spark, G. (1975) *Invisible Loyalties*, New York: Harper & Row.
Franckel, V. (1959) *Man's Search for Meaning*, New York: Pocket Books.
Green, A. (1975) 'La Mere Morte', in *Narcissisme de vie. Narcissisme de Mort*, Paris: Editions de Minuit.
Hilgard, J. (1955) *The Anniversary Syndrome*, New York.
Holmes, T. and Rahe, R. (1967) 'The social readjustment rating scale', *Journal of Psychosomatic Medicine* (11) (republished in the *New York Times*, 10 June 1973).
Jacobson, E. (1938) *Progressive Relaxation*, Chicago: Chicago University Press.
LeShan, L. (1977) *You Can Fight for Your Life*, New York: Evans, (Fr. tr. *Vous pouvez lutter pour votre vie, les facteurs psychiques dans l'origine du cancer*, Paris: Laffont.)
Moreno, J.L. (1953) *Who Shall Survive?*, New York: Beacon House.
Rosenthal, R. and Jacobson, L. (1966) *Experimental Effect in Behavioural Research*, New York: Appleton, Century, Croft.
Rosenthal, R. and Jacobson, L. (1968) *Pygmalion in the Classroom* (the Pygmalion or Rosenthal effect). (Fr. Tr. (1971) *Pygmalion à l'ecole*, Paris: Casterman.)
Seligman, M.E.P. (1975) *Helplessness: on Depression, Development and Death*, San Francisco: Freeman.
Siegel, B. (1986) *Love, Medicine and Miracle*, New York: Harper & Row.
Simonton, C.O. and Simonton, M.S. (1975) 'Belief systems and management of the emotional aspects of malignancy', *Journal of Transpersonal Psychology* 7(1): 29–47.

Simonton, C.O., Simonton, M.S. and Creighton, J. (1978) *Getting Well Again*, Los Angeles: Torcher.

Solomon, G.F. (1985) 'The emerging field of psychoimmunology', *Advances* 2(1).

Solomon, G.F. (1989) 'Psychoneuroimmunology: interaction between central nervous system and immune system', *Journal of Neuroscience Research*, in press.

Solomon, G.F. and Moos, R.H. (1964) 'Emotions, immaturity and disease, *Archives of General Psychiatry* 11: 657.

Further reading

Ancelin Schützenberger, A. (1980) *Le Jeu de Rôle*, Paris: E.S.F.

Ancelin Schützenberger, A. (1989) *Introduction à la Psycho-thérapie Trans-generationnelle*, La psycho-genealogie, en préparation.

Bahnson, C.B. (1968) 'Basic epistemologic problems regarding the psychosomatic process', paper presented at First Congress on High Nervous Activity, Milan.

Berne, E. (1964) *Games People Play*, Fr. tr. *Des Jeux et Des Hommes*, Paris: Stock, 1980.

Bowen, M. (1978) *La Différenciation du Soi: les Triangles et les Systèmes Émotifs Familiaux*, Paris: E.S.F., 1984.

Bowen, M. (1978) *Family Therapy and Clinical Practice*, New York: Jason Aronson.

Cameron, E. and Pauling, L. (1979) *La Vitamine C Contre le Cancer (Vitamin C Against Cancer)*, Montréal: L'Etincelle.

Carter, E.A. and McGoldrick, M. (1980) (eds) *The Family Life Cycle: A Framework For Family Therapy*, New York: Gormer Press.

Cousins, N. (1990) *Head First: The Biology of Hope*, New York: Dutton.

Davis, J. (1984) *The Kennedys: Dynasty and Disaster 1848–1983*, New York: Columbia University Press.

Dunbar, F. (1954) *Emotions and Bodily Changes: A Survey of Literature – Psychosomatic Interrelationship, 1910–1953*, New York: Columbia University Press.

Engel, G. (1975) 'The death of a twin: mourning and anniversary reactions; fragments of 10 years of self analysis', *International Journal of Psychoanalysis* 56 (1): 23–40.

Gaulejac, V. de (1988) *La Neurose de Class*, Paris: Hommes et Groupes.

Glasser, R. (1976) *The Body is the Hero* (French translation (1978): *C'est le Corps Qui Triomphe*, Paris: Laffont).

Holland, J. and Frei, E. (1982) *Cancer Medicine*, 3rd edn, New York: Lead & Seburger.

Holmes, T.H. and Masuda, M. (1974) 'Life changes and illness susceptibility', in B.S. Dohrenwend *et al.* (eds) *Stressful Life Events: Their Nature and Effects*, New York: Wiley.

Kogasa, S. (1979) 'The hardy personality: towards a social psychology of stress on health', in G.S. Sanders (ed.) *Social Psychology of Health and Illness*, Hillsdale, New York: L. Erlbaum.

Kubler-Ross, E. (1975) *Les Derniers Instants de la Vie*, Genève: Labor & Fides.

Kubler-Ross, E. (1976) *La Mort, Dernière Étape de la Croissance*, Ottawa: Ed. Québec-Amerique.

Kubler-Ross, E. (1981) *Living with Death and Dying*, New York: Macmillan.

Leutz, G. (1985) *Mettre sa Vie en Scène: le Psychodrame*, Paris: EPI. (Including preface by Prof. Didier Anzieu and afterword by Prof. A. Ancelin Schützenberger.)

Masson, O. (1983) 'Les personnes et leurs roles dans les systèmes familiaux morphostatiques', *Bulletin de Psychologie*, Paris: Sorbonne, n° special de psychologie clinique Vi, XXXVI, n° 360, juin.

Minuchin, S. (1974) *Families and Family Therapy*, Cambridge, Mass.: Harvard University Press.

Moreno, J.L. (1946) *Psychodrama* I, II and III, Beacon, NY: Beacon House.

Satir, V. (1975) *Thérapie du Couple et de la Famille*, Paris: EPI.

Siebert, L.A. (1983) 'The survivor personality', paper presented at the Western Association of Psychology Convention, quoted in Siegel 1986.

Walsh, S. (1975) 'Living for the dead? Schizophrenia and three generations of family relations', paper, 38th annual meeting, American Psychological Association. Abstract.

Chapter fourteen

Healing the healers

Psychodrama with therapists

Barbara Jean Quin

Introduction

This chapter looks at the use of psychodrama with people in the mental health professions and other related disciplines. At first sight it may seem that this is not a group requiring a specialised approach but appearances can be deceptive. Working with psychological distress is not easy and at times can be extremely painful and people who do this have substantial and legitimate needs for support and stimulus. They are also a unique group in the sense that both the providers and the receivers of support will be therapists of some sort. The healers must heal themselves – or at least other members of their own population. This reflexiveness, that is, the application of a theory to oneself or one's own, makes therapists exciting people to work with but also brings its own difficulties. The first part of the chapter explores these issues.

It then goes on to look at the special place that psychodrama can occupy in the process of staff support. Psychodrama has many advantages for working with mental health professionals. It's fun, powerful, inspiring, involves sharing. It has its own well-developed theory but is compatible with other schools of therapy. The sessions do not require the group members to formally analyse themselves or each other, so therapists can relax into the method and leave their working roles behind. It can get round some defences gently and helpfully. It is also specially appropriate at this time in this country as it is a school of therapy where qualified practitioners are aware of the process from both sides of the fence. They have experienced the method from all points of view, as director, as protagonist and as group member. In this, it is like the psychoanalytic therapies.

In keeping with a topic where reflexiveness is a major factor, I am starting my exploration with an account of my own journey through the issues of staff support and psychodrama.

On a personal note

My personal interest in the link between psychodrama and working with healers goes back to 1973. I was one year into my training in clinical psychology and, partly because of the effort required to cope with the course, I was feeling tired and stressed. As part of the training, I attended a psychodrama group with my fellow trainees and, during its course, rediscovered the simple pleasures of touching, being recognised, and sharing my feelings with other people who were sharing their feelings with me. This experience stood out as one of the very few moments in our training when my fellow students and I were encouraged to acknowledge our common humanity and relate to each other as people first and clinicians second. It set me off on a course that led me through humanistic psychology, encounter groups and other experiential methods and especially further experiences of psychodrama. It seemed self-evident to me that enactment was a powerful therapeutic tool and I could never really understand why a method that holds this as a central process was not right at the centre of my training and that of most other mental health professionals.

Another important experience during my training was hearing a lecture given by Don Bannister, then visiting lecturer at the University of Surrey. He introduced us to the idea of reflexiveness in an academic way. This dictates that one key part in the process of judging the quality of any psychological theory or piece of research should be to consider how much sense it would make if applied to ourselves. This idea has informed my thinking ever since. It helps me to reach decisions about which methods of therapy to pursue on the basis of considering which ones I would be willing to contemplate being applied to myself, my family or my friends. It has also helped me to test out questions about other therapists on myself. Two clear examples of this are my attitudes to supervision and to stress. As colleagues began to ask me to supervise their work, I began to wonder about who should be supervising mine – a relatively common question now but quite unusual in my profession until quite recently. Similarly, as colleagues began to talk about stress and burn-out and to ask me to run support groups, I began to wonder what I did with my own stress and what sort of support I could benefit from receiving.

A major step in my efforts to build up my own professional support network came in my discovery of the Holwell Centre for Psychodrama and Sociodrama, England, and this brought me full circle by taking me back to psychodrama, which I had drifted away from in the preceding few years. This chapter comes out of my thinking since then about how to enhance the quality and quantity of support available to both my colleagues and myself in the work setting and as a routine part of the process of work, and the special place that, in my view, psychodrama should occupy in this process.

The psychological needs of mental health workers

To set the scene for the more general discussion of the use of psychodrama in supporting therapists in our work, it might be helpful to look at the case for developing support networks for our colleagues and ourselves.

At the most basic level, it is helpful to remember that therapists are also people, living lives not dissimilar to those of everyone else. We go through the same basic life cycle as other people and we have no special immunity to the stresses that are a normal part of living. We all grow up and receive some sort of education. We may get married and/or have children. We may move house and we are likely to change job. Later on we may be involved in caring for an elderly relative. Many of us will also go through the traumas of divorce, bereavement or serious illness in ourselves or someone near to us. Sadly, many of us will experience or will have experienced more severe traumas, either in our own lives or in someone in our immediate family; traumas such as alcohol or drug addiction, physical, sexual or emotional abuse in childhood, rape, physical assault or battering in adulthood or similar.

If this last list sounds overdramatic, I can only say that I have worked with skilled and sensitive therapists who have been through these experiences. The following are examples (all names and professions have been changed in examples in this chapter, to protect confidentiality):

Mary is a doctor who was grievously abused sexually by a mentally retarded older boy in her neighbourhood as a child. She thinks her parents may have suspected but they did nothing. She told no-one till she was professional, trying to work with adult patients who had been sexually abused as children.

Charles is a psychologist whose mother, a single parent, disciplined him with a whip till he was old enough to stop her. He hesitated for a whole year in a support group before revealing this to his colleagues and allowing some of the feelings connected with his childhood to emerge. He had been in practice for nearly twenty years and this was the first opportunity for sharing he had experienced that felt safe enough for him to work.

Katy, a social worker, was raped as a teenager. She had never disclosed it to anyone except for the colleague who found her at the time. It welled up and overwhelmed her when she tried to take on a rape victim for individual counselling.

Many similar examples can be found in *Wounded Healers* (Rippere and Williams 1985), a collection of the experiences of depression of mental health workers. Their stories illustrate some of the difficulties that come with the work but they also show clearly the breadth of negative experiences that can be suffered by a group of sad people in their home lives. It seems to be one of the more impressive virtues of our species that some of our members can be so grievously hurt by life and yet emerge as giving and caring people.

Many of the specific sources of stress that come with the work are discussed at length in Guy's book exploring the personal life of the psychotherapist (Guy 1987). Though his book focuses on psychotherapists, his definition is broad and most of the points he makes would relate equally well to other therapists. He lays particular stress on the physical and psychic isolation that can come with the work. In exploring the psychological aspects, he looks at the effects of withholding personal information, setting aside personal concerns, emotional control, one-way intimacy, maintaining the interpretive stance, idealisation and omnipotence, devaluation and attack, goals of treatment (i.e. saying goodbye to the patient), professional competition and public perception. All these sources of stress, which are specific to the task of being a therapist, affect not only the therapist but also all her or his relationships, especially with those closest to her or him.

Expressed in another way, the task of the mental health professional is to work with people in deep distress. This means that all therapists, however they organise their work, will spend much of their time either thinking about or being directly confronted by the most painful aspects of the human condition. Their major tool in working with all this pain is themselves – their thinking, feeling and acting informed by their own memories and studies and the therapeutic models they employ.

Inevitably, choosing to work with such pain requires the therapist to develop strategies, either conscious or unconscious, to keep it at bay and prevent it becoming totally overwhelming. Some of these strategies seem to be healthy and sensible, like following a system of caseload management, working in teams or with co-therapists, seeking supervision or further training, reducing direct patient contact by becoming involved in giving supervision to or training other therapists or moving into management and, of course, seeking formal or informal support.

Other strategies that are commonplace amongst healers seem less healthy or sensible, like trying to compensate for the limited amount that any one of us can do by chronically overworking and taking work home or cutting off from the patients at a feeling level altogether and pretending that the pain is not really there.

Who heals the healers?

A major problem facing many mental health professionals is the difficulty of finding the right support when the going does get rough. Therapists who have poor support networks, for example, as a result of a job change, can be faced with a really difficult and in some ways paradoxical task. Assuming that they have reached the stage of realising that they need outside help, where do they go? They might wonder if there is any point in consulting someone too like themselves in approach as that might not offer anything new. If the approach suggested any solutions, they would already have thought of them. On the other hand, each therapist has chosen an approach to therapy presumably on the basis that they consider it to be the most efficacious approach. That being the case, they might wonder if there is any point in asking for help from someone with a different approach? The paradox is more imaginary than real, as support is more about people and feelings than it is about technique, but the stuck therapist can readily lose sight of that in the fear of 'getting it wrong' and asking for support from someone who turns out not to suit them.

This problem can be further exacerbated by the particular discipline from which the therapist comes. Although some schools of therapy in this country include an experience of personal therapy in their training, few mental health professions require that their trainees undertake personal therapy. For example, it is not obligatory for qualifications in psychiatric medicine, psychiatric nursing, clinical psychology or social work in the field of mental health. Thus it is possible for someone to enter a mental health profession, train, qualify and practise with severe earlier trauma neither disclosed nor worked with, waiting to be triggered by a parallel experience in a patient, and for that person to have no experience of personal therapy at all. Simply entertaining the idea that help could be useful and acceptable can be a major difficulty for such a person. Mary, Charles and Katy, described above, all had this problem.

These are examples of extreme difficulties, but my belief is that none of us should be so short of professional and personal support in the normal course of our work that we reach these extremes. Opportunities to share our work and the impact it has on us should be routine. To use a metaphor, no-one would expect a rally driver to keep on driving a car without getting it serviced frequently and fine-tuning it to a high level of performance. For therapists, their 'car' is their own person and to expect it to run and run without adequate servicing, let alone fine tuning, seems absurd and dreadfully wasteful.

Why psychodrama?

Psychodrama offers a way of meeting the needs for support of mental health workers and in my opinion it is one of the best available. I am aware of at least ten specific aspects of psychodrama that make it a good choice and though some of the reasons are not exclusive to the method, especially those that would apply to any action-based technique, together I think they constitute a powerful argument for encouraging directors of psychodrama to devote at least some of their time and talents to working with their colleagues in supportive contexts. This type of work does create some specific problems for directors and I deal with these in subsequent sections.

1. *Psychodrama is fun.* This almost seems too obvious to state, but it is a distinguishing feature of the method that it is not only acceptable to allow laughter in groups but is positively encouraged. Instead of being seen as a distraction from the main business of the group, it can sometimes become its focal point. A catharsis of laughter can be a great release for the whole group. Also, the dramatic aspect of psychodrama dictates that a good director will take account of comedy as well as tragedy.
2. *Psychodrama is powerful.* The sheer power to create new emotional and intellectual understanding that can be released in a psychodrama session is a major recommendation when working with therapists. We are

usually busy people and many of us can feel tired and jaded but the impact of a psychodrama session can break through that distractedness and tiredness strongly enough to reach people who are well used to working with feelings, especially negative ones.

3. *Psychodrama can be inspiring.* A psychodrama session at its best will be creative and imaginative and will release the spontaneity of the group as well as of the protagonist and director. Therapists especially need to be energised and inspired if they are to go on giving of themselves to others without serious damage to themselves.

4. *Psychodrama involves sharing.* As already noted, therapists can lead very isolated and isolating lives, so the simple affirmation of common humanity built into each classical psychodrama session in the sharing is particularly valuable in this context.

5. *Psychodrama directors have experienced the method themselves.* This point has the same validity and power in relation to staff groups as it has in relation to patient and other groups. In this context, it has the further advantage of 'normalising' the experience. While therapists may be quite happy to admit intellectually that stress is a fact of life and support ought to be one too, they may have more trouble convincing themselves emotionally.

6. *Psychodrama has its own well-developed theory.* Psychodrama has a long and respectable academic history. Moreno himself was a prolific author and many others have since developed his ideas. Whole schools of therapy have come from the combination of psychodramatic ideas with the new and unique creativity of other therapists. This can be very reassuring to professionals whose orientation is different and who may feel less than confident about putting themselves in the role of group member.

7. *The method is compatible with many theoretical approaches.* While psychodrama has its own theoretical underpinning, the process that occurs during a psychodrama group could readily be understood from a number of different theoretical perspectives. For example, the process of enacting a scene from early childhood is similar to the psychoanalytical concept of regression and though tele is a broader concept than transference and countertransference, they are clearly related ideas (see Blatner 1973: 37–8). A behaviour therapist would be quite comfortable with the notion of examining the exact behaviour that has occurred in a difficult situation and would be likely to find the idea of enacting that behaviour a helpful addition to the more usual verbal process of behavioural analysis. Also, the idea of repeating the scene at the end of the drama using different behaviour is typical of the sort of behavioural rehearsal that goes on in, for example, assertiveness training groups (see, for example, Herbert 1987: 169–75).

A systemic family therapist would be likely to regret the absence of real family members but can readily see the usefulness of exploring family interactions using auxiliaries if the real people cannot be present. Such a therapist might also be comfortable with the idea of looking for sources of difficulty in the past as it fits in with ideas of the family life cycle and the notion that family dysfunction can result from failure to negotiate the transition to new stages in the life cycle (see, for example, Falicov 1988: 3 ff.).

I am not trying to suggest that there are no areas where the psychodrama method is radically different from a specific other orientation. The point I am making is that while there are differences from other models, there are enough areas of overlap for therapists of most persuasions to find familiarity with at least some of the events in the psychodrama group.

8. *Psychodrama can sidestep some defences.* Therapists spend much of their time focusing on the difficulties of other people and routinely fending off inquiries about their own lives, feelings, needs, etc. It can be difficult for us to move out of this position into one where a more personal level of relating is appropriate. Psychodrama can facilitate this in two specific ways. First, it is an action-based method, so that most of the verbal habits built up by therapists to avoid self-revelation are simply not activated. This can be particularly powerful at the warm-up stage of the process.

Second, the process of setting up and enacting a scene brings the protagonist into as close a contact with the reality of what happened as possible after the event. The verisimilitude can help to engage the therapist on her or his own account and can help overcome the natural resistance to allowing full emotional recall of painful events.

9. *Psychodrama sessions do not include formal analysis.* This relates again to the importance of enabling therapists to forget their therapeutic roles for the duration of the session and to engage with the process at a more personal level. Many schools of group therapy encourage group members to share their thoughts about each other's problems during the session. While a psychodrama director will occasionally ask the group what they think might be going on for the protagonist during the session, it is not a routine part of the groupwork and is explicitly discouraged in the sharing stage, when the protagonist is particularly vulnerable. It can be a very liberating experience for a therapist to be able to 'switch off' the critical faculty for the duration of a session and just 'go with the flow'.

10. *Psychodrama avoids labels.* There is no place in a psychodrama group for diagnostic labels. Not only are they avoided in the actual session, but the theory of psychodrama places emphasis on exploring situations in their unique context and looking for spontaneity and creativity, rather than on describing pathology. For therapists, this is helpful in

normalising their experiences and thus concentrating on health rather than a model of sickness. It shares this attribute with other humanistic therapies.

The special problems of using psychodrama with therapists

In the previous section, I suggested a number of ways in which psychodrama can be especially useful in working with groups of therapists. In this section, I would like to look at some of the ways in which these groups can be different from groups of patients and explore their implications for the method.

When working with groups of patients, there is at least an implicit assumption and usually an explicit one that the task of the group is to help the members solve psychological dilemmas that they perceive as disabling. In groups of therapists, this is not the case. Each group member will have her or his own expectations about the purpose of the group and the degree of personal revelation consistent with that purpose. At one extreme, there may be members who hope and expect to be able to use the group to work on deeply personal issues with roots buried deep in the past. At the other may be members who regard any discussion of personal information as inappropriately intrusive. The first stage in exploring how to deal with this wide range is to clarify the context in which the group is meeting.

Issues of group context

Staff groups come in many shapes and sizes. They might meet once weekly for a term or indefinitely. The members might be in training for or fully qualified in a number of different professions. They might know each other closely, by sight or not at all. And so on.

From the director's point of view, it is helpful to clarify as much as possible about the group membership and its purpose in meeting with her or him in advance, in order to gain some idea of the level of safety and support available to the members during and after the group and hence to make plans about the type and level of work appropriate to the group.

The demonstration group

The most limited context is probably the request for a one-off demonstration of the method. The members may know each other quite well and work together and they may have a history of personal sharing. On the other hand, they may not know each other at all. Also, some group members may be employed in contexts that allow for little or no sharing of the distress engendered by the work. For them, such one-off sessions may seem like heaven-sent opportunities for exploring some of the difficulties they face professionally. Whatever the combination of members, the director will not be there in person to follow up the session so a degree of caution is appropriate.

The team support group

A more robust context is the team 'support group'. Here, the membership come together specifically with the task of taking care of each other and sharing difficulties. I put in the inverted commas because my experience of groups carrying this label is that they can end up being quite the reverse unless they are set up extremely carefully. Staff teams who are overstressed and in internal conflict can often decide that a support group is the ideal way forward in resolving their difficulties. Even if there is a high level of covert or overt conflict in the group, the support group at least has the advantage that the membership know each other, probably quite well, and expect to go on working together for the immediate future.

The special interest group

Another version of the support group is the type of group that comes together around a particular topic, way of working or professional group. Examples from my own practice are the child-abuse support group, the local branch of the Association for Family Therapy and the special-interest group for clinical psychologists working with children, adolescents and their families. There are no rules for the composition of these types of groups, so they can come together in a wide range of formats and some may choose to work psychodramatically, either all the time using an external director or just for some sessions, using an outside director brought in for the session or one of the membership, who has that skill.

The training group using psychodrama

Some training courses include an element of psychodrama as part of a broader training. For example, I recently ran a two-day workshop for clinical psychologists in training to introduce them to the techniques and philosophy of psychodrama.

The psychodrama training group

From the director's point of view, these are the most robust types of groups where therapists work on themselves. Even new members will have some expectation of working on themselves and there will almost certainly be some group members besides the group director who have experience of personal work using psychodrama.

A local example of a training group is our psychodrama support group. The purpose of the group is to draw together local people with an interest in psychodrama and provide a setting in which we can learn about psychodrama and practise our skills and also have a chance to work on ourselves. Feedback from the membership of the group is very positive and some members go on to register formally for training in psychodrama. The only serious difficulties we face are structural. Qualified staff in the district have difficulty in finding the time to make a commitment to a regular group so it contains rather more students than staff and while this is not in itself a problem, it rather defeats one of our aims, which is to encourage qualified staff to venture into psychodrama.

Issues of technique

All the contexts described previously involve therapists in some degree of personal work. The special issues arising out of this that may need extra care by the director revolve around power, consent and confidentiality.

The method itself is extremely powerful and while this is one of its major strengths, it also carries its own risks. It is easy for a director who is used to patient groups to fall into the trap of assuming that because the group members are fellow professionals, they will be well able to cope with the deepest of sessions and the most powerful of catharses. My own experience is that this is not the case, especially in the one-off workshop setting. Some mental health professions have little or no history of personal work and others involve only verbal work. Thus some highly competent and committed therapists can come to a workshop with little previous exposure to any sort of action-based work and the shock can be quite profound. The power of a psychodrama session can also leave both protagonist and group members feeling overexposed and vulnerable, especially if they have felt and shown strong feelings. This is not likely to be a problem in the session but could well be a source of embarrassment the day after, if the display of feeling was out of character.

> A recent example of this from my own practice was the first session of a regular support group I held with a group of nurses on a post-registration course. I used the 'two-chair' technique to explore the issue of support with them by inviting them to each meet up with the person who was their strongest source of support in life at that time. The session involved no scene setting and only used role reversal to explore the relationships a little. Despite the simplicity of the technique, the session was both powerful and moving. Only one of the group members had done anything like this before, though they had all met role playing at one time or another.

Probably the greatest risk arising out of the power of the method is of an individual being so unbalanced by an experience of psychodrama that she or he feels unable to continue functioning as a therapist in the immediate aftermath. While this might not be too much of a problem in the context of a residential training week, it could create severe difficulties in the context of a session followed by an immediate return to work, with no follow-up and no support system.

> This problem arose locally a while ago when I was involved in setting up a one-off session for a staff member who became deeply distressed following a group where she had rediscovered her feelings about her own experiences of child abuse.

Another issue that the director of a staff group needs to take into account is the real power relationships existing between members of the group, both formally and informally. At the formal level, some members may be managerially accountable to others and this can have an inhibiting effect on both sides. It is difficult to let go and admit to serious weaknesses and errors in front of someone you have to give orders to or someone who will write your references when you leave! In a group that works together as a team, there will also be a whole network of informal relationships based on personal style, skills, length of time in the team, profession, gender, friendship, etc. that may inhibit some members from free expression.

If the director is a member of the team or a colleague working closely with some, but not all, members of the group, that introduces a whole extra layer of complexity. While the director of a psychodrama session cannot take literal responsibility for the experience of each and every member of the group, the role does carry overall responsibility for the process of the group and is quite clearly differentiated from the roles of protagonist, auxiliary ego or group member. Groups that are used to working psychodramatically will find it quite easy to cope with a member dropping into and out of the director's role, assuming that there is more than one director available to the group, but the experience will be quite different in a group that is new to the method and it may be quite difficult for both the director and some of the group members to allow the role to be laid aside after the session.

A final risk area for a director in a group of therapists is the one that comes from the reflexiveness of the situation, and this is the risk that increases with the therapeutic competence of the group members. In a group of professionals, both the director and the members are experienced in working with people. There may be group members who have experience of training therapists. The group may even include psychodrama trainers. It will often happen that some of the members are more experienced than the director. While in the real world this should not be a problem as the experienced therapists are there by choice and can be presumed to be supportive and open to the experience in a positive way, in the internal world of the director this can easily restimulate fears of being judged and found to be inadequate. The commonness of these fears was brought home to me at a workshop exploring the process of psychodrama. Virtually every member of the workshop owned up to 'stage fright' when directing in front of their psychodrama trainers.

We all have to find ways of dealing with our own performance anxiety. The problem with staff groups is that when directing a group of one's peers, these fears are likely to be nearer to the surface than usual, so if the group is not directly supervised, we need to be especially watchful for our own personal patterns of defence against anxiety.

The process of a typical session

There is no 'right way' to conduct a psychodrama session with fellow mental health professionals, but careful attention to issues of consent and confidentiality and a healthy degree of caution can help in dealing with the problem areas outlined previously. What follows are the guidelines I use myself in setting up and running staff groups. They are culled from conversations with fellow psychodramatists (especially Marcia Karp and Ken Sprague), from conversations with other therapists involved in running support groups or staff training groups, from my own experience and from my own thoughts and reflections on the process to date.

Preparation

Before taking on work with a group of therapists, I try to find out key information about the composition of the group. I check with the group convenor (if other than myself) whether the members work together and if so, what are their formal relationships, what they are likely to know about psychodrama and what they expect to get out of the group. If the group is to meet with me only once or twice, I also try to find out in advance if the members are likely to have other sources of support in the work setting, for example, do they belong to a support group or do they all have personal supervision? Armed with this information, I decide in advance how I will structure the group. In particular, I plan the warm-up stage of the group in some detail and plan out roughly how long each stage of the group will take. I also decide whether I will work with vignettes or two scene dramas, possibly with more than one protagonist, or whether I will seek a protagonist for a full core psychodrama.

If the group is likely to include members with little experience of action methods, I will plan to use more than one simple physical warm-up to establish a degree of relaxation with non-verbal methods. I will also plan to warm up more than one protagonist to an issue that is clearly work-related.

Director's warm-up

Before starting work with a group of fellow therapists, I will go through my plan in my mind and make sure I am happy with it. I will then go through a brief relaxation routine and take time to remind myself that therapists are people and I am a person and that more joins us together than divides us. As one of my own risks is to overcompensate for my anxiety by getting overconfident, I will also remind myself that I do not have to be perfect!

Contract with the group

If this is my first session with this group, I will take time to explain briefly the pattern I expect the session to take and talk about confidentiality. All therapists will be used to the concept in relation to patients but they may well not have thought through what it means in the context of personal work in a group of colleagues. They are very likely to want to share their own work with friends, spouses or absent colleagues and they are also likely to want to feel free to discuss the techniques. It can be useful to think about how they can do both these things without breaching the confidentiality of other group members' work.

I will also raise the issues of personal revelation and consent. In a patient group, it is reasonable to suppose that in time, every member will decide to reveal a little of themselves in order to achieve the benefit of attending. In groups of therapists, this cannot always be assumed. For example, at worst, a member of a team who attends a support group because ordered to by a superior but who neither wishes to attend, nor has any belief that attending will have any personal benefits, is likely to work hard not to reveal anything personal. It is important that the director knows that person's position and accepts it unconditionally. I also feel it is important that the degree of self-revelation is fairly similar for all group members. If some members are prepared for self-disclosure while others wish to exclude their home lives from the business of the group, it will be difficult to create an atmosphere of trust and co-operation and the less revealing members may feel themselves to be under undue pressure to go beyond the limits they judge to be safe.

Group warm-up

Once these points have been aired, I will proceed with the warm-up as planned (or as amended in the light of my first contact with the group). When the protagonist warm-up is reached, I will explain that the protagonist works on behalf of the group and will again indicate what that is likely to involve.

In an ongoing group, all the above issues will already have been covered but I have found it helpful to raise the issue of consent from time to time in order to allow the members of the group to see if they have changed in any way.

Psychodrama or sociodrama?

If the group is a one-off demonstration, I will already know if the brief is to work sociodramatically or psychodramatically. If it is a long-standing group, the decision should emerge out of the warm-up. Groups of staff who work together may want to explore issues of group dynamics or issues relating to their roles in the wider system. In either case, sociodrama may be a more effective method than psychodrama and I would switch between the two as seemed appropriate.

The psychodrama itself

Once a protagonist has emerged, I would proceed as in any other psychodrama session, with only one specific proviso. I would have already decided at the planning stage whether I would be aiming for a vignette, a brief psychodrama or a full core psychodrama. At the contract stage, I would explain the limits of the session clearly to the protagonist. If the aim was to demonstrate the technique, I would explain that I would normally be looking to trace back the problem to an earlier time in the protagonist's life but as the situation was only a demonstration, I would stop at any points where I thought a change of scene might be indicated and check that perception out with the protagonist. The option of going back would be explored briefly, verbally, but not taken up.

Sharing

The sharing stage of a psychodrama session will be completely unfamiliar to many therapists. Once the action stops and they are invited to talk, they are quite likely to assume that their task is to offer an analysis of the protagonist's work. This is not too surprising as that may well be what they would do in their own groupwork. I usually invite people to share by using the metaphor of a journey. The protagonist has taken us all on a journey through her or his life and I would like us to share with each other, and especially with the protagonist, what journeys this has reminded us of through our own histories. By emphasising the personal nature of sharing, I cut down the risk of the protagonist being assailed by the combined therapeutic interpretations of a highly sophisticated group of people but I have to confess that I still find it harder to control this stage than any other in working with therapists. However much a group of professionals become emotionally involved in the work of a protagonist, it is inevitable, and appropriate, that they will also think about the process unfolding in the psychodrama. That is their skill. What can be difficult for a group of therapists who are not used to working psychodramatically is the idea that the drama is its own analysis and the sharing is about rejoining the protagonist to the group, rather than continuing the analysis. Therapists are also quite likely to offer analyses of other group members' sharing statements. The only techniques I have found to prevent this process from becoming destructive are a careful initial explanation, frequent reminders and a high level of vigilance!

Closure

The sharing is usually the final stage in a psychodrama session. It is also the stage that aims to achieve closure of the group. It is always important to make sure that both the drama itself and the group achieve a good stopping point. If the group is a one-off group, then this is even more important than usual. If anyone is particularly upset towards the end of the session, I will take time to check out that they can take their distress to a safe person after the group or look within the group for someone who can be supportive for a while afterwards. If necessary, I would delay closing the group till the distress had been worked with enough to make it manageable. I am especially cautious to monitor the level of distress in group members and deal with it as the group goes along if any of the members have to work immediately afterwards. It is not easy to work straight after a powerful psychodrama group. It is even harder to work as a therapist, dealing with someone else's distress and leaving one's own pain to one side.

Inspiration helps

There are two areas involved in working with mental health professionals where no amount of technique will help and it is in these areas that spontaneity and creativity are especially important. It is also in these areas that the special excitements of working with therapists shine through.

Therapists can become overloaded with pain

This phenomenon can most easily be seen at residential courses but it can also be in evidence in therapist groups that meet weekly over more than a few sessions or in groups where the membership are themselves involved in psychodrama directing in between sessions. It can also happen in any other type of staff group. It is the awful feeling that at least some of the group members have run out of empathy. I have certainly experienced this sensation myself and discussed it with other therapists who are regularly in training or support groups. While one part of me still wants to reach out to the protagonist and support her or his work, another part of me is simply too tired to care any more. I have seen too much abuse or death or desertion and for the time being, I have shut off. The same feeling can assail me if I see too many clients with similar problems in a short time. In my head, I know that each one is unique and individual, but I cannot find the right note to respond in my heart.

The most obvious solution to this dilemma is simply to call a halt for a while. It may also be helpful for the group to do something different together, such as silly warm-ups or going for a walk right away from the theatre or group room. The time when these tactics will not help is when a group is drawing to a close and there are members waiting to work as protagonist, especially if those members have stood down to let others go first. At these times, what is needed is a little magic! It does not come on tap but it is there to be found if the director is brave enough to trust the method and the group. Some of the most magical sessions I have been involved in as a group member have come late in a week-long course, when the members are tired but close. The group tele has been strong and a new way through a particular dilemma has been found.

Therapists can be skilled at resisting

My experience of working with mental health professionals as protagonists is that they can be creative, exciting and courageous in the risks that they will take but that when they become stuck, they do so with great thoroughness. Skilled and sensitive people will suddenly start crying 'crocodile tears' and avoiding the real distress, or sidetracking the director, maybe using talking to avoid action, or allowing themselves to be led down well-known pathways rather than face the unknown areas. Sometimes the director can spot these self-defeating tactics but at other times, the avoidance only becomes clear to the protagonist and the group

241

after the end of the session, when the only remedy is to go away and think through the process and try not to avoid the difficult bit next time. This process of resistance must be familiar to all therapists in one form or another. What seems to me to make the resistance of fellow professionals different is the sheer range and subtlety of defensive tactics that can apparently be deployed with no conscious thought.

To understand this observation, I first set about trying to learn from my own experience as a protagonist. When I reflected on my own sessions, the aspect that most impressed and most depressed me was the effort I would put into resisting the director. I would pull defensive tactics out of the hat in great profusion and the closer the session came to opening up areas of deep pain, the harder I would resist. I discussed earlier in the chapter the advantages of psychodrama as a method that can get round defences but the shadow side of that is that those defences that remain are deeply ingrained and can be quite unconscious. I know that at a conscious level, the last thing I wanted to do in my own sessions was resist direction, but I still did it.

The why of my resistance was easy to understand (and with understanding, forgive). Defences were built up in the first place to protect against intolerable pain, often at an age when understanding was not sufficiently developed to be of much help, or to provide workable methods of dealing with conflicts that had been beyond my power to resolve at the time. They had been refined and repeated in similar situations for years.

What was not so clear was how I had come by such a wide range of defensive tactics. The solution to this question that I would like to offer does not seem easy to test but it has the advantages of fitting my own experience and of being theoretically sound.

Therapists spend much of their time trying to help people who have dysfunctional responses to situations to find new and creative ways of dealing with them. One of the methods we use, drawn from social learning theory, is modelling. We behave in the way we want the patients to behave and invite them to use us as an exemplar. The logical corollary of that situation is that we are exposed to models of dysfunctional behaviour of all shapes and sizes and it seems reasonable to suppose that when we are under pressure, we should call on those models to add depth and complexity to our own defences. We would not need to think out that process any more than the child copying the parent's behaviour would need to do so consciously.

Even if this idea is rejected, it seems reasonable to suppose that therapists as a group are people who have thought long and hard about how people function in the world. We are an articulate, well-educated group and our defences will be correspondingly articulate and sophisticated.

One further thought about the vigour with which mental health professionals defend themselves in groups: patients will usually go only as far as they need to release their creativity in their area of maximum difficulty. Therapists, on the other hand, need to be reasonably sure that they can function in most problem areas without getting snarled up in their own unfinished business. A by-product of this is that they may feel they need to go deeper in working on themselves than they would ask their patients to go. Thus the problems they bring to training or support groups may be vaguer and/or located earlier in their history, where memories are fewer.

All the aforementioned ideas add up to attempts to explain my own resistance as a protagonist and the resistance I have observed and worked with in fellow therapists. More important is where to look for solutions. As with the first problem area, I have no magical solutions to offer but I have experienced magic, as director, as protagonist and as group member. As director, I have found that the most fruitful approach is to try to hold my attention on a 'wide' band when I begin to feel that the protagonist is blocking and to look for the next step in any and all of the elements of the drama. I will try to find my own creativity but I will also be happy to go with the creativity in the auxiliaries or in the other group members. Psychodrama is a group method and it is at times like these that it is most important to remember that. I will not exclude looking for solutions directly with the protagonist but I will be aware that she or he is swimming against an internal tide of resistance and may not be able to be creative at such moments in the session.

Above all, I try to remember to trust the method!

Conclusion

I have tried to show in this chapter how therapists need and deserve formal support sessions as a routine part of their work and why I feel so strongly that psychodrama is the method of choice for these types of sessions. As I have reflected on these themes in order to write the chapter, I have been reminded of more and more examples of them intertwining in my own history as a therapist. I remember, for instance, writing about how to support residential social workers working in secure units for disturbed children and the psychodrama sessions with the staff group that stimulated the piece. I remember using sociodrama with a group of staff in an adolescent unit to help us understand the problems in the staff group.

There are many other memories and if I try to survey them as a group, what strikes me most strongly is that these are some of the richest and most rewarding experiences I have had as a therapist, a group leader and a psychodrama director. All mental health professionals, including psychodramatists, have some choice about where they put in their effort. I believe in the importance of this work with a passion that surprises me and if one outcome of writing this chapter is that more therapists enjoy more psychodrama, I will regard the effort as well spent!

References

Blatner, H.E. (1973) *Acting In: Practical Applications of Psychodramatic Methods*, New York: Springer Publishing.

Falicov, C.J. (ed.) (1988) *Family Transitions: Continuity and Change over the Family Life Cycle*, New York: Guildford.

Guy, J.D. (1987) *The Personal Life of the Psychotherapist*, New York: John Wiley and Sons.

Herbert, M. (1987) *Behavioural Treatment of Children with Problems*, London: Academic Press.

Rippere, V. and Williams, R. (eds) (1985) *Wounded Healers: Mental Health Workers' Experience of Depression*, Chichester: John Wiley and Sons.

Name index

Abraham, Nicholas 217
Ackerman, Nathan 215
Ader, R. 203, 207
Ancelin Schützenberger, Anne 3, 204, 205, 206, 215, 216
Arroyave, Fernando 167, 176
Axline, Virginia 91

Bahnson, C.B. 203, 207
Baker, A.W. and Duncan, S.P. 78
Bannister, Anne 5
Bannister, Don 228
Benward, J. and Gerber, J.D. 80
Bhanji, S. 139
Bianco, P.J. 139
Bion, W.R. 122
Black, C. 180
Blane, H.T. 158
Blatner, Adam 80, 87
Blatner, Adam and Blatner, Alec 7, 10, 11
Blatner, H.E. 232
Blos, P. 119
Boszormenyi-Nagy, I. 215
Bowlby, John 4, 191–2, 193
Brook, Peter 118
Bruch, Hilde 139

Canetti, E. 133
Clarkson, Petrūska 97
Cohen, A. 191
Coln, H. 198
Colwell, Maria 78
Combes, Susie 35
Conway, A. and Clarkson, P. 97
Coué, Dr. 211

Dali, Salvador 218
Danielson, Claire 35

Davies, G. 79
de Beauvoir, Simone 215
Donne, John 29

Einstein Albert 50
Eliot, T.S. 28
Eller Goldman, Elaine 5
Eller Goldman, E. and Morrison, D.S. 10, 12
Ellwood, J. and Oke, M. 119
Erikson, E. 116

Falicov, C.J. 233
Feldmar, Andrew 99
Finkelhor, D. 78
Foulkes, S.H. 116, 117, 122, 129, 139, 151
Foulkes, S.H. and Anthony, E.J. 116, 117, 128
Fox, J. 10
Franckel, V. 209
Freud, Sigmund 84, 97–9, 129, 160

Galen 221
Gelinas, D. 79
Giarretto, H. and Giarretto, A. 92
Goodwin, J. 79
Gravitz, H. and Bowden, J. 182, 184
Green, André 218
Green, R. and Murray, E. 191
Greenberg, I. 166
Greenson, R.R. 160
Groth, A.N. and Birnbaum, H.J. 79
Guy, J.D. 229

Haworth, Peter 35
Heawood, Maureen 112
Henderson, A. 191

Herbert, M. 232
Herman, J.L 78
Hewitt, J. 191
Hilgard, J. 206
Holmes, T. and Rahe, R. 206, 207, 208–9
Howells, J.G. 74

Jacobson, E. 210
James, J. and Meyerding, J. 80
Jefferies, Jinnie 4, 99, 199
Jewitt, Claudia 83
Jones, D.P. and McGraw, J.M. 79
Jones, Ernest 22, 24
Jones, M. 138
Jung, C.G. 30

Kaplin, H. 191
Karp, Marcia 2, 9, 12, 175, 238
Karpel, M.A. and Strauss, E.S. 53, 65
Keats, John 28
Kessel, N. and Walton, T. 156
Klein, M. 131

Laing, R.D. 104
Lange, S.G. and Hartgers, M.J.W. 152
Laufer, M. and Laufer, M.E. 131
Lerner, R. 180
LeShan, L. 206, 209
Levi, Jacob Moreno *see* Moreno, J.L.
Lewin, K. 116
Long, Suzanne: 'Sexual abuse of young children' 91–2

McCord, W. and McCord, J. 156
MacFarlane, K. and Waterman, J. 78, 79, 91
MacKenzie, Midge 103, 112
Main, T. 159, 175
Malan, D. 127
Meillo, Joke 138, 149
Menninger, Karl: *Man Against Himself* 156–7
Miller, Alice 45, 80, 81, 84, 92, 100, 104; *The Drama of Being a Child* 101, 102; *For Your Own Good* 102; *Thou Shalt Not Be Aware* 102
Millet, J.-F. 218
Molnos, Angela 117, 127
Moore, Henry 92
Moreno, J.L 53, 96, 140; on enactment 83; 'life method' 33–4; on need for controls 49; and network effect 53; on

personality 15–16, 17, 186; and purpose of psychodrama 7–8, 13, 77, 106, 180, 232; on reversal strategy 165; and role of director 7–8, 175; on role of protagonist 28; on sharing process 12; and sociodrama 117–18; and sociometry 215; on spontaneity 2, 129–30; and 'surplus reality' 213; on tele 81, 92, 160; *Who Shall Survive?* 97–9
Moreno, Zerka 12, 13, 65, 72, 103

Oaklander, Violet 91
On Becoming a Psychotherapist 101

Pitzele, Peter 3
Plato, *The Republic* 29

Quin, Barbara Jean 3

Rank, Otto 73
Rippere, V. and Williams, R., *Wounded Healers* 229
Rosenbaum, M. and de Charms, R. 191
Rosenthal, R. and Jacobson, L. 204, 206, 213
Ruscombe-King, Gillie 4–5
Rutan, J.S. and Alonso, A. 152–3

Sandler, J., Dare, C. and Holder, A. 160
Sartre, Jean-Paul 215
Schatzberg, A.F., Lobis, R.A. and Westfall, M.P. 151
Seligman, M.E.P. 204
Sgroi, Suzanne, *Handbook of Clinical Intervention in Child Sexual Abuse* 79–80
Shakespeare, William: *Hamlet* 22–3, 24–5, 29
Siegel, Bernie: *Love, Medicine and Miracle* 203–4, 206
Simonton, M.O. and Simonton, C.S. 203–4, 205, 206, 214, 219
Simonton, M.O., Simonton, C.S. and Creighton, J.: *Getting Well Again* 220
Solomon, G.F. 203, 207
Solomon, G.F. and Moos, R.H. 203
Spark, G. 215
Sprague, Ken 3, 4, 101, 112, 238
Storr, A. 175

Torok, M. 217

Treadwell, T., Stein, S. and Kumar, V. 162

Van Gogh, Theo 218
Van Gogh, Vincent 218

Watzlawick, P. 72

Wegscheider, S. 180
Willis, Sarah T. 3, 4, 122
Wilson, Kit 5
Winnicott, D.W. 118, 119–20

Yalom, I.D. 81, 160

Subject index

ACOAs (adult children of alcoholics) 179–86
acting, in intrapsychic psychodrama 23
acting-out 124–5, 129, 132; in group-work with adolescents 120, 122; in psychotherapeutic community 139
action, dangers of in therapy 132–3; defensive use of 132; as focus of psychodrama 160–1; movement away from in group-analytic drama (GAD) 126; and psychoanalysis 129
action sociogram 182
action techniques, for children of alcoholics 180
Actuality (BBC Radio 4) 196–7, 199
adolescents 15–30; adolescent sexual matrix 132; characteristics after background of abuse 118–19, 123; difficult to help 1–2; and group-analytic drama 115–33; and *Hamlet* 22; and individual therapy 115–16; initiation rites 29–30; length of session 90; in psychiatric hospital 17–18; and psychodrama 3, 4; in psychotherapeutic community 137–53; rehearsal for future 89; resistance 115–16; and sexual abuse 17, 79, 84–5; and sociodrama 89; and substance abuse 17; techniques for group-work with 120–2
alcoholism 155–76; and case profiles in psychodrama 161–74; definition of 155; difficult in treating 1, 2; effect on children 5, 67–8, 141–2, 150–1; family disease concept 179; origins and development 156–8; and personality traits 156; physical symptoms 155,

158; and rediscovery of potential through psychodrama 176; and resistance in psychodrama 160–1
American Humane Society 78
anger 20, 27–8; after child sexual abuse 83, 99, 197; in alcoholics 156, 169; blocking of 100; expression of 11, 109, 169; providing safe channels for 197–8
anniversary syndrome 206, 207, 214–15; and replacement child 217–18
anorexia nervosa 4; case history 140–2; difficult to help 1, 2; individual psychotherapy for 141, 142, 144, 146–7, 148, 149, 150, 152–3; problems in treatment of 139–40; and use of psychodrama 142–53
anxiety 25, 124–5; of adolescents 120, 121, 131; in alcoholics 161, 162; about catharsis 170–1; about losing control 197–8; performance anxiety 237; sexual 126, 131–2
art work, with abused children 90; for autistic young people 41–2; contribution to psychodrama 33; and Down's group 35–8; in work with cancer patients 211
assertiveness training 232
attachment theory 191, 199
attention, adolescent attitudes to 121
audience, role of 8
authority issues, in group-work with adolescents 121–2
autistic young people 3, 4, 40–3; art work with 41–2; and Down's group 43–4; and psychodrama 33; warm-up for 40–1
auxiliary egos 11, 19–20, 109–10, 117, 130–1; and child sexual abuse 92;

deroling 12; in group work with alcoholics 164–5, 168–9; role of 8, 10, 98

Beacon Hospital, New York 7, 8
behaviour patterns, early establishment of 192
behaviour therapy 232; and anorexia nervosa 139
'blind walk' (trust exercise) 181
body, influenced by mind 203
body image, and psychodrama 148–9
boredom 18–19; in group-work with adolescents 120
breathing exercises 210; in group-work with adolescents 121, 124
Britain, child sexual abuse in 78–9

cancer, and attitudes of patients 204–6; improving life of patients 203–4; and stress 206–10
catharsis 11; anxiety about 170–1; in group work with alcoholics 165–7, 170
character-playing see role-playing
chemical dependency, characteristics 179–80
child abuse, physical 78, 79, 107, 119
child sexual abuse 5, 77, 119; adult recovery from 95–112; among therapists 229; confrontation of abusers 88–9; effects of 77–8, 79–80; feelings of powerlessness 81–2; gender differences 78; and homosexuality 78; need for 'advocate' for child 100; need for professional treatment 79; perpetuation of 192; and prostitution 80; and repetition 84; role of mother 83, 89, 91, 92; and runaways 80; statistics 78–9; and substance abuse 80; truthfulness of children 79; under-reporting of 78; use of anatomically correct dolls 82–3, 85–6; uses of psychodrama 80–1
children, of alcoholics 5, 179–86; assessment of developmental level by therapist 90–1; early establishment of behaviour patterns 192; effects of neglect 80, 119; emotional abuse 79; need to mourn death of 217–18; and parents' alcoholism 141–2; physical abuse of 78, 79, 107, 119; preparing for operation 220–1; 'replacement child'

217–18; use of teddy bear in rehearsal work 220–1
choosing 185–6
classical psychodrama, stages of 8–13
Cleveland child sexual abuse crisis (1987) 79
closed groups 161–2
closure (completion) of psychodrama 12, 240
co-dependency 180
communication, acting-out as 129; exploration of, in group-analytic drama 128
conductor see director
confidence, and alcoholism 155, 157; and negative behaviour 193
confidentiality, in psychodrama for therapists 238–9
contract in psychodrama 9, 238
control, by director 139, 159; fear of losing 197–8; lack of in abused adolescents 119
coping strategies 21; among therapists 230; for children of alcoholics 180
creativity 129; in work with therapists 241–3
criminal activities, and childhood abuse 119, 124; see also child sexual abuse; prisoners; rape
crying, and healing 83

death, and 'anniversary syndrome' 206, 207, 214–15, 217–18; and psychodrama 3, 206, 209–10, 211–13
defence mechanisms, of alcoholics 174, 175; and psychodrama 233, 241–3; of therapists 175, 241–3
democracy, and psychodrama 49–50
demonstration group 234
denial, of alcoholism 159, 170, 181; and anorexia nervosa 139–40
dependency, chemical 179–80; repression of 156–7; see also alcoholism; anorexia nervosa
deroling 12, 58
desensitisation 106; and re-enactment 87
director, negative feelings of 124; role of 2–5, 8, 9, 122, 127–8; role in psychodrama for therapists 237; see also therapists
divorce and effects 57–63
dolls, anatomically correct 82–3, 85–6

doubling 11, 147–8, 150, 195; in group-analytic drama 130–1; *see also* auxiliary egos
Down's group, and art classes 35–8; and psychodrama 33
drama 9–10; and power of changing behaviour patterns 133

Education Act (1981), and special educational needs 34
ego, Moreno's challenging of 15; 'observing ego' 28–9
emergent awareness 182
emotional abuse of children 79
empathy, development of in adolescents 131–2; therapist 'running out of' 241
empty space, concept of 118
enactment 8, 9–12, 232; importance of 228; in psychodrama for child sexual abuse 83–7
encounter groups 8, 228
energy channelling, in group-work with adolescents 120–1
externalisation 132

failure, perception of 47–8
family, acceptance of good elements 109–10; and anorexia nervosa 141–2, 144, 146, 149–51; conflicts within 56–7; effects of alcoholism upon 180; explored in psychodrama 146–7, 152; 'family account books' 215; influence of father 156, 157; and origins of alcoholism 156–7, 163–4, 165; over-protective 157; patterns revealed in genosociogram 215–17, 218, and role structure 65
'family account books' 215
family sculpting 28
family therapy 53, 232–3; and psychodrama 73–4
Family Therapy, Association for 235
fantasy 16–17; and child sexual abuse 84, 85–6; and group-analytic drama 130–1
fear *see* anxiety
feelings, acting out of in re-enactment 87; containment of in chemically dependent family 183; expression of 11, 83; mistrust of after child sexual abuse 88; repression of 11
field theory 116
Four Winds Hospital, New York 17–18

free-floating discussion 117, 128
future projection technique 89

GAD *see* group-analytic drama (GAD)
gender role reversal 131
genograms 215
genosociograms 204, 207, 215–17, 218
gestalt 91, 116
Grendon Prison, psychodrama in 189–99
grief, containment of in chemically dependent family 183; need for after death of child 217–18
group analysis, and group-analytic drama (GAD) 116–17
'group as a whole' concept 128
group-analytic drama (GAD) 116–33; and group analysis 116–17; and psychodrama 117, 127, 128–33; and sociodrama 117–18; and theatre 116, 118; use of mirroring 130
groups 20–1, 23–4, 234–6; democracy within 49–50, 102–3; demonstration group 234; importance of in psychodrama 4, 145; not for small children 85; role in group-analytic drama (GAD) 129; and role training 23–4; special interest group 235; support of 106, 107; team support group 235; training groups 235–6; value for adolescents 84–5, 115–16, 129

handicapped people, psychodrama with 3
happiness, cultivation of in cancer patients 219–20
healing, and crying 83
Holwell Centre for Psychodrama and Sociodrama 40–2, 95–112, 228
homosexuality, and child sexual abuse 78
humour, in psychodrama 130, 231
hypnotic induction (unconscious command) 97, 108

identification 117; 'distorted' 160
identity, and adult children of alcoholics 186; polyvalent nature of 15–16; and social nature of man 116
individual psychotherapy, for anorexia nervosa 141, 142, 144, 146–7, 148, 149, 150, 152–3; and small children 85; unsuitability for adolescents 129
initiation rites, for adolescents 29–30

inspiration in psychodrama 2–4, 7, 241–3
interpersonal psychodrama 23–4
interpretation, when not useful 12, 240
intrapsychic psychodrama 15–30;
    definition 16–17; and elaboration 24–5;
    and *Hamlet* 22–5
'invented drama' 118, 121, 127
isolation 107; of adolescents 119–20,
    131; and alcoholism 155; among
    therapists 229–30, 232; of prisoners 189

JPS (Juvenile Psychiatric Service) 141

language, adolescent use of 119
learning difficulties, and art classes 35–8;
    and psychodrama 33
letter writing 183–4
limits, setting of in psychotherapeutic
    community 139; in treatment of
    alcoholism 159
Los Angeles, child sexual abuse in 79

magic shop 70, 172, 186
masks, defensive use of 17–22; *see also*
    resistance
matrix, use of in group analysis 116–17
mental institutions, background 34
mind, influence on body 203
mirroring 12, 184–5; in group-analytic
    drama 130
mother, and child sexual abuse 83, 89, 91,
    92; 'dead' after death of child 218; not
    acknowledging children's sexuality 97,
    99; and 'replacement child' 217–18

National Society for the Prevention of
    Cruelty to Children (NSPCC) 78
negative transference 197
neglect of children 80, 119
neurotransmittors, and health 203, 207,
    220
non-action techniques 122, 129, 132–3;
    see also group-analytic drama (GAD)
non-verbal signals 128
nurturing, adolescent need for in
    group-analytic drama 120, 122

On Becoming Psychotherapist 101–2
openness, dangers of 73; difficulty of in
    family therapy 73

part-playing *see* role-playing

peace movement 33, 35
permissiveness, in psychotherapeutic
    community 138–9
personality, based on childhood
    attachments 191
physical abuse, among therapists 229
physical exercise 124, 206, 219; in
    group-work with adolescents 120–1
playfulness, and adult children of
    alcoholics 185; in group-work with
    adolescents 120; psychotherapy
    encouraging 118, 129–30
power relationships, among therapists 237
powerlessness, in child sexual abuse 81–2
'predictions' of cancer patients 205–6, 207
prisoners 4, 189–99; background of abuse
    190–1; failings of punishment 199;
    hostility towards 197; isolation of 189
projection, and alcoholism 159, 161; by
    therapist 175
promiscuity 119
props in psychodrama 10, 107–8
prostitution 119; and child sexual abuse
    80
protagonist, role of 8–9; and 'sculpting'
    28–9; selection of 9
psychiatric disorders, classification of 137
psychiatric hospitals, psychodrama in 34;
    treatment of anorexia nervosa 137–53
psychoanalysis, and action 129; and
    anorexia nervosa 139; combination
    with psychodrama 4; group analysis
    116–17; Moreno's criticism of 98; and
    sexuality 98–9
psychodrama, action-based 233; and
    adolescents 3, 4; for adult children of
    alcoholics 184; and art teaching 33;
    avoids formal analysis 233–4, 240;
    basic elements of 7–8; and body image
    148–9; of cancer 210–11; and child
    sexual abuse 80–1, 83–7; classical 2,
    7–13; and death 3, 206, 209–10,
    211–13; and democracy 49–50; and
    eating 144–5, 152; exploring time and
    space 73–4; and family therapy 73–4,
    146–7; and feelings of shame 147–8;
    and group relationships 143–4; and
    group-analytic drama (GAD) 117, 127,
    128–33; group-analytic frame of
    reference 151–2; guidelines for
    working with disabled 3, 50; and
    illness 3, 206, 209–10, 211–13; and

importance of group 4; and individual work 73, 85; as initiation rite for adolescents 29–30; inspiration 2–4, 7, 241–3; and interpersonal reality 16; intrapsychic 15–30; as life method 33–4; and needs of mental health workers 231–7; overlaps with other therapy models 232–3; to prepare for cancer treatment 211–13; pressurising resistance of client 151–2; in prison 189–99; process of with mental health workers 238–40; and psychoanalysis 4; in psychotherapeutic community 138–53; and recovery of potential in alcoholic 176; and recreation of reality 10; to re-enter past 45; and seriously ill 203–22; and sexual behaviour 47–8; spontaneity 2–4; surreal 16–17; theory 232–3; as therapy of relationships 106; use with therapists 227–44; *see also* director; techniques

psychotherapeutic community, for disturbed adolescents 137–53

psychotherapist, difficult cases for 1–2; personal difficulties 2; support for 3; and transference 4–5

psychotherapy, in psychotherapeutic community 138

puberty, and abused children 119

puppets, use of by sexually abused children 77, 81, 84, 86, 92

rape 192–3, 229

reassurance, as warm-up in psychodrama with children 81–3

re-enactment 143, 147–8; and child sexual abuse 83–7; and desensitisation 87

regression 83, 232; in group-work with adolescents 120; and spontaneity 129

rehearsal 10–11; psychodrama as 211–14; in psychodrama with child sexual abuse 87–90; with sick children 220–1

rehearsal work, for adult children of alcoholics 184–5; in group work with alcoholics 167–8

rejection, coping with 107, 195

relationships, central to psychodrama 106; and effect of alcoholism 155, 157–8

relaxation exercises 206, 210, 222

repetition, by victims of child sexual abuse 84

rescue, sought by alcoholic 175

resentment, overcoming 219

resistance 126–7; acting-out as 129; by adolescents 115–16; by alcoholics in psychodrama 161; and pressure of psychodrama 151–2; in psychodrama with therapists 241–3

resonance 117

risk-taking 3–4

rites of passage, for adolescents 29–30

role reversal 11, 25–6, 67–8, 71, 73, 85, 194; and GAD 131; and gender 131; in group work with alcoholics 164–5, 168–9

role structure, in family 65

role-playing 15–17, 88–9; in group work with alcoholics 170; and *Hamlet* 22–3; masks as 17–22; and resistance 126–8; for seriously ill 210–14, 220–1, 222; by sexually abused children 80; and spontaneity 108–10

role-testing 44–5

role-training 24, 43, 44

'rule 43' 189

runaways, and child sexual abuse 80

'secondary benefits' of illness 206

self 28; adolescent sense of 131–2; definition of 15–16, 17

self-control, development of 11

self-disclosure, adolescent fear of 121

self-esteem, lack of 107

self-mutilation 131

Session, The (BBC TV) 99–100

sexual abuse 5; and adolescents 17; as betrayal of trust 77–8

sexuality, adolescent sexual matrix 132; anxiety over 126, 131–2; fear of 97, 98–9, 147–8, 157; and psychoanalysis 98–9

shame, explored in psychodrama 147–8

sharing 8, 12–13; at end of psychodrama 89–90

'significant other' 183; in group-analytic drama (GAD) 130–1; *see also* auxiliary egos

sociodrama 43, 44; and adolescents 89; and group-analytic drama (GAD) 117–18; in work with therapists 239, 243

sociograms 55–6, 182

sociometry 27–9, 71–2; genosociogram
215–17, 218
sociotherapy, in psychotherapeutic
community 138
soliloquy 61, 71
solioquy, in intrapsychic psychodrama 23
special educational needs 34
special interest group 235
splitting manoeuvres (between different
therapies) 144
spontaneity 2–4, 9, 18, 129–30; creating
conditions for 38–9; and fulfilment
100; lack of in adult children of
alcoholics 185; in Moreno's work 97,
98; and role-playing 108–10; in work
with therapists 241–3
spontaneous remissions of cancer 204
stage, role of 8
staging 105
Stegreiftheater, Die (Theatre of
Spontaneity) 7
story playing 185
stress, among therapists 228, 229–30; and
cancer 206–10; combatting 210,
221–2; identifying 210
substance abuse 119; and adolescents 17;
and child sexual abuse 80
suicide 84–5, 119, 141, 142, 144, 191
supervision, of therapists 228, 229
surplus reality 10, 11–12, 16–17, 71, 84,
195–6, 213
surreal psychodrama 16–17
symbolic distance technique 87–8
symbolism 80–1, 86
systems theory 91–2

team support group 235
techniques 2, 4–5, 7; artwork 33, 41–2,
90; breathing exercises 210; empty
chair 183; for group-work with
adolescents 120–2; letter writing
183–4; non-action 117, 118; and
'operations' 131; in psychodrama for
therapists 236–7; relaxation exercises
206, 210, 222; visualisation 206, 222
'tele' 10, 81, 92, 108, 160, 232
territorial imperative 65–7
theatre 125–7; and group-analytic drama
(GAD) 116, 118
Theatre of Spontaneity (Die
Stegreiftheater) 7
therapists, acknowledgement of

tele/transference 160; assessment of
developmental level of child 90–1;
attitude in psychodrama for alcoholics
175–6; background 228–9; coping
strategies 230; defence mechanisms
175; 241–3; difficulties in seeking help
230–1, 236–7; feelings aroused by
child sexual abuse 86–7; importance of
relationship with client (tele) 81;
isolation of 230, 232; need for control
of personal feelings 86–7, 90; need to
look from childlike point of view 91–2;
need to set limits with sexually abused
children 81; On Becoming a
Psychotherapist 101–2; and personal
therapy 231; problems in dealing with
alcoholics 156; role of in work with
children 82; and stress 228, 229–30;
use of psychodrama with 227–44; work
with abusers 91
touching 104, 105, 228; in group-work
with adolescents 120–1
training groups 235–6
transactional analysis 91
transference 4–5, 81, 153, 160, 232; and
disturbed adolescents 149; negative
115–16, 197
Transport and General Workers Union 35
trust 79, 81, 88, 99; for adult children of
alcoholics 180–1; establishment of 96;
need to trust child in psychodrama 92;
in psychodrama with alcoholics 162;
and sexual abuse 77–8; in warm-up 96
trust exercises, in group-work with
adolescents 120

violence 106–7, 189–99
visualisation 206, 222
vulnerability, acceptance of 84–5

warm-ups 2, 8–9, 19; action-method 35;
for adult children of alcoholics 181; for
autistic young people 40–1; in
group-work with adolescents 120–1,
126–7; miming disabilities 38–9;
protagonist-centred 169; in
psychodrama for alcoholics 162–4; in
psychodrama for therapists 238–9; as
'reassurance' in psychodrama with
children 81–3
'working-through' 152
World Health Organisation 155